Homer's
Odyssey

Charles Weiss

CAMBRIDGE UNIVERSITY PRESS
Cambridge, New York, Melbourne, Madrid, Cape Town,
Singapore, São Paulo, Delhi, Tokyo, Mexico City

Cambridge University Press
The Edinburgh Building, Cambridge CB2 8RU, UK

www.cambridge.org
Information on this title: www.cambridge.org/9780521137737

First published 2012

Printed in India by Replika Press Pvt. Ltd

A catalogue record for this publication is available from the British Library

ISBN 978-0-521-13773-7 Paperback

Contents

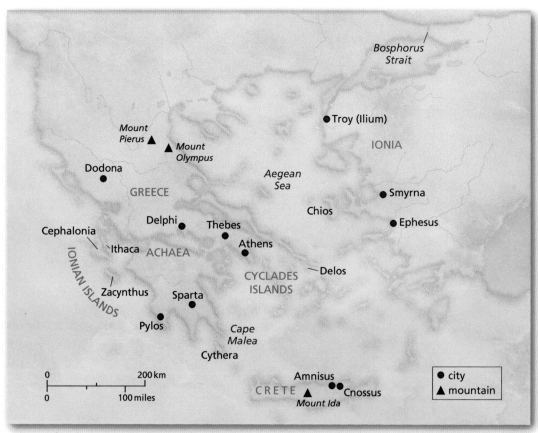

Greece and Ionia: ancient sites mentioned in the text.

Introduction

The poet

We must start on a sceptical note: we know next to nothing about Homer. Although in the ancient world the *Iliad* and *Odyssey* were almost universally attributed to someone by the name of 'Homer', many now doubt that there ever existed an individual poet who composed either of the poems, let alone both. These questions of authorship of the poems and of the identity of 'Homer' are collectively referred to as 'The Homeric Question'. What we do know is that by the end of the seventh century BC other poets seem to have knowledge of the poems, and there seems little reason to doubt that they existed largely as we have them today by 650 BC or so. Some scholars, on the other hand, believe that there were multiple competing (and conflicting) versions of the poems all the way into the Hellenistic period of the third century BC (e.g. Nagy 2004), but there is room for debate here, and we will probably never know the truth of the matter for sure. Homer is the most well-researched author of classical antiquity, and a glimpse at practically any item on the list of further reading (pp. 183–7) will indicate the enormous effort that has gone into understanding him; yet much remains uncertain.

For Greeks of the Classical period (and onwards) Homer was simply 'the Poet', much in the way that for centuries in the Western tradition the Hebrew and Christian Scriptures were 'the Book'. Homer came to dominate the Greek literary and cultural tradition (Graziosi 2002 and Nagy 2009) and it is difficult to understand ancient Greek culture without knowing his poetry. Because of Homer's popularity in antiquity several cities boasted that they were his place of birth; most of these cities (e.g. Ephesus and Smyrna) were in Ionia, the west coast of modern-day Turkey; this coheres with the particular ancient Greek dialect of the poems, largely Ionic, and on these grounds it makes sense to think that Homer, if he existed, was born somewhere in Ionia, or perhaps on an island in the Aegean (Chios also claimed to be his birthplace) sometime around 700 BC. We may also deduce from the geographical information in the *Odyssey* that Homer must have been somewhat familiar with at least portions of mainland Greece, perhaps even the western Ionian islands, where Odysseus' Ithaca is, yet there are as many different opinions about the geography of the *Odyssey* as there are scholars. Scepticism existed already in antiquity: the Hellenistic geographer Eratosthenes (quoted in Strabo's *Geography* 1.2.15), referring to an episode in *Odyssey* 10, cynically quipped that 'you could discover where Odysseus wandered when you discover the cobbler who made the bag of winds'.

All of this begs the question: did Homer actually exist? The poems clearly belong to what scholars today call an oral tradition: that is, they show signs of being composed within an **oral** and **performative** context. Comparison with such poetry across the world shows that the very definition of authorship is elusive, with poets frequently inheriting material and in turn adapting and expanding it. We have evidence that the poems of Homer were routinely performed by **rhapsodes**, probably 'song stitchers' in Greek, men who would recite the poems or portions of them to an audience. (The conditions of performance are unclear, but read Plato's *Ion* for a tantalizing glimpse; see the beginning of Book 22, p. 160.) Was Homer simply one of these rhapsodes, reciting poetry that had been passed down to him? Again, we possess only the name 'Homer', and we have very few names of any rhapsodes: if he was a member of such a profession he must have been very good at what he was doing.

The complications now multiply: was this Homer literate? We have evidence that the Greeks were literate by 700 BC at the latest (see Powell 1997). How could he have performed such monumentally long poems? Most oral poems from other cultures are much shorter: perhaps the *Odyssey* grew by a process of accretion by which stories of independent origin (e.g. Telemachus' story, or the Polyphemus story) came to be fused together. What would Homer's audience be like? How old was the poetry that preceded Homer? Who created *that*? We have essentially nothing in Greek before Homer, only guesswork: it is as though we possessed the works of a Da Vinci or a Michelangelo without having any art from the Middle Ages.

The short answer to such questions is that we simply don't know very much for sure, though for centuries now Homeric scholarship has tried to answer them, with varying success. In brief it seems safe to assume that Homer – or perhaps we should now say these poems – stands at the end of a long oral tradition. In light of the aesthetic complexity and sophistication of the *Iliad* and the *Odyssey*, the longer this tradition was, the better.

There is a tradition that Homer was blind, like the court poet Demodocus in *Odyssey* Book 8, but this detail and all of the colourful biographies of Homer from the ancient world that survive (see M. L. West 2003) were composed hundreds of years or more after his putative birth and must be discounted in the light of what we know about such ancient biographical information: much of it was fabricated out of the information available only in the poems themselves (see Lefkowitz 1981).

The poem

Naturally, one of the important elements of a long narrative poem is the plot, or central action, and for this we can turn to no less of an authority than Aristotle for a summary, taken from his fourth-century BC *Poetics* (1455b):

> A man is away from home for many years and jealously watched by Poseidon and has lost his followers; moreover at home his affairs are such that his property is being wasted by suitors and plots laid against his son; he comes home in dire distress and after disclosing himself makes an attack and destroys his enemies without being killed himself.
>
> (Translated by Hubbard in Russell and Winterbottom 1972)

The *Odyssey* seems urgently propelled forward by this central question of Odysseus' homecoming (*nostos*): how will he make it back home and how will he avenge himself on the suitors when he returns? Parallels for this core plot can be found in the mythology and folklore of various cultures. There are interesting similarities with the heroic journey of the great Mesopotamian hero Gilgamesh described in the *Epic of Gilgamesh*, the oldest surviving work of poetry, whose origins date back to the third millennium BC (see M. L. West 1997, chapter 8; for folktale elements in Homer, see Hansen 1997 and Page 1973). By contrast we may compare the plot of the *Iliad* (which is likely to pre-date the *Odyssey*): it is arguably more subtle and complex, built around a purely emotional experience: Achilles' anger and its consequences. Yes, there is bloody fighting and there are vivid war scenes, but these are **episodes** and not actually necessary for the narrative core. When it came to selecting his material, we imagine that Homer may have been under constraint as an **epic** poet to narrate the 'deeds of man and god', as Penelope famously says (**1.338**). Yet we can presume that all of Greek myth and legend lay before Homer as potential subject-material, and his choice to focus so narrowly on such relatively short spans of time (the action of each of the *Iliad* and the *Odyssey* transpires over some 40 days) could very well have been one novelty that distinguished his poetry from the rest. It has been held that such subtlety in the *Iliad*, in fact, should be credited to Homer's dissatisfaction with his poetic precedent – all action and little depth – and indeed it is normally believed that his poems were such an improvement on preceding poetry (which seems to have mainly treated the Trojan War and is known as the 'epic cycle' because it 'encircles' the *Iliad* and *Odyssey*) that they simply wiped out the competition.

Is the *Odyssey* a simple folkloric tale of revenge? Naturally the answer to this question will depend on one's aesthetic judgement. One of my goals will be to suggest that the poem exhibits the highest calibre of poetic sophistication and artistry, and that the ways in which it problematizes the plot itself and challenges our expectations as readers are some of its most exciting features. Given what little we know, however, about the conditions of composition, there is always room for debate. It is important not to read too much into our author, but at the same time we must not underestimate him; Homer has been poorly served for centuries by a kind of scholarship that has seemed more interested in what lay behind him than in the poems themselves. The tide has turned to some degree (as can be seen by comparing the three 'companion' volumes, Wace and Stubbings 1962; Morris and Powell 1997; Fowler 2004); but still, there remains a great deal of controversy about the nature of Homeric poetry.

We have, then, our central plot; yet look at just a few things Homer does to subvert its simplicity:

- We do not meet our hero in person until Book 5.
- Some of the most exciting portions of the narrative (Books 9–12) are put in the mouth of our hero as a flashback sequence (there are other flashbacks as well, notably in Books 3, 4 and 19).
- Seven years of potential narrative are completely glossed over in near silence (i.e. Odysseus' time with Calypso).
- In the words of most students, 'nothing happens' for some eight out of the 24 books of the epic (Books 13–20).
- Many readers, from antiquity up to today, find the slaughter of the suitors in Book 22 and the sudden resolution in Book 24 surprising, if not unsettling.

Just a brief catalogue, but even this glimpse suggests the complexity of the poem. As with the *Iliad*, Homer has exercised a principle of selectivity in creating the plot: just as we do not get the full story of the Trojan War in the *Iliad* (literally 'Troy Poem' in Greek; the names 'Troy' and 'Ilium' refer to the same city), so we do not actually get the full story of Odysseus and his journey home in the *Odyssey* (literally 'Odysseus Poem'). Despite this complexity, however, many patterns are discernible in the *Odyssey*. Scholars disagree on just how much patterning is present or significant, but structural complexity is one of the distinctive features of this poem. Though we remain in doubt whether to ascribe to Homer the book divisions of the *Odyssey* (see Olson 1995), it is relatively easy to discern six major narrative units in the poem, each consisting of four books:

1 Books 1–4: The 'Telemachy' (as it was known in antiquity): the scene-setting story of Odysseus' son, Telemachus, in Ithaca.
2 Books 5–8: Odysseus' journey to and arrival in Phaeacia.
3 Books 9–12: Odysseus' first-person flashback narrative of his wanderings before arriving in Phaeacia.
4 Books 13–16: Odysseus' arrival in Ithaca (in disguise as an old beggar) and reunion with his son.
5 Books 17–20: Odysseus' experiences (still in disguise) in his own palace, preparing his attack on the suitors.
6 Books 21–24: Odysseus' final self-disclosure, slaughter of the suitors, and reunion with Penelope and his father, Laertes.

In this book I have divided the poem into five parts: sections 4 and 5 in this list can be conveniently collapsed into one.

What else can we expect to find in our text? Two of the greatest constituent elements of the poem will become immediately apparent: **episodic narrative** and **direct speech**. Homer does much more 'showing' than 'telling', in the classic distinction developed by Wayne Booth (1983): he lets us see things happening rather than simply summarizing, and he seldom discloses his own opinion. It is chiefly in fact through direct speech that Homer characterizes the people of his poetry; very rarely will he tell us directly what to think of someone (roughly 50 per cent of Homeric epic consists of direct speech). At times the text will actually read like a script and demand an oral performance of its own: it is easy to see intimations of Greek drama in Homer, and you may find that reading passages aloud will help to capture some of the nuances and subtleties of the speeches. In ancient literary criticism, Homeric poetry was known for its vividness and its imitative, or mimetic quality – and it is easy to see why. These two elements of narrative and speech, at any rate, will form the core of any segment or separable 'story' within the poem.

One of the most dynamic features of the poem, however, is the way in which Homer will invite us to compare one segment or story with another segment within the poem (items compared in this way are traditionally called 'foils' or 'pendants') – this can be achieved through a variety of similarities (e.g. theme, shared character or linguistic parallels), and result in an enhanced understanding of both segments: two (or more, for that matter) stories act, as it were, upon one another and manage to suggest things that are unspoken directly in either. Homer's similes are another means of inviting the audience to imagine and work out meaning for themselves: they are always more suggestive than they seem on first reading and deserve more than a passing glance. Similarly, Homer frequently leaves it up to us to establish points of contact between digressions and the main narrative; at the least we can say that Homeric poetry exhibits a huge range of narrative pace, and this can only enrich the reader's experience. All of these phenomena fall within the field of what scholars call today 'narratology', or study of narrative technique: it is no accident that the *Odyssey* is particularly well served by such studies (see De Jong 2001).

The success of contemporary prose translations of the *Odyssey* into English shows that the story itself is compelling: it draws us in, despite the gulf of time and culture that separates us from Homer. But one vital element of Homeric poetry is of course the verse itself. Though much of the effect of the original Greek will be lost in translation, some characteristics are discernible even in the most straightforward of translations (as this one purports to be), and in order to give you a better feel for what the original is like it will be worthwhile expanding on this here.

Homer was a traditional poet who inherited much of his material and his poetic technique. Just as it is impossible to make a comprehensive judgement as to the originality of Homer's treatment of particular stories since so much comparative evidence has disappeared, in the same way it is difficult to judge the quality of the verse accurately. Yet a few observations can be made.

It is evident that before the lifetime of Homer Greeks already enjoyed some form of poetry, but we have only a vague idea of what it was like. At the least Homer thought it believable to depict the bard (*aoidos*) Demodocus singing some form of epic at Alcinous' palace in *Odyssey* 8; similarly, Phemius entertains the suitors in Ithaca throughout the *Odyssey*, and even a hero such as Achilles sings at *Iliad* 9.186–9. It is reasonable to believe that pre-Homeric poetry concerned gods and heroes, and that therefore Homer has actually done nothing out of the ordinary here. Verse, it was felt, was not only somehow appropriate for such elevated subject-matter, it was also (and still is today) memorable because of its rhythm, and the right medium in which to recount things worth remembering.

The particular kind of verse Homer uses, furthermore, is clearly traditional: it is called **dactylic hexameter** and we assume it was in use long before these particular poems were composed. Homer's near-contemporaries such as Hesiod used it, and later poets (e.g. Apollonius of Rhodes, whose third-century BC epic about Jason and the Argonauts, the *Argonautica*, remains popular) came to use it too. The metre passed into Roman epic and was adopted by the likes of Virgil and Ovid.

Each line of this hexameter consists of 'six measures' (*hex-* + *metron*) of syllables, and each of these measures consists of one of two possible combinations:

1 a long syllable (represented here as ¯) + two short syllables (represented here as ˘ ˘), called a *dactyl*, Greek for 'finger', because it resembles the left-hand index finger as viewed on its side: ¯ ˘ ˘

2 a long syllable + another long syllable, called a *spondee*, perhaps because it was normally used at *spondai* (libations): ¯ ¯

The whole line looks like this:

1	2	3	4	5	6
¯ ˘ ˘	¯ ˘ ˘	¯ ˘ ˘	¯ ˘ ˘	¯ ˘ ˘	¯ ¯
or	or	or	or	or	or
¯ ¯	¯ ¯	¯ ¯	¯ ¯	¯ ¯	¯ ˘

Any line of hexameter can therefore have between 12 (i.e. if only spondees) and 17 syllables (i.e. if the first five feet are dactyls), and it is this kind of variety, as well as a host of other possible patterns, that keeps the line from being monotonous in the original Greek (for a good idea of the aesthetics involved even in translation see Edwards 2002).

All classical Greek metres are in fact based on syllable *length* and not on *stress*, as in English poetry (i.e. the way we pronounce particular words in a line of poetry emphatically). At the cost of strict accuracy, however, some idea of the Greek hexameter can be felt in the English hexameter, as in this opening line from Longfellow's *Evangeline* of 1847 (the stress-marks printed here are of course not original):

> Thís is the fórest priméval. The múrmuring pínes and the hémlocks

The line reads or 'scans' as five dactyls plus a final spondee: can you make out the rhythm? The Victorian English poet and critic Matthew Arnold famously recommended the English hexameter as the best metre for rendering Homer and offered a few lines of his own as a sample translation; here is Achilles' horse Xanthus addressing his master at a dramatic moment in *Iliad* 19.408–10:

> Trúly, yét this tíme will we sáve thee, míghty Achílles!
>
> Bút thy dáy of déath is at hánd; nor shall wé be the reáson –
>
> Nó, but the wíll of Heáven, and Fáte's invíncible pówer.

Arnold's lectures *On Translating Homer* (published in 1861) remain worth reading, particularly for those interested in the problems of rendering Homer poetically within the English poetic tradition. There will be no attempt to translate Homer metrically here, though I have tried to preserve the units of sense and sentence-patterns of the original poem, so that the line numbers used here correspond to the Greek. Other translators have attempted poetic renderings, however, and any translation should in fact be compared with others in order to get a better idea of the original (see Steiner 2004 for a good overview of different translations of Homer).

Two features of Homeric verse will strike even modern English readers as odd: 1) conventional or 'fixed' **epithets** (or adjectives) that sometimes seem to have no bearing on the immediate context (e.g. why are Homeric ships *always* 'hollow' or 'black', and why is Penelope *always* 'shrewd'?); and 2) the **repetition** of individual words, lines, sentences, speeches, scenes (e.g. the coming of dawn or feasting), even whole themes (all of these can be called 'formulae', Latin for 'little patterns'): on one calculation, for instance, every fifth line of the *Iliad* and *Odyssey* taken together can be found to be repeated in some way; other ways of calculating can fix the rate of repetition even higher.

The origin of these features was traced in a famous series of studies initiated in the 1920s by Milman Parry (see the 1971 collection) and carried forward by his student Albert B. Lord (2000 (1960)). By comparing Homer to contemporary south Slavic poetry created and sung by non-literate poets, they discovered striking similarities that demonstrated clearly that Homeric poetry is an **oral poetry** passed down from poet to poet and that the conventional epithets and formulae reveal a kind of building-block system used by a performing oral poet as a means of manipulating his material for extempore performance (recordings of these poets can now be accessed online; as of my writing this in October 2011 they can be found at the Milman Parry Collection online at http://chs119.harvard. edu/mpc; Lord 2000 [1960] comes with a CD). Further research since then (see e.g. J. M. Foley 1999) suggests that these epithets and formulae are not merely ways for poets to fill lines, but that they provide a wide variety of interpretive possibilities to a contemporary audience that is accustomed to the system. A good example of this can be found in the last line of the *Iliad*, where Hector, who is being buried, is called (as so often) 'tamer of horses' (*hippodamos*). The epithet seems unnecessary and irrelevant to the context, yet as Edwards points out (1997), the epithet poignantly echoes Patroclus' last words to Achilles in *Iliad* 16.854, where Patroclus ironically uses the verb 'to tame', and one of Achilles' traditional epithets falls in exactly the same place in the line as Hector's. I have in fact at times varied the translation of a given epithet based on context; Penelope's epithet 'clever' or 'shrewd' (*periphrōn*) is almost exclusively hers (it is used once of Queen Arete and four times of the slave Euryclea). Telemachus' epithet 'shrewd' (*pepnumenos*) is also used sparingly of others and is almost exclusively his. For Odysseus see note on **1.1**.

A third element that stands out to the reader with Greek is the nature of the language used in the poems: it is difficult or perhaps impossible to replicate in English but it deserves mention here because it is so characteristic of Homer. The language is not merely 'Greek' but an astonishing mix of forms that come from a wide variety of Greek dialects from all over the Aegean world (chiefly East Ionic, Aeolic, Arcado-Cypriot and Attic-Ionic), and from different stages in the development of these languages (see Horrocks 1997, with Janko 1998). This mix has been called in German scholarship a *Kunstsprache* or 'art language'; it has been well defined as 'an artificial idiom constructed out of archaic, dialectal and invented forms, used both for their metrical utility and to give the effect of distancing the poetic language from everyday speech' (Chadwick 1990). The result is a variety whose richness stands unrivalled in classical poetry; it has often been observed that it is the inspiration for the experimental use of language in James Joyce's *Ulysses*. Homer's use of language, particularly in the *Odyssey*, stands out as highly self-conscious and at times even quite playful. There are, in fact, colloquial elements in Homeric Greek, further proof that these poems seem designed to be spoken out loud. What may be missing for the modern reader is an extensive use of metaphor, so common in our own poetry. Yet it must be remembered that this is above all **narrative** poetry, and whatever we may lose in the close verbal metaphor we are accustomed to, we gain in Homer's deft manipulation of epithets, formulae and foils.

A brief word on the major characters you will meet in the *Odyssey*:

- **Odysseus** will certainly live up to his epithets 'long-suffering' and 'clever', but there are complexities here: his qualities as a hero and leader will come under scrutiny throughout the poem and ultimately it must be asked, if Odysseus wants to come home so badly, why does he take so long in doing so?

- **Penelope**, his wife, will play a prominent role in Parts 4 and 5 and she will similarly live up to her epithet, 'shrewd'. Much contemporary debate swirls around just how shrewd she is, but I will suggest in the notes that we ought to give her the benefit of the doubt: she is her husband's equal and, in my opinion, steals the show towards the end of the poem.

- **Telemachus** ('Far-fighter'), their twenty-something-year-old son, seems highly strung and anxious, not unlike his father; he seems to live in his father's shadow and is keen to prove himself, yet is never quite given the chance; he is the star of the first four books and frequently serves as a clever plot-device for Homer.

- The goddess **Athena** is Odysseus' attentive patroness; her interference in human affairs, however, is rarely direct and mainly motivational, hence her frequent appearance in human guise. She is a colourful character in her own right (see especially Book 13), yet it is easy to see how readers through the ages have taken her as an allegory for wisdom.

- The **suitors** are largely nasty pieces of work but they are not merely 'the bad guys': there is a great deal at stake in winning Penelope's hand and after 19 years of waiting for Odysseus they seem justified in the attempt; Antinous and Eurymachus are the chief suitors and though much of the narrative dealing with them is included only in summary form here, Homer takes pains to delineate their characterization.

- Among the secondary characters, **Calypso**, **Nausicaa** and **Circe** will all stand out as intriguing foils to Penelope, **Alcinous** and **Polyphemus** could not be more strongly contrasted in terms of hospitality, and the loyal **Eumaeus** and **Euryclea** will lend a touch of rustic charm to the poem.

Bear in mind just how much the largely domestic setting of our poem contrasts with what we can take as the norm of epic poetry: the world of heroes and fighting. Special attention should in fact be drawn to the representation of women in the *Odyssey*: they have such important roles to play (see especially Penelope in Parts 4 and 5) in the poem that the Victorian critic Samuel Butler famously argued that the *Odyssey* must have been composed by a woman – and their importance has guided my selection of books for translation here. Good studies on women in the *Odyssey* include Cohen 1995 and Clayton 2004.

Finally, a few themes to watch out for. Odysseus' **family unit** (*oikos*, also 'house') is of central interest: its current state of disrepair at the beginning of the poem and subsequent restoration at the end is, along with Odysseus' *nostos*, the very spine of the narrative. Restoration of the *oikos* is in larger terms a matter of **civilization** and **justice**: we will find several domestic settings along the way (e.g. *chez* Nestor, Menelaus, Circe, Alcinous, Polyphemus) and all will invite comparison with the situation in Ithaca. **Hospitality** (*xeinia*) will emerge as a key concept here. But exactly how is justice to be restored? Odysseus is above all clever, and his patron goddess is Athena, goddess of wisdom: with Penelope's help they do come up with a solution – and a bloody one at that. If they are all so clever, is such violence necessary? Many scholars think Homer is attempting to deal with the weighty matters of right and wrong in the *Odyssey*, almost like a philosopher (e.g. Bernadete 1997 and Deneen 2000), and there can be no doubt that Greek drama draws heavily on the *deus ex machina* (literally 'god from a machine', i.e. a stage crane) of Athena's sudden intervention in Book 24. The immortals, too, are frequently felt to be more interested in right and wrong here than in the *Iliad*. But what about all the lying? Is **deception** really justified in the *Odyssey*? Certainly deception is what Odysseus was best known for: he invented the Trojan Horse, the final means by which the Greeks defeated Troy, and it is only natural that Homer would have to deal with this aspect of Odysseus' character in the poem. Yet deception may involve self-concealment, a motif that stands in strong contrast to Odysseus' passion to be known, to be recognized as the great hero of the Trojan War, to have his *kleos* – his 'great deeds' or 'fame' – acknowledged. **Acknowledgement** and **recognition** are great themes of the *Odyssey* (see Murnaghan 1987). Yet in all of this we will repeatedly find one extra layer of interpretation – the *Odyssey* is an incredibly self-reflecting or **metapoetic** poem: Homer constantly seems to find ways of reminding us that this epic is also about poetry itself. There are singing bards, there are singing birds, there are singing women weaving, there is constant allusion, in my opinion, to the *Iliad* – in a stunning *tour de force* we find Agamemnon referring to the *Odyssey* itself (24.194–8):

> 'Perfect Penelope, daughter of Icarius!
>
> What a mind! *You* never forgot your wedded husband
>
> Odysseus. And now people won't forget her and what she's done –
>
> ever! The gods will give mortals
>
> a poem, one that will elevate and delight sharp Penelope!'

We are told what will happen from the outset of the poem – much as so many characters within the poem are given oracles and prophecies about the future – and yet we, like they, find ourselves content to wait it out and see how it all comes together. Homer is an extraordinarily self-confident author, and such self-confidence and concern with calling attention to the poem per se sit well with what we understand to be the competitive or 'agonistic' nature of poetic performance in ancient Greece (see Gentili 1988 and Edmunds and Wallace 1997). Homer's bards work for a living, and powerful men depend on them to spread, preserve, and indeed create their *kleos*.

Conventions used in the text and notes

Cross-references that appear in bold type (e.g. **1.1**) refer to passages of the *Odyssey* that are included in this book. Long vowel markings (macra) are included the first time a Greek word appears.

Works mentioned in the notes are cited by author and date; the full reference can be found in the list on pp. 184–7. Except where noted, references to the Oxford commentary are all ad loc., i.e. in S. West 1988, Hainsworth 1988, Heubeck 1989 and 1992, Russo 1992 and Fernández-Galiano 1992 the reference corresponds exactly to the line number in my translation.

In Archelaos' Apotheosis of Homer *(third century BC), the poet is crowned by Time and the World, as little personifications of the* Iliad *and* Odyssey *crouch by his side. The Olympians occupy the top row, with the Muses and other figures coming in between. Note Homer's resemblance to Zeus: the relief makes clear the status of Homer in the Greek world.*

Part One (Books 1–4): The 'Telemachy'

Book 1

1.1–10   **Tell me, Muse**, of the **ingenious and much-travelled man** who wandered
so far off course after he sacked the sacred citadel of **Troy**!
He saw the cities of many men and he understood their minds;
while attempting to stay alive and see his men home safely
he suffered great pain on the sea – and in his heart –   1.5
but despite this effort he did not save them.
No, they perished as the result of their own recklessness: they consumed
the cows of Hyperion the Sun God, **the fools!** –

Tell me, Muse   taken literally these words form a prayer or invocation to a divinity: in keeping with the representation of divine knowledge elsewhere in the poem, Homer as narrator here admits his dependence on a superior power for things no mortal can possibly know in full. This admission may also be taken more suggestively to highlight the quality of the poem – songs and poets are regularly 'divine' in Homer. The traditional number of nine Muses appears in Book 24 (lines 60–2), at Achilles' funeral; otherwise the unspecified 'Muse' appears elsewhere only in Book 8: she 'loves' and 'has instructed' the court poet Demodocus. The mythological traditions about the Muses vary widely; Homer has left his treatment of them much vaguer than his contemporary Hesiod in his *Theogony*, where they are the daughters of Zeus and Mnemosune (Memory).

ingenious and much-travelled   the Greek word here (*polutropos*) is used only once again of Odysseus at **10.330** (see question 2 on p. 96); Greeks themselves in antiquity debated as to its interpretation and it is translated twice here to capture its ambiguity. It must mean something like 'much-turned' but the meaning of 'turned' here is open to interpretation. (See Peradotto 1990 for an intriguing exploration of some of the possibilities.) Odysseus' most common epithets are 'long-suffering' (*polutlas*) and 'crafty' (*polumetis*); both are used frequently of him in the *Iliad*.

man   in Greek, it is *andra* (man) that is famously and most emphatically the first word of the poem (we may compare 'anger', the first word of the *Iliad*), yet we do not learn the name of this man until line 21. Virgil acknowledged Homer's influence by following this pattern in the first three words of the *Aeneid*: *arma uirumque cano*, 'arms and the man I sing': his poem will contain both the martial element of the *Iliad* and the story of a hero's voyage from the *Odyssey*.

Troy   Odysseus can be credited with the sacking of the city (traditionally dated to 1184 BC) because he devised the plan of the Trojan Horse (see note on **4.272**).

the fools   Homer seems to be disclosing his opinion to his audience, not a common phenomenon. Odysseus' men will consume the cows in Book 12.

A Muse plays the cithara (from which we get our word 'guitar') on Mount Helicon, one of the traditional homes of the Muses (vase-painting, fifth century BC).

and in return that god took from them the day of their homecoming.
Start your story **somewhere here**, goddess – you are the daughter of Zeus!
Do for my audience and me **as you have done for others.**   1.10

For most readers these first ten lines form a prologue or preface to the *Odyssey*, much in the same way that the *Iliad* starts. Some readers have taken the preface to extend to line 21.

---

somewhere here   a unique word in all of Homer (such words are referred to as *hapax legomena*), it draws attention to Homer's dependence on his Muse – the poet has no idea where to begin – and it ironically gives an almost casual quality to what is a very carefully planned unfolding of narrative complexity. Homer closes this section as he began it, with direct address to the Muse, a device typical of oral poetry known as 'ring composition', which helps articulate the divisions of the narrative for the listener.

as you have done for others   the Greek here seems to suggest that Homer is again coming across as a self-deprecating human narrator in need of divine help; he also hints at the fact that other poets have treated similar material.

1. The focus of lines 4–9 is on Odysseus' relations with his companions. While this is a significant theme it can hardly be said to be the major theme of the poem. For some scholars these lines jar so much that they must have belonged to a different poem originally. Do you think these lines make sense as an introduction to the poem?

2. Why might Homer wish to excuse Odysseus from blame in the deaths of his men?

3. What do we learn about Odysseus in these opening lines?

4. Traditionally these lines have been felt to be symptomatic of Homer's narrative bias in favour of his protagonist. Can you make a case for a more subtle or even ironic authorial attitude towards Odysseus?

1.11–95

Though all the others who had escaped utter destruction at Troy
were home after surviving the war and the sea,
the nymph, Lady **Calypso**, resplendent goddess, kept him back
in hollow caves, isolated. He longed
to come home and return to his wife, but Calypso wanted him to
        be her husband.   1.15
Yet just when in the roll of time a year had come and gone,
the gods spun fate for him and ordained a **homecoming**
to Ithaca (yet not even then had he and those dear to him
escaped conflict): all the gods pitied him
except for Poseidon. This god was constantly enraged with   1.20
godlike **Odysseus** as he made his journey home.
But now **Poseidon** had gone to visit the distant

Calypso we won't meet Calypso (whose name resembles the Greek for 'I will conceal') and Odysseus until Book 5: Homer tantalizes us here but makes us wait while he builds up narrative tension over the next four books.

homecoming the Greek word is *nostos*; it gives us our word 'nostalgia', literally 'pain for a return home'. Much of the Greek epic cycle (see p. 3), now largely lost, concerned the homecomings (*nostoi*) of other Greek heroes as they returned from Troy (mentioned in lines 11–12). Menelaus narrates his own *nostos* to Telemachus in Book 4. Note that the gods 'spin' a homecoming for Odysseus: on the spinning and weaving motif see note on line **1.238**. The rapid scene-change to a divine decision-making council at line 26 will be familiar to audiences and readers of the *Iliad*; here, as there, the gods look down on human action.

Odysseus the 'man' of line 1 is finally named here for the first time: the delay is typical of the Homeric style and appropriate in a text so concerned with the themes of concealment and identity. The Latin name for Odysseus, *Vlixes* (hence our Ulysses today), probably comes via the Etruscan language.

Poseidon his anger will be explained at line **68**. As the god of the sea he can obstruct Odysseus' *nostos* (Poseidon's brother Zeus is god of the sky and their brother Hades is god of the Underworld). Homer's gods are fond of the pious and far-flung Ethiopians: in the first book of the *Iliad* they all go to visit them. Note how Homer typically digresses here.

Ethiopians (who live at the far edge of humanity and fall into two groups:
those who live at the setting of the sun and those at its rising)
to accept a sacrifice of bulls and rams,   1.25
and there he took his seat as guest and delighted himself with the feast.
                                                    Now the other gods
assembled together in the palace of Olympian Zeus.
The father of men and gods began to speak to them;
he remembered in his heart the handsome Aegisthus,
whom **Orestes**, son of far-famed Agamemnon, had put to death.   1.30
With him in mind he addressed the immortals:
'The *outrage*! Mortals are now beginning to blame us gods
and say that misfortune comes from us! And yet it's they themselves,
as a result of their own **recklessness**, who create such unnecessary suffering!
Case in point: just now Aegisthus married Agamemnon's wedded wife   1.35
– an act of excess! – and he killed him when he arrived home from Troy.
He planned his utter destruction even after we had told him in advance
not to kill him nor to court his wife
by sending Hermes, Watchful **Slayer of Argus**:
"Revenge is bound to come from Orestes, grandson of Atreus,   1.40
the moment he reaches manhood and begins to miss his homeland."
That's what Hermes told him and yet despite this advice
he failed to persuade Aegisthus and now the man has paid for it in full.'
Then Bright-eyed goddess Athena replied:
'Son of Cronus, father, supreme among the gods,   1.45
surely that man lies dead in a death he deserved –
and anyone else who acts like that should die like that.
But as for warlike Odysseus, my heart burns with anguish
for this unlucky creature, who has been suffering for such a long time
                                                    apart from those he loves
on a sea-girt island in the centre of the ocean.   1.50
A goddess has her palace there, on this wooded isle,

Orestes   made famous in Greek literature by Aeschylus' *Oresteia* trilogy, he and his family story are held up here (and see line 298) as a paradigm, or parallel for Telemachus; what went wrong with his family constantly looms ominously in the background: Aegisthus kills Agamemnon on his homecoming: what will happen to Odysseus on his *nostos*? Note that in Homer's version of the story Aegisthus, and not Clytemnestra, is the murderer; he forms a better parallel with the suitors – he is Agamemnon's cousin – than she, as his wife, would.

recklessness   the Greek is *atasthalia*, an important concept for the *Odyssey* since this is what the suitors are guilty of, as well as Odysseus' men (see line 7). The central idea is failure to pay heed to a warning, as here with Aegisthus.

Slayer of Argus   for details of Hermes' defeat of this many-eyed monster see note on **5.43**. Hermes serves as the messenger of the gods in the *Odyssey*, as Iris does in the *Iliad*.

the daughter of baleful **Atlas**, the god who knows
the depths of the entire sea, and who supports the massive
pillars that encompass earth and sky.
It's his daughter who's detaining my weeping, wretched man;   1.55
with her soft and seductive words she constantly
charms him so that he won't remember Ithaca. And meanwhile Odysseus,
who yearns to see even just a puff of smoke rise
from his fatherland, wants to die! Are you still not moved
in your heart for him, Olympian? Didn't Odysseus   1.60
bring you some pleasure in the sacrifices he made by the Argive ships
at wide Troy? Why in fact have you **become so angry** with him, Zeus?'
In reply Cloud-gatherer addressed her:
'My child, what's this that you've let slip from your mouth?
How could I have overlooked godlike Odysseus?   1.65
He's abundantly clever among mortals and he has given abundantly in sacrifices
to us immortal gods who hold wide heaven.
It's Poseidon, Stayer of Earth, who has become so resolutely
angry with him over the Cyclops whom Odysseus deprived of sight,
godlike **Polyphemus**, whose might is greatest   1.70
among all the Cyclopes. Now it was the nymph Thoosa who give birth to him,
daughter of Phorcys, master of the barren sea,
after making love to Poseidon in hollow caves.
This is why Earth-shaker Poseidon is driving him back from his ancestral
land though he has not, of course, managed to put Odysseus to death.   1.75
Come on, then, let's all of us discuss here and now
how Odysseus is to achieve his homecoming. Poseidon will let go of
his anger: he certainly won't be able to maintain this quarrel
all on his own, contrary to the wishes of all the immortals!'

Then Bright-eyed goddess Athena replied: 1.80
'Son of Cronus, father, supreme among the gods,

Atlas one of the Titans and brother of Prometheus, he fought against Zeus and was made to hold up the world as his punishment; his daughter is Calypso. His connection with the sea here is curious: S. West 1988 explains this by reference to the Hittite mythological monster Upelluri, who lives in the sea and upon whom the world is built. For further connections between Greek myth and the Near East, see M. L. West 1997 and 2007.

become so angry the Greek word here is *ōdusao*, highly reminiscent of Odysseus' name; in Book 19 (**19.407–9**) Odysseus' grandfather Autolycus explicitly connects the concept of anger to our hero (see also **5.340**). The actual origin of Odysseus' name is unclear, yet Homer is fond of such puns (see Silk 2004), and particularly of suggestive names.

Polyphemus we will meet the Cyclops Polyphemus fully in Book 9; with the mention of the obscure Thoosa we find Homer (and Zeus!) typically digressing and displaying his erudition in conventional epic style.

if in fact the blessed gods now want this,
my shrewd Odysseus' homecoming,
then let's urge Conductor Hermes, Slayer of Argus,
to go to the island of Ogygia and speedily tell   1.85
the fair-haired nymph our sure decree:
great-hearted Odysseus is coming home.
Meanwhile I'll make for Ithaca so that I can
encourage **his son** and put some strength in his heart:
he'll assemble the long-haired **Achaeans**   1.90
and give full notice to all these suitors who are constantly
slaughtering his thronging sheep and fine horned oxen.
I will send him to Sparta and sandy Pylos
so that he can make enquiries about his father's homecoming –
                                         if anyone will talk to him –
and thereby acquire a good **reputation** among mortals.'   1.95

> 1   What is achieved by starting the poem with the Olympian gods?
>
> 2   What are your first impressions of the gods and their interactions as they are
>   presented in the poem?
>
> 3   Can you think of other myths – even modern ones – in which the son of a
>   hero is sent on a mission to find his father?

1.96–143   With these words Athena tied her fine sandals beneath her feet;
immortal and golden, they carried her over sea
and endless land with the breath of the wind.
She took with her a stout spear with a sharp bronze edge,
heavy, long and sturdy – the one she uses to subdue the ranks of fighting   1.100
men whenever in all her might as Zeus' daughter her anger is roused –
Athena sped down from the heights of Mount Olympus
and came to stand at the front door of Odysseus' house in Ithaca,

---

his son   Athena's words now open and at the same time summarize the 'Telemachy', or
'story of Telemachus', as the first four books of the epic are frequently called. By calling
his fellow Greeks to a formal assembly (*agorē*), Telemachus can highlight for the reader
as well as his countrymen just how difficult the situation with the suitors has become –
and arguably Odysseus' revenge is thereby more justified. In Sparta Telemachus will meet
Menelaus (Book 4) and in Pylos he will meet Nestor (Book 3).

Achaeans   the Greeks who go to fight at Troy are variously named in Homer as
'Achaeans', 'Argives', 'Danaans' and 'sons of Danaus': all these terms will be confusing to
a first-time reader but they are largely synonymous.

reputation   a good reputation, or 'fame' (*kleos*) is what the typical epic hero craves and
it is what motivates Odysseus in our tale. According to Athena, Telemachus needs to be
educated in the concept.

right on the threshold of the courtyard. Bronze spear in hand
she made herself resemble Odysseus' Ithacan ally **Mentes**, leader
of the Taphians.   1.105

And there she found the **mighty** suitors. They
sat before the doorway, happily rolling their dice and
sitting on the hides of the cows they had slaughtered.
Their messengers and nimble attendants were on hand:
some were mixing wine and water in the large bowls,   1.110
others were cleaning the tables carefully with sponges
and setting them up, while others set about divvying up the abundant meat.
      Godlike Telemachus was the very first to spot Athena;
he sat among the suitors grieving in his heart,
looking in hope for his noble father, that he might come   1.115
and rout the suitors there in the palace,
regain his honour and rule as king over what was his.
      Sitting with these thoughts in mind Telemachus saw Athena
and made straight for the courtyard, angered in his heart that
a **stranger** had stood outside for so long. He stood close to her,   1.120
grasped her right hand, and took the bronze spear.
As he addressed her the words flew from his mouth:
'Greetings, stranger and guest, you will find hospitality here: then after
dining you can tell me what you've come to say.'
With these words he led her in and Pallas Athena followed.   1.125
Once they were within the lofty hall

Mentes   Athena makes her first appearance on earth disguised as Mentes. As Odysseus' patron goddess it is no surprise to find her concealing herself and, in effect, lying. Mentes is an outsider, not a native Ithacan, and as S. West 1988 notes, 'the shocked reaction of a stranger is more effective than any words which could be put in the mouth of Mentor' (Telemachus' next major adviser, whom we meet in Book 2, and from whose name we get our word 'mentor'). Note the subtlety of the intervention: just as earlier she appealed to Zeus' sense of justice, here Athena merely appeals to Telemachus' desire for fame and a good reputation to get him moving.

mighty   the suitors are routinely given positive epithets like 'mighty', even in the mouths of their enemies. The reader is cautioned not to read too much into the significance of these epithets, which belong to the fixed repertoire of epic language (see p. 7). They do not necessarily represent an endorsement of the suitors, but simply characterize them as powerful and the leading men of the region.

Their messengers and nimble attendants   these are freeborn men, not slaves, who perform a variety of tasks for their lords, just as they do for the heroes of the *Iliad*.

stranger   *xeinos* can also be translated 'guest' or 'host'; hospitality (*xeinia*) is based on the same word; it is a key concept in Odysseus' world and will feature prominently in the poem (e.g. in Book 9). Telemachus' concern for his guest here contrasts strongly with the suitors, whose extended stay and bad behaviour have violated the norms of hospitality.

he took her spear and stood it next to a large column
within a polished spear-case, where in fact many
other spears stood that belonged to great-hearted Odysseus.
He led her to a chair and seated her, spreading fine cloth in the seat;   1.130
the chair was beautifully made and underneath was a stool for her feet.
Next to her he drew up a fine couch. They sat apart
from the suitors so that Telemachus' guest would not be annoyed at their noise
and lose interest in the meal; she had come to the company of arrogant men
and she was there to ask Telemachus about his absent father.   1.135
　　　　A slave-girl brought a water jug made out of beautiful gold
and poured water over their hands, holding a silver basin below
so that they could rinse them clean. Nearby them she laid out a table
　　　　　　　　　　　　　　　　　　　　　　　　　　of carved wood.
A dutiful steward then brought the food and put it before them;
there was a good deal of it and she gave generously of what she had.   1.140
A carver brought platters of all kinds of meat and put it
before them; he also brought golden goblets,
while one of the messengers immediately approached them to pour some wine.

> 1   Why does Homer have Athena appear in disguise? Wouldn't a direct divine
>   appearance (i.e. an epiphany) be more effective?
>
> 2   Why does Homer mention that Telemachus was the first to notice Athena /
>   Mentes?
>
> 3   Why does Homer mention Odysseus' spears in line 129?

1.144–77　　Then the proud suitors all entered the hall. As they
took their seats, rank and file, among the couches and chairs,   1.145
the messengers poured water over their hands,
slave-girls heaped up the food in baskets,
and boys filled their bowls to the brim with drink.
The suitors then started on the food that had been placed before them,
and once they had had enough food   1.150
and drink, other concerns occupied their minds:
song and dance – the crowning glories of a meal.
One of the messengers put a fine lyre into the hands
of **Phemius**, whom the suitors forced to sing.

Phemius   with the introduction of Phemius we find Homer's playful self-consciousness
at work; we are inevitably invited to compare the singers of the *Odyssey* with Homer
himself, and indeed, these audiences with ourselves (see Segal 1994, chapters 6–8); note
that Phemius is spared when Odysseus kills the suitors in Book 22. His name is based on
the word 'report', or 'talk', even 'rumour' (*phēmē*): his job is to spread the fame of gods
and men.

Just as he put his hands to the instrument and began his fine song,   1.155
Telemachus addressed Bright-eyed Athena,
leaning in close to her head so that the others couldn't hear him:
'Friend and guest, if I were to say something would it anger you?
Music and poetry: that's all these men care
about – and it's easy enough for them – they are consuming the livelihood
                                                    of another   1.160
without fear of reprisal! Meanwhile his white bones lie rotting in the rain
somewhere on land – or ocean waves wash over them in the sea!
If these men were to see him return to Ithaca
they would all pray for more speed to make a getaway
than for more money to spend on fancy clothes.   1.165
But as it is, this man has died horribly, and even if some mortal were to tell us
that he's on his way back, it will hardly bring
us any comfort: his day of return is gone.
But come now, tell me this and speak truly:
who are you and who is your father? Where is your city and what is
                                                    your family line?   1.170
What sort of ship did you come in? How did the sailors
bring you to Ithaca? Who in fact did they profess to be?
I suspect that you didn't get here on foot!
Answer me truly so that I can know
whether you are visiting us for the first time or are one of my father's   1.175
guest-friends. Many men have come to our
home and he was fond of visiting others.'

> 1 Why does Telemachus wait for Phemius to start singing before he speaks to
>   Athena / Mentes?
> 2 What do you make of Telemachus' attitude in this conversation?
> 3 What do we learn about the suitors at their first appearance?

1.178–266   Bright-eyed goddess Athena replied to Telemachus:
'I will then speak truly about what you ask:
I contend that I am Mentes, son of wise   1.180
Anchialus, and I am king of the oar-loving Taphians.
That's how I got here: with my companions and our ship.
I was sailing over the wine-dark sea among foreigners
to Temesa, in search of bronze, and I'm shipping ruddy iron.

Homeric society and history

Athena's mention of bronze and iron neatly encapsulates the fictional world of the *Odyssey*. The poem portrays elements of life drawn from the Bronze Age (2000–1100 BC) as well as the Iron Age (1100–800 BC) of Greece. So, for example, the weapons are bronze but we also find the more recently developed and tougher iron in use (compare **9.393**). It is therefore over-simplifying matters to think of Homeric society as representing a particular time-period; some details may reflect realities of Homer's own day, while others hearken back to an earlier period – perhaps because they are deliberately and nostalgically setting the poem in an age of heroes or because the oral tradition stretches back to a time when weapons were still made out of bronze. Scholars differ widely on exactly how to relate a given element of Homeric society to the realities of Homer's own day or earlier periods (see Osborne 2004 and Morris 1997 for useful overviews), yet surely the mention of shipping here reflects the realities of expanding trade in early Greece, and it lends an element of realism to our epic. Temesa may refer to Tamassos on the island of Cyprus, a well-known source of copper, used in the production of bronze. Other people (Taphians) and places (Rheithrum, Neium) cannot be located geographically.

My ship stands out in the countryside, away from the city,   1.185
in the port of Rheithrum, just under the woods of Neium.
We contend that we have been guest-friends of your father, and he of us,
from the beginning: go and ask aged Lord
Laertes – I've heard that he no longer comes
into town but rather lives out in the countryside, suffering,   1.190
his only company being the old slave-woman who brings him his food
and drink when exhaustion lays hold of his limbs
as he shuffles along the hills of his fruitful vineyard.
So, here I am. People were telling me that he was here at home,
your father, but it seems the gods are keeping him from his journey.   1.195
But our splendid Odysseus has not died somewhere on land:
he is being detained somewhere out on the wide sea,
on some sea-girt island, where harsh men are holding him captive;
some savages are keeping him somewhere against his will.
But let me hazard a guess as to what the immortals   1.200
are aiming at and how I think this story will end,
though I am certainly no seer and have no knowledge of augury.
Odysseus will not, I am sure, be far away from his beloved
fatherland, not even if chains of iron hold him now.
He is resourceful: he will be contemplating how to make his return.   1.205
But come now, speak and tell me truthfully:
are you Odysseus' child? You are the right size,

and there is a strong resemblance in your eyes
and face. He and I met quite often
before he sailed for Troy, where other   1.210
fine Argives went as well, sailing in the hollow ships.
But since then I have not seen Odysseus, nor he me.'
       Shrewd Telemachus then replied to her in turn:
'Well then, dear guest, I too will speak truly:
My mother says that I am his son, but I   1.215
don't know – no one can prove his paternity.
How I wish I were the son of a lucky
man – one whom old age overtakes while still in charge of his possessions.
But as it is, since this is what you're asking,
the man they say was my father was the unluckiest of all men.'   1.220
       Bright-eyed goddess Athena then replied:
'The gods have certainly not given you a family meant to be inglorious,
not with Penelope as your mother, at least!
But come now, tell me this and speak truly:
What's this thronging feast for? And how are you involved?   1.225
Has someone funded a special banquet, or was there a wedding? This is no
                                   potluck supper:
these creatures seem so arrogant to me,
feasting everywhere in the palace. Any person of sense
coming in here would be outraged to see such shamelessness!'
       Shrewd Telemachus then replied to her in turn: 1.230
'If this is in fact the object of your enquiry, my friend and guest,
then let me speak: at one point this house was meant to be wealthy,
meant to be perfect – as long as that man was still resident.
But as it is, the gods wanted something else: a plan of misfortune.
They have wiped out all knowledge of him – more than any   1.235
other man – by making it impossible for me even to grieve for his death:
if he had fallen with his companions among the Trojans
or died in the company of those he loved after **winding off** the thread of war,
then all of Greece would have made him a burial mound,
and he would have won a glorious future for his son.   1.240
But, as it is, the storm winds have snatched him away without a trace!
He's gone: unknown, unheard of, leaving me only pain
and sorrow. But now I find myself crying these tears not just for him

---

winding off the verb literally means 'to wind up a ball of thread'; the imagery of
weaving abounds in the *Odyssey* (see Clayton 2004, especially chapter 2): gods, men,
women and poets are all portrayed as weaving in one way or another; the image works
particularly well for the narrative 'strands' of the epic.

alone: the gods have fashioned more heartache for me:
all the chief men in power over the islands of   1.245
Dulichium and Samé and woody Zacynthus,
as well as those in power throughout rocky Ithaca,
each one of these men is pursuing my mother's hand in marriage
                        and grinding down this house.
Meanwhile she does nothing to put off such a loathsome union nor is she
capable of bringing things to a conclusion, and they continue feasting and
                               destroying   1.250
my house. Soon they will do me in too!'
In indignation Pallas Athena then addressed Telemachus:
'This is terrible! You *do* need your missing
Odysseus: he would attack these shameful suitors!
How I wish he could come here and stand at the entrance   1.255
to this hall, with a helmet, a shield and two spears,
being just the man he was when I first came to know him:
he drank with me at my house and enjoyed himself there –
he was making his way from Ephyra after leaving **Ilus**, son of Mermerus.
Odysseus had gone there in his swift ship   1.260
in pursuit of deadly poison, something to
smear on his bronze-tipped arrows. But Ilus
didn't give him any, out of reverence for the immortal gods,
but my father did give him some: he was terribly fond of Odysseus!
But *that's* the kind of man Odysseus would be among these suitors: 1.265
they would all meet a quick end and regret these wedding plans of theirs.

---

1   Why do you think Athena feels the need to cook up this elaborate lie?

2   What is the effect of the frequent mention of the absent Odysseus?

Dulichium   there is debate about the relationship of these islands as described in the epic to modern-day Ithaca and surrounding islands (see Graziosi 2008). Attempts at locating places described in the *Odyssey* were already common in ancient times and continue to this day; however, poets rarely allow their imagination to be restricted by reality, not least in a work as full of fantasy as the *Odyssey*.

Ilus   he is not known elsewhere and Athena could, of course, be inventing him herself. Note that we find Odysseus connected to archery here right at the outset of the epic (so important for the conclusion), whereas in the *Iliad* he does not use a bow at all. Archery is frequently thought to be less heroic than manly, Iliadic hand-to-hand fighting (compare *Iliad* 11.385 and Sutherland 2001); to use poison would be particularly unheroic, hence Ilus' refusal here.

1.267–364   But you know, Telemachus, it lies completely in the lap of the gods
whether or not Odysseus will return and avenge himself
here in his palace. In the meantime, I urge you to think hard
about how you can drive these suitors out of here.   1.270
Come now, listen carefully to what I have to say:
call the Greek warriors to an assembly tomorrow
and make a proclamation to all of them, with the gods as your witnesses:
command the suitors to disperse and go back to their own homes
and tell your mother that if she is intent on marrying   1.275
she should go back home to her powerful father.
Her parents will lay on a wedding with all the right
gifts, just the right things for a beloved daughter.
Now as for you, I have a clever suggestion, if you'll listen:
set sail in your finest twenty-oared ship   1.280
and make a journey to find out about your long-absent father.
See if anyone can tell you anything or if you can find some news,
a report, anything – this kind of thing can confer distinction on you.

    First go to **Pylos** and talk to resplendent Nestor,
then go from there to Sparta and to fair-haired Menelaus: 1.285
he was the last of the bronze-mailed Achaeans to reach home.
If you hear that your father is alive and making his way home,
you could endure another year here, despite this stress;
but if you hear that he is dead and no longer with us,
then come back here to your beloved fatherland,   1.290
make a memorial monument and lay on a large funeral
for him, one that would be appropriate, and find a husband for your mother.
Then once you've carried out these tasks
next think deeply in your heart and mind
about how to put the suitors to death, here in your palace.   1.295
Are you going to use a trap or do it in the open? Your age, after all, is no longer
that of a child, and you must not behave like one.
Surely you've heard how resplendent Orestes met with unanimous
                                          approval and
glory when he killed his father's murderer:

Pylos Bronze Age Pylos (see map, p. iv) has yielded rich archaeological discoveries attesting to Mycenaean civilization (Sparta less so), including a palace that has been dubbed 'Nestor's palace' containing storerooms and some clay tablets written in the Mycenaean script known as Linear B that served as records of wares (see Shelmerdine 2008 and Cline 2010 for surveys). The general picture of palace life we gain from archaeology confirms that possessions were an important marker of status in Bronze Age Mycenaean society, and underscores why the depletion of the family's supplies is seen by Penelope, Telemachus and Odysseus as such a problem.

wily Aegisthus had killed his famous father!   1.300
And you, my friend, be brave – I can see you're fit, handsome and in good
fighting form: let those who come after us speak well of you.
But as for now I'll go back to my swift ship
and companions: they are probably fed up with waiting for me.
But think about what I've said, Telemachus: think carefully.'   1.305
            Shrewd Telemachus then addressed her in turn:
'Guest and friend: it's clear to me that what you say is meant with
                                                    genuine kindness –
towards both father and son – and I won't forget this.
But come now, stay with me here: I know you want to be on your way,
but have a bath, take some refreshment for yourself,   1.310
enjoy yourself and accept a gift from me before you return to your ship:
I've got something good in mind, something beautiful, something
that you will want to pass down, just the sort of thing that guest-friends
                                                    exchange with one another.'
            Bright-eyed goddess Athena then replied to him:
'Don't detain me any longer now: I am quite keen to start my journey.   1.315
As for your gift: give this object of beauty to me
to take home when I return – give me whatever
your heart desires – and you will have a gift in exchange that is equal in value.'
            With these words Bright-eyed Athena departed:
she flew upwards, just like a bird. But she put   1.320
strength and courage in Telemachus' heart, and she made him think of his
                                                    father
more than ever before. He felt this in his heart
and was deeply **surprised**: it occurred to him that Mentes was a god,
and godlike he now made straight for the suitors.
At that moment the well-known poet was performing for his audience,
                                                    and they sat   1.325
listening in silence. He was singing about the homecoming of the Achaeans
that Pallas Athena had inflicted upon them and how painful and pitiful it was.
            Clever Penelope, daughter of Icarius,
contemplated the god-sent music as she sat in her room above the hall
and not alone did she descend the high palace   1.330
staircase: two attendants followed her.
In feminine splendour she reached the suitors

---

surprised amazement is routinely the human reaction to divine appearances and
interventions in Greek literature. Note the irony of the situation: while Athena has
been conversing with Telemachus, Phemius has been performing the *nostoi*-song, now
described in the following lines – the very misery she herself created (line 327; see 4.502)!
Such irony is frequent in the *Odyssey*.

and stood next to the finely wrought central pillar of the palace,
holding a sleek and shiny veil over her cheeks.
Her trusted attendants took their place on either side.   1.335
In tears she then addressed the inspired poet:
'Phemius, seeing that you know much other material that can charm
                                                men's minds,
those deeds of man and god that poets make famous,
take your seat and sing something from this for the men as they drink
                                               their wine
in silence. But stop singing this sad   1.340
song that always breaks my
heart: unforgettable grief hits me particularly hard.
When you put me in this state of mind I always think of my husband, and I
miss him: all of Greece and Argos know his story.'
        Shrewd Telemachus then addressed her in turn: 1.345
'Mother, why do you insist that a poet who is loyal to our family
not give pleasure to others and go wherever his mind takes him? Poets are
not guilty here: it's Zeus, I think you'll find, who's responsible: he controls
humble mortal life however it suits him.
Don't be angry with Phemius for singing about the disasters that have
                                      befallen the sons of Danaus.   1.350
People talk more about a poem
when it concerns **what's new**.
Be strong in your heart and dare to listen:
Odysseus was not after all the only man to lose his day of homecoming
in Troy: many other men died.   1.355
Go back to your rooms and get back to your work
at spinning and weaving wool, and tell your attendants
to do the same. **Talk** is for us menfolk,
all of us, and particularly me, since I'm the one in charge of Odysseus' palace.'
Penelope was taken aback at this and retreated back to her rooms,   1.360
contemplating carefully the shrewd words of her son.
Once she and her attendants were upstairs
she then wept for her beloved husband Odysseus until Bright-eyed
Athena enveloped her eyes with sweet sleep.

what's new as S. West 1988 observes: 'since much modern writing on oral epic emphasizes the importance of the familiar and traditional, it is interesting to find the poet stressing the value of novelty'. In the fictional context the *nostoi* of the Greek leaders are indeed recent history.

Talk the last four lines of Telemachus' speech are nearly identical with Hector's famous last words to Andromache in the *Iliad* (6.490–3); the only difference is that 'talk' here replaces the word 'war' in the *Iliad* passage.

1 Why does finding his father's body seem to be so important for Telemachus?

2 What can we learn about the circumstances in which poems like the *Odyssey* were performed from the description of Phemius in action?

3 How is Penelope characterized in her first appearance? Why might she cover her face with a veil?

4 Is Telemachus being too hard on Penelope in his response to her comment? What might Homer be trying to show through this incident?

5 What do you think Penelope feels about Telemachus' 'shrewd words' as she thinks them over?

6 What do you make of Athena's interference? Does it make Telemachus seem more heroic (in that he is visited by a goddess) or less so?

7 Telemachus' narrative strand in the *Odyssey* is frequently thought of as portraying the young man's coming of age. As you follow his character through the poem, do you agree with this assessment?

1.365–411

The suitors, meanwhile, filled the dark hall with their loud chatter.   1.365
They clamoured for sleep, and bed.
Shrewd Telemachus began to speak to them:
'You insufferably arrogant creatures, all after my mother's hand in marriage,
for the moment let's enjoy our feasting and put an end to this
shouting: we ought to listen to this fine   1.370
poet: he has the voice of a god.
But in the morning let's all sit down and meet
in an assembly, where I will issue you an explicit proclamation of
eviction – you have devoured all that we own and
it's time to find your meals and residence elsewhere.   1.375
But if you decide that you prefer wiping out a solitary
man's livelihood without consequence,
fine – keep fleecing me. But if Zeus ever permits acts of vengeance,
I will call upon the everlasting gods for their help,
and you will die, here within the palace, with no one to avenge you.'   1.380
        After these words all the suitors, bit their lips in deep
shock at Telemachus, who had addressed them so courageously.
Antinous, son of Eupeithes, replied:
'Only the gods, Telemachus, could have taught you
to brag like this and speak so courageously.   1.385
I pray that the Son of Cronus won't make you king over sea-girt
Ithaca just because it should come to you by birth.'
        Shrewd Telemachus then addressed him in turn:
'Though what I have to say will anger you, Antinous,
I would in fact like to take the kingship if Zeus will give it to me.   1.390
Or is it that you feel kingship is an evil in itself?
It cannot be a bad thing: it immediately brings you a wealthy
home and it brings you more fame and distinction.

There are already princes among the Achaeans, and there are
plenty of them here in sea-girt Ithaca, both young and old –   1.395
any of these could become king here now that resplendent Odysseus is dead.
But I will become king over the **house** that belongs to us,
and king over our slaves, the ones that resplendent Odysseus captured
                                                              and left for me.'
Then Eurymachus, son of Polybus, addressed him in reply:
'As to who will rule over the Achaeans in sea-girt Ithaca, Telemachus,   1.400
these matters are really for the gods to decide.
But as for you and your possessions and this palace: you should in fact
                                                              rule here.
As long as Ithaca still stands we must not allow anyone to come
and deprive you of your possessions by force and violence.
But I want to ask you, my good man, about your guest: 1.405
where was this man from? What country did he lay claim
to hail from? And where does he trace his family line and fatherland?
Was he here to convey some news about your father's return?
Or was he here to pursue some business of his own?
It's a shame he left so quickly: we didn't have time   1.410
to recognize him, and he seemed distinguished.'

- Antinous is the chief suitor and Eurymachus is his closest competition.
  Though we will only get a glimpse of them in this partial translation of the
  poem, how might you contrast them based on these two speeches alone?

1.412–44   Shrewd Telemachus then addressed him in turn:
'You know, Eurymachus, that my father's homecoming is a lost cause.
I no longer believe the reports – if in fact they still come in –
and should my mother summon and question   1.415
a prophet here I do not care for what he has to say.
The man was an old guest-friend of my father's, from Taphos,
and said he was Mentes, son of wise

---

house   it has been argued that Homer's presentation of the power-structure on Ithaca
is muddled, possibly the result of a mixture of source material. The Greek word used in
line 394 of the suitors ('princes') is the same as that translated as 'king' in 396 and 397, i.e.
basileus: it is clearly a term with varying meanings, referring to important local chieftains,
who each as local *basileus* controls his own house and territory, and who seem to be
vying for overall dominance (i.e. to be head *basileus*) now that Odysseus is dead. It would
seem that Odysseus' house (*oikos*) is of central importance and that marriage to Penelope
would convey to the successful suitor a distinct advantage in the power struggle. At the
same time, Telemachus seems to be staking his own claim to control of the house. For a
good overview of Homeric society as it can be constructed from the *Iliad* and *Odyssey*,
see Raaflaub 1997.

*Greeks at play in a typical symposium; the atmosphere here cannot be far from that in Odysseus' palace (**1.421–2**); paintings from the Tomb of the Diver, Paestum, fifth century BC.*

Anchialus and king of the oar-loving Taphians.'

Thus Telemachus spoke, though he knew in his heart that Mentes
was in fact Athena.   1.420

Meanwhile the suitors turned to the pleasures of
dance and the charms of poetry and song as they waited for nightfall.
Eventually black evening came as they revelled,
then each left for home in search of sleep.

Meanwhile Telemachus went off to bed with a great deal on
his mind.   1.425

His bedroom sat high in the beautiful palace
courtyard, with a commanding view.
True-hearted Euryclea, daughter of Ops (who was son of Peisenor),
followed him and carried torches that burned brightly.
Laertes had long ago purchased Euryclea for his estate   1.430
at a time when she was still on the cusp of adolescence. He gave twenty
oxen for her,
and he honoured her in the palace as though she were his wife.
Yet he never bedded her – he sought instead to avoid his wife's anger.

Euryclea slave-women such as Euryclea were usually taken as spoils of war or through kidnapping or piracy, and fulfilled a variety of duties in the household. These sometimes included serving as the concubine of their master – in Book 4, for example, we witness the wedding preparations for Megapenthes, Menelaus' son by a slave-woman (4.11–12). Euryclea's treatment by Laertes, therefore, is singled out for comment here; it introduces a strand that runs through the poem in which sexual *mores* are symptomatic of a character's ethics. S. West 1988 notes that the patronymic 'daughter of Ops' here is 'markedly honorific' for Euryclea – slaves do not normally have lines of descent in Homer.

It was this Euryclea who followed Telemachus and carried the bright
                                              torches. Of all the slaves
she particularly loved him: she had raised him from a baby.   1.435
He opened the door of his artfully made bedchamber,
sat himself on the bed, and removed his fine soft tunic
and put it in the hands of the careful old woman.
She smoothed it over and folded it,
then hung it on a peg next to the inlaid bed.   1.440
On leaving the bedroom she closed the door by the curved silver
handle and stretched the strap over the bolt.
Telemachus covered himself in his fine wool blanket and thought deeply
the whole night long about the path that Athena had shown him.

> With the close of the day we find the close of the book, a common epic pattern.
> We as readers find ourselves exactly in Telemachus' position; he is pondering
> what will happen just as we are. He is a sort of stand-in for the reader.

1 Are you sympathetic towards Telemachus? How has Homer communicated
   his character?
2 How successful is Book 1 as an introduction for the epic?

Book 2

In Book 2 the great debate in the assembly is held: in colourful and emotional
speeches Telemachus makes his case and then the suitors make theirs. The
latter complain that Penelope has been deceiving them by unravelling Laertes'
funereal shroud (Book 19 reveals the full story) and assert that they will not leave
until she has chosen a husband. Despite an omen from Zeus that is favourable
to Telemachus (two eagles fly close by), the suitors jeer and refuse to budge.
Odysseus' friend Mentor then stands up to speak, finding fault with the present
company for allowing the suitors to get away with their behaviour. The suitor
Leocritus dismisses him scornfully and claims that even if Odysseus does come
back, he will have a difficult time fighting the suitors on his own. Leocritus then
breaks up the assembly and the suitors return to the palace.

Telemachus goes to the beach and prays to Athena to help him make his journey.
Athena then appears in the guise of Mentor and tells him that (s)he expects great
things of him, that the suitors will soon die, and that (s)he will prepare him a ship
and accompany him on the journey that very night. Telemachus then returns
to the palace to get things ready. Antinous approaches, telling him to relax and
join the feasting. He promises Telemachus that the suitors will supply him with a
ship. Telemachus becomes angry, refuses to join in the feasting, and threatens to

'bring destruction' on the suitors in time, asserting that he will indeed go to Pylos, even though his resources are limited. The suitors mock him and note his express intention to kill them. Telemachus visits the storeroom – set to play a significant role at the end of the epic – and asks Euryclea to prepare 12 jars of wine for his journey (the wine has been preserved all this time for the return of Odysseus). She is to keep all this a secret from Penelope. Euryclea protests that he will die either out at sea or, on returning, at the hands of the suitors; Telemachus tells her not to fear and not to tell Penelope. Euryclea swears she will do all this.

Athena then gets involved in the action again by transforming herself into the likeness of Telemachus. In this disguise she instructs 'all the men of Ithaca' to meet at Telemachus' ship that evening. She then prepares the ship and its crew, and causes the suitors and the Ithacans all to fall into a deep sleep. She assumes the guise of Mentor again and hurries Telemachus along, leading him down to the sea; everyone boards, Athena sends a favourable wind, and the crew push off and pour a libation to all the gods – 'in particular to the Grey-eyed daughter of Zeus'. With the closing line of the book we see the ship sailing quickly through the night.

Book 3

Book 3 opens with the sunrise as Telemachus reaches Pylos, where the inhabitants are making a huge sacrifice to Poseidon. Athena, still in the guise of Mentor, encourages Telemachus, who is feeling shy, to approach Nestor. Pisistratus, one of Nestor's sons, greets them warmly and asks them to join the sacrifice. After the sacrifices Nestor enquires after his guests: do they mean good or ill? Athena puts courage into Telemachus as he asks about his missing father.

Nestor, true to his reputation, delivers a long-winded reply: not even if he had five or six years could he recall all the sufferings of the Greeks at Troy! He recalls the magnificent Odysseus and in particular how the two of them worked as a pair and were looked to for advice. Nestor lays the blame for the Greeks' disastrous homecoming squarely at Athena's feet, ironically enough: she had caused a quarrel between Menelaus and Agamemnon; the former wanted to set sail immediately but the latter wanted to sacrifice to Athena before leaving, in order to placate her anger. Homer does not at this point indicate why Athena is angry but we can assume this was due to Neoptolemus' rape of Cassandra in the temple of Athena at Troy. Nestor then relates how he departed with Menelaus the next day. Odysseus joined them, but then decided to return to Troy and Agamemnon. Nestor details some of the stops along the way, but his journey back to Pylos was quick and painless. He has heard some reports since reaching home: Achilles' troops, Philoctetes and Idomeneus all returned home safely, and we all know what happened to Agamemnon and Aegisthus; Nestor flatters Telemachus by comparing him directly to Orestes.

The death of Agamemnon was a popular theme throughout antiquity; this neoclassical rendition by Pierre Narcisse Guérin (1774–1833) follows the version where Clytemnestra, not Aegisthus, kills the king (see Odyssey 4.512–37).

Telemachus accepts the compliment and explains the situation in Ithaca, of which Nestor has apparently caught wind. He hopes that Athena will look after Telemachus just as she used to look after Odysseus at Troy and help him take revenge on the suitors. Telemachus feels overwhelmed at the prospect, but now Athena/Mentor ironically butts in and tells Telemachus that with a god on your side you can do anything. Telemachus, however, remains gloomy: Odysseus will never return; he changes the subject by asking Nestor for more detail on the fates of Agamemnon and Menelaus.

Nestor explains that the wicked Aegisthus seduced Clytemnestra. Agamemnon had even left a poet (!) to keep an eye on her, but Aegisthus did away with him. Meanwhile, he (Nestor) and Menelaus were at that time sailing home together, but they became separated when Zeus sent a storm. Menelaus then wandered abroad but collected much wealth. Aegisthus was king of Mycenae for seven years but Orestes killed him in the eighth year in revenge for his father's death. Menelaus reached home at that same time. Nestor advises Telemachus not to be far from home for too long, but recommends that he visit Menelaus and offers his own horses and sons as travelling companions.

As the sun sets, Athena/Mentor urges the company to sacrifice to Poseidon. After they do so, Telemachus and Athena/Mentor make for their ship, to sleep on board, but Nestor generously refuses this. Athena/Mentor then cunningly suggests that Telemachus alone should stay while he sets sail at dawn on a private mission. Athena then suddenly transforms herself into a vulture and flies away, stunning the entire company. Nestor, excited, assures Telemachus of his future and promises a special sacrifice to Athena.

In the morning Nestor holds an assembly with his six sons and Telemachus. He is keen to prepare a magnificent sacrifice for Athena. The goddess is present as the elaborate ritual takes place. The youngest daughter of Nestor then bathes Telemachus, who comes out looking like a god, then the feasting begins. At the close of the meal, Nestor arranges for his son Pisistratus to travel by horse and chariot with Telemachus to see Menelaus in Sparta. They travel all day long with Pisistratus at the reins, spend the night with a friend, and travel all day long again; as the book closes they have reached Sparta.

Book 4

As Book 4 opens, Menelaus and his wife Helen welcome Telemachus to their palace in Sparta. Menelaus' memories of Odysseus in Troy provoke Telemachus to tears and the entire company is seen crying; Helen now intriguingly puts a drug in everyone's wine to keep them from crying, and then confidently joins the storytelling herself.

4.235–89   'Menelaus, Zeus-cherished son of Atreus, and you,   4.235
fine sons of fine fathers: Zeus, in all his divinity, gives
both good and bad; sometimes to us, sometimes to others: he can do anything.
Sit now at our table, dine in our palace,
and enjoy one another's conversation – and I too will tell of things that
                                       suit the occasion.
         I could not comprehensively recount   4.240
all of great-hearted Odysseus' accomplishments,
but I will tell you what that mighty man dared to do
at Troy, where you Achaeans came to grief.
He punched himself in the face to disfigure himself;
he then dressed in filthy rags to look like a slave,   4.245
and then took to the wide avenues of a hostile city.
He concealed his identity and made himself look like
a beggar, someone who could bear no resemblance to the man he was
                                     among the Greek ships.

In this disguise he entered Troy, where no one
spotted him except for me: out of them all **I alone recognized** who he was.   4.250
I began asking him questions, but he cunningly evaded me.
          After I had **bathed him** and anointed him with oil
I put some clothes on him and swore on no uncertain terms
that I would not reveal him to the Trojans
before he could make it back to the swift Greek ships and their huts
                                    on the beach.   4.255
He then explained to me what the Achaean forces had in mind,
and after killing many Trojans with his sharp bronze sword
he made it back to the Argives and disclosed a great deal of information
                                    to them.
While the rest of the Trojan women cried out in lamentation, I was
delighted. I had had a change of heart and wanted to come   4.260
back home, and I regretted that **destructive infatuation**, that *thing* that
                                    Aphrodite
had gifted me when she took me there, away from my beloved fatherland,
separated from my daughter, my husband, and our relationship –
this man lacks nothing, neither in intelligence or looks.'
Handsome Menelaus then addressed her and replied: 4.265
'Well put, my wife: all of what you've said is good.
I have learned a great deal about how fighting men think
and how they act, and I've seen much of this world.
But these eyes have yet to behold anyone
like my beloved great-hearted Odysseus –   4.270

I alone recognized   Helen's story of Odysseus concealing himself as a beggar fits Odysseus like a glove and foreshadows what he will come to do once he lands on Ithaca; her claim that she alone recognized him provokes a comparison between her and Penelope, and raises the question of whether the latter will recognize him. It is worth noting that Odysseus was originally one of Helen's many suitors before she married Menelaus; the theme was treated in Hesiod's now-lost *Suitors of Helen*.

bathed him   bathing guests is a common token of hospitality in epic and is described in formulaic language that we find repeated from one scene to the next; we may compare Calypso's (Book 5), Nausicaa's (Book 6) and ultimately Penelope's (Books 19 and 23) treatment of Odysseus. Even in these formulaic scenes, however, there is remarkable variation in how the scenes are put to use in advancing the plot. Spreading oil on skin after a bath was common in the ancient Mediterranean.

destructive infatuation   Helen's claims that Aphrodite, the goddess of love, sent her destructive infatuation (Greek *atē*), another key concept in the world of Homer (see especially Dodds 1951, chapter 1), might be taken as a way of absolving herself of some of the responsibility (see 4.503 and **23.222**). The question of whether Helen was responsible for causing the Trojan War was variously answered in ancient literature.

and what that mighty man dared to do
in the **Wooden Horse**. We all were sitting there inside – the finest Greek
fighters – bringing death and doom to Troy.
Then you, Helen, approached us – some god
probably summoned you, one that wanted to give the Trojans a chance

at glory.   4.275

Godlike **Deiphobus** followed you out as you came towards us.
You walked around that hollow trap three times, feeling all along its sides,
and you called out for each of us, the finest Danaans, naming us one by one,
in perfect imitation of each Argive's wife.
Diomedes, the magnificent Odysseus and I,   4.280
we were sitting in the centre of the horse and we heard you clearly.
Two of us you upset deeply: we became anxious:
should we get right out or keep listening secretly from inside?
But Odysseus kept us from acting on impulse,
and at this point all the other sons of Achaea also fell silent,   4.285
though **Anticlus** alone wanted to reply
to you. But Odysseus mercilessly squeezed
his mouth shut in his mighty hands – and thereby saved all the Achaeans.
He held him tight until Pallas Athene led you away.'

---

1   Many of the lines from 276 to 289 were criticized in antiquity as spurious and un-Homeric: what do you think of Helen's actions here? Is she being loyal to the Greeks or the Trojans?

2   What do you make of the fact that Menelaus reminisces over a story that could put his wife in a bad light? Can you detect any hostility between the king and queen? How might this be relevant for the overall story of the *Odyssey*?

3   In what ways does Helen's story differ from that of Menelaus in its focus?

Wooden Horse   this is of course the Trojan Horse, Odysseus' invention and the means by which the Greeks were able to infiltrate Troy and defeat the Trojans; see the end of Book 8 and **9.20** for more details, including Odysseus' role in devising the plan.

Deiphobus   one of the Trojan king Priam's sons and a great warrior in the *Iliad*, he became Helen's husband after the death of Paris. (In Book 6 of Virgil's *Aeneid* the ghost of Deiphobus relates that Helen betrayed him during the sack of Troy, and led Menelaus to his bedroom, where he killed him.)

Diomedes   he is one of the greatest of the Greek heroes in the *Iliad*, where Books 5 and 6 are largely given over to his exploits. *Iliad* 10 describes his joint venture with Odysseus in which they sneak into the Trojan camp at night and wreak havoc.

Anticlus   he is not known otherwise, but this scene foreshadows the climactic moment when Odysseus silences Euryclea in Book 19.

4.290–5

Shrewd Telemachus then replied in turn: 4.290
'Menelaus, Zeus-cherished son of Atreus, leader of armies,
this story makes the situation even more painful. This bravery didn't keep
                                                  the poor man from dying –
even if he had a heart of pure iron he would have died.
But come now, show us the way to bed so we can enjoy
some rest and the sweetness of sleep.'   4.295

296–847 (end)

With these words Helen looks after the guests' sleeping arrangements and the company goes to bed. In the morning Menelaus finds Telemachus and asks him exactly why he's come. Telemachus explains that he's after news of his father and he describes the situation with the suitors; Menelaus responds with surprise that the suitors would attempt such folly – surely Odysseus will return and kill them all. Menelaus now relates how on his way home he was detained in Egypt because he hadn't performed the requisite sacrifices to the gods. The goddess Eidothea, daughter of the Old Man of the Sea (a magical shape-shifter a.k.a. Proteus), pities him and explains a way out: he must capture her father, who will tell him what he needs to know – and more. She devises a trick to help Menelaus; on the next morning they execute their curious plan: Menelaus and his men hide in sealskins supplied by Eidothea; when the Old Man of the Sea appears, Menelaus traps him and learns the fate of his fellow Greeks, including his now-murdered brother Agamemnon. Odysseus, it is revealed, is being held by force on the island of Calypso. Menelaus concludes his narrative of how he made it home safely and invites his guests to stay with him. Telemachus politely declines; he is keen to get home. Homer now changes the scene back to Ithaca, where we find the suitors learning that Telemachus has made for Pylos and Sparta. The report infuriates them and they plan to ambush Telemachus and put him to death on his way back. Medon the herald overhears the suitors' plans and loyally informs Penelope; she is shocked to learn that her son has left on this mission and fears he will be lost out on the sea, just like Odysseus. She tries to sleep but can't out of anxiety for her son; when she finally does, Athena sends a comforting dream; the book closes with the suitors installed in their ambush. We won't see Telemachus again, however, until Book 15: we have reached the end of the 'Telemachy'.

---

1   What parallels can you detect between Menelaus and Odysseus?

2   It has long been a popular view to see Telemachus as maturing over the course of the *Odyssey*, probably under the influence of the French novelist Fénelon's romanticizing *Les aventures de Télémaque*, published in 1699. How has Telemachus matured (if at all) over the course of these books?

Part Two (Books 5–8): Ingenious Odysseus

Book 5

5.1–91   Dawn arose from the bed she shared with noble
Tithonus so that she could bring light to immortal and mortal alike.
The gods went to sit in their thrones and among them was
Zeus, High Thunderer, whose might is supreme.
Athena sought to address them, preoccupied with the many troubles   5.5
of Odysseus. The fact that he was in the palace of Lady Calypso made
                                                                                her anxious.
'Father Zeus and you other blessed gods who live eternally,
let no human king in power be kind, mild or gentle
any more! Let there be no more room for justice in his heart!
Rather let kings be harsh, let them commit acts of injustice!   5.10
Why? Because out of all his former subjects not a single one can remember
divine Odysseus – and how gentle he was with them.
Meanwhile he lies out on some island suffering wretchedly
in the palace of Lady Calypso: she's keeping him there
by force and he cannot return to his fatherland.   5.15
He has no ships nor men to sail them there;
no one can send him on his way over the broad back of the sea.
And now they actually want to kill his beloved son
on his return journey! He went to holy Pylos and resplendent
Sparta to get information about his father.'   5.20
In reply Cloud-gatherer Zeus addressed her:

Tithonus   the book opens with the coming of Dawn (Eos), as frequently in the epic, yet uniquely here we also find mention of Tithonus, Dawn's consort. The detail is fitting: the goddess was so deeply in love with this mortal that she made him immortal (but famously and unfortunately neglected to make him unageing); he forms a suitable comparison for Odysseus, whom Calypso wishes to make immortal (though she in his case does intend to make him unageing, see **5.136**).

Athena sought to address   Athena now addresses a second divine council; the words she uses here (lines 8–12) are an exact echo of words Telemachus uses in the assembly of Book 2 (lines 230–4). Some critics find this second council unnecessary in the light of the first one (**1.26–95**) and therefore evidence of interpolation (i.e. a later addition), yet it sets the stage afresh and adds an element of gravity: we are just about to meet our hero for the first time in person. The practice of initiating a sequence of narrative, interrupting it, then resuming it again is referred to as 'ring composition'; it is characteristic of Homeric technique and will be seen again, e.g. in the framing of Books 9–12.

'What an extraordinary thing to say, my child!
Isn't this what you planned? Didn't you actually mean for
Odysseus to take revenge on them on his return?
Now go and send Telemachus home – do it carefully: you can manage this – 5.25
get him back to his fatherland completely unscathed,
and get the suitors and their ships back home as well.'
As he spoke he then addressed Hermes, his dear son:
'You, Hermes, are my messenger, and I need you to do this for me.
Tell the beautiful Lady Calypso my infallible decree: 5.30
great-hearted Odysseus is coming home,
and no god or mortal man is to send him on his way.
No: on the twentieth day of suffering on a tightly fitted boat
he will come to the shores of fertile **Scheria**,
land of the Phaeacians, near and dear to the gods.   5.35
They will revere him greatly in their hearts – like a god –
and they will send him on a ship to his beloved fatherland,
with many gifts of bronze, gold and fine garments;
they will give him more than he could ever have taken from Troy
had he come home safe with his fair share of the **war-booty**.   5.40
It is Odysseus' **destiny** to see his loved ones and reach
his fine home and fatherland.'
Messenger Hermes, **Slayer of Argus**, acted swiftly in obedience

What an extraordinary thing to say   the Greek here is literally 'what sort of word has escaped the fence of your teeth'; the phrase is reminiscent of the 'winged words' that I have translated as 'vigorous language' etc. (e.g. **9.409**). Such phrases are archaic and vivid but also formulaic and frequently repeated; I have opted for something in English that captures the tone of the context.

Scheria   on Scheria and the Phaeacians, see note on **6.4**.

war-booty   this and treasure in general, like fame (*kleos*), is of fundamental importance to a Homeric hero; it is an indication of status.

destiny   unlike so much of our experience with, say, contemporary fiction, we have known since **1.17** that it is Odysseus' destiny to make it home; what matters in the Homeric narrative is evidently not so much *suspense* as *how* the story unfolds. We might compare ancient Greek tragedy: normally the audience already knows much of what will happen through the mythical tradition, passed down in childhood; what matters is how the action unfolds and how the characters experience it. There is some debate among scholars as to the relationship of the gods and destiny (or fate) in Homer, yet it makes good sense (in my opinion) to take destiny as identical to the will of the gods – especially that of Zeus: see box on p. 43.

Slayer of Argus   the epithet (encountered at **1.39** and **1.84**) refers to the myth of Io: Hera, in a jealous rage, had set the watchful Argus over Zeus' beloved Io (whom she had transformed into a cow); Argus had several eyes (in some versions up to one hundred!) and Hermes craftily used his wand, described here, to lull him to sleep and kill him, at Zeus' behest.

to Zeus' orders and bound fine sandals beneath his feet –
divine, golden sandals – which took him over both endless land   5.45
and sea on the breezes of the wind.
He also took the wand he uses to cast a spell over human eyes –
all are prey to him – and he rouses them from sleep as well.
With this in hand the strong Slayer of Argus took flight.
As he descended from sky to sea he touched on the mountains of **Pieria**.   5.50
He skirted over the waves like a seagull
hunting for fish among the treacherous folds of the barren sea
and dipping his flapping wings in the sea-water –
that's how Hermes made his way over the many waves.
When he reached the distant **island**   5.55
he came out of the purple-dark sea and made for
the shore. He reached a large cave, the home of
the Fair-tressed Lady, and found her within.
There was a huge fire on the open hearth and the scent of burning
cedar (perfect for firewood), and citron wood perfumed   5.60
the entire island. Within the cave **Calypso** was **singing** – she had a
                                                      beautiful voice.
She was working at the loom, weaving with a golden shuttle.
The woodland encircling the cave was in full bloom:
alder, poplar and fragrant cypress.
Birds were gliding throughout the wood to nest for the night: 5.65
horned owls, falcons and long-tongued
sea-crows, the ones always down by the shore.
Cultivated vines encircled the hollow cave;
they were at their best, luxuriant with clusters of grapes,
and four springs, one after the other, burbled clear water.   5.70
They sat close together and streamed now this way, now that.
Soft patches of grass around the cave were full of violets
and wild celery. Even an immortal would have gazed in admiration
and sheer delight on entering this scene.
Messenger Hermes stood there in amazement.   5.75

Pieria   an area dominated by Mount Pierus, one of the traditional homes of the Muses.

island   the island of Ogygia lies in the fantasy-land outer regions of the world (to the west), beyond the reach of normal humans – where all of the action for Part Two and Part Three will take place. The geography here, like that of Ithaca (see p. 1), is of course obscure and, like **Calypso** herself, best regarded as poetic invention (her name is intriguingly connected to the Greek for 'to conceal'). Note that Calypso's **singing** subtly connects weaving to poetry; see further on Penelope's weaving below (**19.123** ff.). Calypso is a goddess, yet she is a woman, doing women's work. As Hainsworth 1988 notes, the idyllic scene here is beautiful but there is a 'sinister overtone: there are no people in this paradise'; the effect underscores Odysseus' isolation.

Once he had taken it all in
he next went to the wide cave. Magnificent Calypso
saw him standing there and recognized him fully.
The immortal gods recognize one
another no matter how far apart they live.   5.80
Now Hermes did not find great-hearted Odysseus inside;
no: he was sitting on the beach in tears – he had been there for some time –
vexing his own heart with weeping, lamentation and pain
as he gazed at the barren sea and cried.
As she took to her bright and shining throne,   5.85
magnificent Calypso asked Hermes:
'What's this? Why have you come, wand and all, Hermes? Tell me.
You are a friend and I respect you. Yet you don't come here often.
Tell me what your intentions are. You will have my full compliance,
if I can do it – and if it is something that can actually be done.   5.90
But first come inside and let me prepare something for you. You are
                                                                my guest.'

---

1   Why does Homer describe Hermes' journey and the island of Ogygia in such
    detail?

2   Do you find the scene sinister, as Hainsworth does? How does Hermes react
    to what he sees?

3   Calypso's questioning of her guest before serving him food contravenes
    the normal rules of hospitality (*xeinia*): contrast Telemachus' reception of
    Athena in Book 1. What does this tell us about Calypso's state of mind?

5.92–144   With these words the goddess put a small table before him,
filled it with **ambrosia** and mixed some red nectar.
Messenger Hermes, Slayer of Argus, drank and ate.
He was hungry, and on finishing the satisfying meal   5.95
he replied to Calypso with these words:
            'We are both gods, and now you ask me why I've come. Since
                                                    you've requested
an answer I'll tell you exactly the reason why.
Zeus. He ordered me to come here, though I was reluctant.
Who, after all, would *want* to make their way through so much briny
                                                    sea-water?   5.100
It's endless! There's not even a human city nearby, a place where we gods
could obtain sacrifices and the kind of **hecatombs** we've come to expect.

---

ambrosia   the unique food of the gods; nectar is their special drink. The word *ambrosia*
can be taken to mean, literally, 'immortality'.

hecatombs   literally 'sacrifices of 100 oxen'– a grand offering indeed!

Anyway, it's quite impossible for a god to skirt round the plan
of mighty Zeus and disappoint him.
He says there's a man here with you: of all those who fought   5.105
for those nine years over Priam's city,
took it in the tenth, then came home –
he's the worst off. These men **offended Athena** on their way home
and she sent a destructive wind against them – and some very large waves.
Though this storm destroyed all his fine men   5.110
it brought him here and washed him ashore.
Zeus has now ordered you to send this man home as quickly as possible:
his destiny is not to die here, apart from his loved ones,
but rather to see them and return
to his fine home and fatherland.'   5.115
As he spoke, Calypso, resplendent among goddesses, shuddered.
The words flew from her mouth as she replied:
          '**You gods are pitiless!** Of all living creatures you are the most jealous!
If a goddess takes a lover you take issue
with her sharing a bed with him openly.   5.120
That's how it was when Rosy-fingered Dawn took Orion:
you gods, living in such perpetual ease, took issue with her!
Out in Ortygia the lofty and pious Artemis
attacked and killed him with her own quick arrows.
And that's how it was when beautiful Demeter gave in   5.125
to passion and made love to Iasion
out in some farmer's field: Zeus soon knew
every detail and struck Iasion dead with a flash of lightning.
And that's how it is with me now! You gods are jealous that a mortal
                                                          lives with me.
And yet I was the one who saved him. He came all alone,   5.130
clinging to a keel: Zeus had shattered his swift ship
with a flash of lightning out on the wine-dark sea,
and though this storm destroyed all his fine men
it brought him here and washed him ashore.
I loved him and cared for him and told him   5.135
that I would make him immortal and unageing for all the days of his life.

---

offended Athena   for the cause of Athena's anger see Book 3 (p. 31).

You gods are pitiless! Calypso's complaint is highly reminiscent of Apollo's own complaint to the gods at *Iliad* 24.33–54 that they should look after Hector's mutilated body – and, more strikingly, Penelope's complaint at **23.210** ff. In good Homeric fashion Calypso cites mythological examples to make her point. In later legend Calypso bore Odysseus a son (in one version, this is Latinus) or two; see also **10.347** and **19.518**.

But since it's quite impossible for another god to skirt round the plan
of mighty Zeus and disappoint him,
then let him perish out on the fruitless sea if that is where Zeus
is pushing him to go with this decree of his! But I cannot send him: 5.140
I have no ships nor men to sail them
who could send him over the broad back of the sea.
But because I'm happy for him I won't hide him from you: I will surrender him
so that he can reach his fatherland unscathed.'

> * How would you judge the tone of Hermes' speech? And what about
>   Calypso's?

5.145–227   Messenger Hermes in turn addressed her: 5.145
'Prepare to send him off then, and show some respect for the anger of Zeus:
you don't want to upset him or get on the wrong side of his wrath.'
With these words mighty Slayer of Argus departed.
     In obedience to this message from Zeus, Lady Calypso
went to find great-hearted Odysseus.   5.150
She discovered him sitting on the beach. His eyes were, as ever,
wet with tears: the sweetness of life was passing him by
as he mourned for his journey home – and he no longer wanted Lady Calypso.

Arnold Böcklin's Odysseus und Kalypso *(1883). What details in this painting reflect Odysseus
and Calypso's relationship? Böcklin captures Odysseus' isolation effectively here, a theme that
later authors came to develop: the Roman writer Ovid, for instance, frequently figures himself as a
kind of Odysseus in the poetry he composed in exile (*Tristia, Epistulae ex Ponto*).*

The gods

The gods pervade the Homeric poems from beginning to end: the *Iliad* begins with the anger of Apollo and ends with the gods conducting Priam to Achilles and ordering Achilles to yield to him the body of Hector; the *Odyssey* begins with a council of the gods on Olympus and ends with the intervention of Athena. In the case of the *Iliad*, the plot is driven by the constant agency of the divine, while in the *Odyssey*, Odysseus is brought home and protected by Athena. Prophecies and omens sent from the gods function as foreshadowing devices for the plot. But far from being merely a literary device, the gods are also key elements of both poems. In the *Iliad*, Achilles describes the gods as spinning for wretched mortals a life of suffering, while they themselves live a charmed life free from suffering (see *Odyssey* **6.42–5**). Thus the privileged nature of the gods helps bring out what it means to be human. Odysseus (like Achilles) is a hero who suffers and who comes to terms with his mortality. He rejects Calypso's offer of a life of immortal bliss.

Gods in Homeric poetry are fearsome and can act arbitrarily, showing the jealousy and vindictiveness that modern readers might expect in humans but not in gods. Indeed, the Olympian gods are 'anthropomorphic' (literally 'of human shape') and exhibit human emotions and behaviour, though they are much more powerful. Greek religion is in large part concerned with appeasing the gods in order to avoid misfortune. More positively put, the basis of religion is the belief that 'all men have need of the gods' (*Odyssey* 3.48), and that the gods are (usually) responsive to this need if they are duly worshipped. Sacrifice and prayer are the means of seeking their help or appeasing their anger. In comparison with the *Iliad*, the *Odyssey* seems to offer a more moral portrait of the gods, and Zeus especially, as arbiters of right and wrong and enforcers of moral behaviour (e.g. at **1.378–80**). See Griffin 1980b and Kearns 2004 for overviews of the function of the gods in Homeric poetry.

The gods and fate coexist in the Homeric world view and are often described in similar language (e.g. both spin); gods are often mentioned when explaining unusual or marvellous events or ideas (sometimes these are attributed to 'a god' without specifying which, e.g. **23.222**), while fate more frequently is mentioned in reference to the inevitability of events, especially death.

The nights he spent among the hollow caves were slept
under compulsion: she wanted him by her side but he wasn't willing.   5.155
He spent his days among the rocks on the shore,
vexing his own heart with tears, lamentation and pain
as he gazed at the barren sea and cried.
In her magnificence Calypso stood near and spoke:
'Unlucky man, please stop this crying: don't waste your life   5.160

---

vexing his own heart   another evocation of the *Iliad*, where Achilles is seen quite similarly, alone on the beach, vexing his heart in grief over the loss of his friend Patroclus (*Iliad* 23.59–61). We can also compare Achilles' great sulk over losing the slave-girl Briseis which initiates the main action of the *Iliad* (1.330 ff.; the beach appears at line 350).

like this. I am going to be kind to you and send you off.
Come on: cut some long beams, join them together with some bronze,
and make yourself a wide boat. Put a half-deck at the back,
and make it high, so that it can carry you over the mists of the sea.
I will put food and water and red wine   5.165
on board, something nice to keep you from starving,
and I'll put some clothes on you. And I'll send a wind to follow you
so that you can reach your fatherland unscathed –
if, that is, the gods who hold wide heaven are willing:
they are stronger than I when it comes to getting things done.'   5.170
   The godlike and long-suffering Odysseus shuddered at her words
and his reply came flying from his mouth:
'You have something else in mind, goddess, you have no intention to send
                   me off
with this order of yours for me to cross the great gulf of the sea on a boat!
What an impossible thing to do! Not even good ships can   5.175
do this – swift ones, ones that are lucky enough to get a favourable wind
                 from Zeus!
And I'm not about to get on board a boat if it's actually contrary to
                your wishes:
not unless you swear in no uncertain terms, goddess,
that you are not planning some fresh misfortune for me.'
   Calypso, resplendent among goddesses, laughed at his words.   5.180
She caressed him with her hand, then addressed him:
'Wicked man! You're no fool:
what a clever thing to come up with.
No: let the earth know, let wide heaven above and the watery
waves of the Styx know – the most serious   5.185
and most solemn oath available to the blessed gods –
let them know right here and right now that I will not devise some new
                misfortune for you.
I will in fact tell you what I have in mind, every detail
of my plan, when the moment is right.
I am, of course, fair-minded, Odysseus, and my   5.190
heart isn't made of iron. I feel sorry for you.'
   With these words the magnificent goddess led him
quickly back home. Odysseus followed her divine footsteps.
Goddess and man now reached the hollow cave;
as he took his place on the chair on which Hermes had just   5.195
sat, Calypso set about putting all kinds of food before him,
drink as well. It was the sort of food that mortals eat.
She sat across from godlike Odysseus

as her slave-girls put ambrosia and nectar in front of her.
They set their hands to what lay before them   5.200
and when they had had enough to eat and drink
divine Calypso was then the first to speak:
'Son of Laertes, offspring of Zeus, clever Odysseus,
is this how you want to return home to
your beloved fatherland? Right now? Very well then. Goodbye.   5.205
If you understood all the misery that fate
has in store for you before you reach your fatherland
you would stay right here and build a home with me
 – and become immortal. But I know your heart is set on seeing
your wife. You've done nothing but pine for her every day.   5.210
I will, however, assert my claim to being her equal, if not her better,
in looks and stature. It's completely beneath a goddess to compete
with a mortal female in such matters anyway.'
          Odysseus thought carefully about what Calypso was saying and replied:
'My lady, goddess Calypso, don't get angry with me over this. I know   5.215
full well why Penelope, despite her fine mind,
is not your equal in looks and bodily magnificence:
she's mortal. You're immortal and ageless.
Nevertheless every day I've been wanting – desiring –
to go home and see the day of my return.   5.220
If in fact one of the gods is going to make me suffer out on the depths
                                                          of the sea,
then I'm ready for it: I have a brave heart in my chest.
I've already been through hell and suffered a great deal
at Troy and on my journey so far: whatever happens next will be a
                                                          fitting coda.'
          As he spoke the sun sank into the gloom.   5.225
The two of them went to a corner of the hollow cave,
made love, and lingered by one another's side.

1	How fitting is this an introduction to our hero? Why has it been so long delayed?
2	Do the Olympian gods – particularly the males – enjoy a sexual double-standard?
3	How would you characterize the relationship between Odysseus and Calypso?
4	What motivates Odysseus' choice for a return to everyday human life over sharing a life of ease with a goddess?
5	Examine Odysseus' closing speech: how does he craft it in response to what Calypso has just said?

The *Odyssey* and Near Eastern epic

The Mesopotamian hero Gilgamesh and his poem (traditionally dated to the third millennium BC) offer many striking parallels (and differences) to Odysseus and the *Odyssey* (see M. L. West 1997, chapter 8; we might note even with these brief excerpts parallels in the formulaic style of the poetry as well).

He washed his filthy hair, he cleaned his gear,
Shook out his locks over his back,
Threw away his dirty clothes and put on fresh ones.
He clothed himself in robes and tied on a sash.
Gilgamesh put his crown on his head
And Ishtar the princess raised her eyes to the beauty of Gilgamesh.
'Come to me, Gilgamesh, and be my lover!
Bestow on me the gift of your fruit!
You can be my husband, and I can be your wife.
I shall have a chariot of lapis lazuli and gold harnessed for you,
With wheels of gold, and horns of elmēšu-stone
You shall harness ūmu-demons as great mules!
Enter into our house through the fragrance of pine!
When you enter our house
The wonderfully-wrought threshold shall kiss your feet!
Kings, nobles, princes shall bow down beneath you.
The verdure [?] of mountain and country shall bring you produce,
Your goats shall bear triplets, your ewes twins,
Your loaded donkey shall outpace the mule.
Your horses shall run proud at the chariot,
[Your ox] shall be unrivalled at the yoke.'
Gilgamesh made his voice heard and spoke,
He said to Ishtar the princess,
'What could I give you if I possessed you?
I would give you body oil and garments,
I would give you food and sustenance.
Could I provide you with bread fit for gods?
Could I provide you with ale fit for kings?'

Epic of Gilgamesh VI.i (tr. Dalley 1989)

In the following passage, Gilgamesh has just defeated the monster Humbaba and attracted the goddess Ishtar's attentions (she is comparable to the Greek Aphrodite). When, like Odysseus, he comes to reject a goddess, she does not take it sitting down. We can contrast Calypso's acceptance of Odysseus' decision:

> *When Ishtar heard this,*
> *Ishtar was furious, and [went up] to heaven.*
> *Ishtar went up and wept before her father Anu,*
> *Her tears flowed before her mother Antu.*
> *'Father, Gilgamesh has shamed me again and again!*
> *Gilgamesh spelt out to me my dishonour,*
> *My dishonour and my disgrace.'*
> *Anu made his voice heard and spoke,*
> *He said to the princess Ishtar,*
> *'Why [?] didn't you accuse Gilgamesh the king for yourself,*
> *Since Gilgamesh spelt out your dishonour,*
> *Your dishonour and your disgrace?'*
> *Ishtar made her voice heard and spoke,*
> *She said to her father Anu,*
> *'Father, please give me the Bull of Heaven, and let me strike Gilgamesh down!*
> *Let me […] Gilgamesh in his dwelling!*
> *If you don't give me the Bull of Heaven,*
> *I shall strike [?] [   ]*
> *I shall set my face towards the infernal regions,*
> *I shall raise up the dead, and they will eat the living,*
> *I shall make the dead outnumber the living!'*
>
> Epic of Gilgamesh VI.iii (tr. Dalley 1989)
>
> Commentators have drawn parallels between Ishtar's threat here and that
> of Helios at *Odyssey* **12.383**, and more generally to the Greek myth of
> Persephone, who spends half her time in the Underworld. (The brackets and
> gaps in the text printed here show where the clay tablets that preserve the
> *Epic* cannot be deciphered.)

5.228–387

When Early-born Rosy-fingered Dawn appeared
Odysseus immediately put on his tunic and mantle
while Calypso put on her large white robe,   5.230
a fine and pretty piece. Around her waist she put
a beautiful golden belt and on her head she put a head-covering;
she then began to contemplate how to send off brave Odysseus.
        She first gave him a huge axe, one he could hold perfectly in his hands.
It was bronze and double-edged, with a   5.235
very fine olive-wood handle that slotted perfectly into the head.
Next she gave him a polished hatchet. He then set off
for the edge of the island, where the tall trees were:
alder, ash and fir trees that stretched into the sky.
They had been dry for a long time, unusually dry, the kind of wood that would
                                        float perfectly for Odysseus.   5.240

Meanwhile, after she had shown him where these tall trees were,
the magnificent goddess Calypso made her way back home
while he fashioned the trees into beams. He finished the work quickly.
He fetched twenty beams in all and then took his axe to them
and expertly planed them and straightened them with a plumbline.   5.245
Goddess Calypso meanwhile brought him a drill.
He then drilled them and fitted them all together,
and with wooden pegs and cords he fashioned a **boat**.
Just as a sharp and experienced carpenter might plan and
mark out the hull of a wide freight-ship,   5.250
that's how much space Odysseus made for his wide boat.
He slotted together close upright planks and constructed the fore and aft
platforms, finishing them off with broad planks for the surface.
In the middle he placed the mast and fitted it out with a crow's nest.
Next he made an oar for steering   5.255
and then he fenced the boat all about with osier wicker-work
as a defence against the waves. He then covered this with even more wood.
In the meantime magnificent Calypso brought him cloth
so that he could make the sail, and this too he fashioned with skill.
He tied straps, ropes and sheets to it,   5.260
then dragged the boat on rollers down to the bright sea.
He completed it all in four days.
On the fifth day resplendent Calypso bathed him, dressed him
with fresh clothes, and sent him away from her island.
The goddess had put in the ship one skin of red wine for him,   5.265
and another large skin of water, along with a bag full of
other provisions: in this she put an abundant supply of cooked food.
She sent forth a propitious, balmy wind.
Noble Odysseus happily spread his sail to the wind.
He skilfully steered with the oar   5.270
as he sat. No sleep fell upon his eyes
as he gazed at the Pleiades and the slowly-sinking Boötes
and the Bear – they also call this the Wagon.
It turned there before his eyes. He spotted Orion as well,

---

boat note that Odysseus makes a boat, and not a raft, a common misrepresentation.
Odysseus' skill (*technē*) underlines his cleverness, or *mētis*; we will come to see a rather
gruesome application of such skill in Book 9 (see especially **9.384–6**). Calypso fittingly
brings woven cloth for a sail; her assistance adds pathos to the scene, and to a degree,
a touch of humour (especially line 246); we might compare the making of the famous
Shield of Achilles in *Iliad* 18, where the elaborate description of details slows the pace of
the narrative as we prepare for a significant moment in the story.

the one constellation that doesn't sink into the waters of **Ocean**.   5.275
Magnificent Calypso had instructed Odysseus to
make his way across the sea by keeping Orion on the right.
He sailed for seventeen days as he made his way across the sea,
and on the eighteenth the shadowy mountains of Phaeacia
appeared. He was quite close now.   5.280
The island seemed like a shield in the mists of the sea.
Mighty Earth-shaker Poseidon was on his way back from Ethiopia
and saw Odysseus at a distance, from the Solymi mountains. He was clearly
crossing the sea! Poseidon's mind gave way to rage;
he shook his head and addressed himself: 5.285
'Oh no! While I was with the Ethiopians the gods
completely changed their plans for Odysseus!
He's actually close to Phaeacia now, and I can see that's where he's destined
to escape the vast climax of pain that's coming his way.
But I can still give him a fair share of suffering, I swear!'   5.290
        With these words Poseidon collected his clouds, stirred the sea,
and took his trident in hand. He roused every gust
of every possible kind of wind and covered both earth
and sea with cloud. Night sprang from the sky.
The Eurus, the Notus, blustering Zephyr,   5.295
sky-sprung, tidal-wave Boreas – these **winds** crashed down on the sea.
Odysseus trembled with fear throughout his body.
He became agitated and spoke to himself:
'What misery! At last – a new trial to deal with!
No doubt that Calypso said everything truthfully   5.300
when she said that I would have my fill of grief out on the sea
before I could reach home – that's what's happening here!
Just look at the clouds that Zeus is using to crown and deck
the sky! He's stirred up the sea and the gusts of every possible
wind are blowing violently. My doom is safe and secure now!   5.305
It's the Danaans who died back in wide Troy as they served under
the sons of Atreus who are lucky – three, no four times luckier than I.
That's how I ought to have died and fulfilled my fate:
right when all those Trojans hurled their bronze spears

Ocean   in Greek thought Ocean (*Okeanos*), also a god, is conceived of as a river that
runs round the flat circle of the world; as we will see in Book 10 (**10.508**; compare 24.11)
one must cross the river of Ocean to visit the world of the dead. From the constellations
mentioned here it is impossible to judge the season of the year in which Odysseus is
sailing but we can tell that he is headed from west to east.

winds   the winds were worshipped as gods in ancient Greece; Eurus is the east wind,
Notus the south, Zephyr the west, and Boreas the north.

at me as we fought over the **corpse** of the son of Peleus.   5.310
I could have had a proper burial that way, and the Achaeans would now be
                                                    singing my praise.
As it is I was fated to die the death of a wretch!'
Just as he spoke a vast wave crashed down on him from above
with mighty force and shook the boat violently.
Odysseus lost his grip on the steering-oar and was shot   5.315
from the boat. As the winds clashed, a mighty
blast came and split the mast in two, to his dismay.
The winds swept the sail away as the crow's nest crashed into the sea.
Odysseus was then underwater for some time, unable to
surface under the force of the vast waves: 5.320
the garments that Lady Calypso had given him were weighing him down.
In time he finally surfaced, spitting bitter
brine as it gushed out from mouth and nose.
     Despite his exhaustion Odysseus did not forget his boat:
he rushed for it through the waves and held on to it,   5.325
then sat himself down in the middle: he had just escaped death.
Another vast wave then surged and carried the boat this way and that –
it was just as when in late summer Boreas comes and carries the thistle-down
across a field and the down bundles together, thick and fast.
That's how the winds carried the boat across the sea, this way and that.   5.330
Sometimes Notus would let Boreas do the carrying
and sometimes Eurus would allow Zephyr to chase it down.
     The beautiful daughter of Cadmus, Ino, also known as **Leucothea**,
saw Odysseus. She had once been fully mortal
but now her destiny in the depths of the sea was to be revered a goddess.   5.335
She pitied Odysseus: he was lost and suffering.
She rose from the water like a shearwater in flight,
found a place in the boat and addressed him:
     'Poor man! Why is Earth-shaker Poseidon so obviously

---

corpse   this battle over the corpse of Achilles is not in the *Iliad* but it is mentioned again
in *Odyssey* 24.37–42. Odysseus' point is that if he had died at that moment he would now
have maximum fame, *kleos* – and a proper burial with a memorial monument to preserve
that *kleos* for future generations (see note on **12.8** ff.). Achilles says very much the same
thing at *Iliad* 21.279–83, when he faces death in his fight against the River Scamander;
the parallel confirms Odysseus' status here as a hero facing a truly epic struggle.

Leucothea   Menelaus' Eidothea (4.351 ff.) forms an obvious parallel to Leucothea here;
in her incarnation as the human Ino she helped raise the god Dionysus, son of her sister
Semele by Zeus, but Hera caused her death in a jealous rage. Zeus in pity made her
immortal, appropriately enough for the situation here in Book 5 (see note on **5.2**). Note
that Athena is avoiding helping Odysseus out of respect for Poseidon (see **6.329–30**), and
that when Poseidon leaves the scene at the end of this book, she comes to supply help.

and so utterly **angry** with you? All of this is his handiwork, meant just
for you!   5.340
And yet he won't wipe you out completely, no matter how much he wants to.
Come, do exactly as I say – I think you can follow my instructions:
take off these clothes and abandon your ship
to the winds, then swim and aim for a safe arrival
at the land of the Phaeacians: it's where you're destined to escape all this.   5.345
Here: take my **divine veil** and stretch it
across your chest. Don't be afraid: nothing will happen to you and you're
not going to die.

The moment you lay hold of dry land
take it off and throw it back into the depths of the sea,
as far as possible, then turn around and keep well back.'   5.350
With these words the goddess gave him the veil
and plunged back into the billowing sea
like a shearwater. A black wave enveloped her.
Much-suffering, noble Odysseus was in two minds;
he became agitated and addressed himself bravely: 5.355
'Oh no! I hope one of the immortals isn't weaving another plan
to deceive me – she's told me to leap out of my boat!
I won't do it just yet: I can see with my own eyes
that land is near, and that's where she said I could escape.
This is what I'm going to do; it's the best plan: 5.360
as long as the planks stay together all tied up
I'm going to wait right here and endure whatever trouble comes my way.
But the moment that a wave comes and breaks the boat apart
I'll start swimming – I can't think of any better course of action.'
Now when Odysseus was holding this internal debate,   5.365
Earth-shaker Poseidon stirred a vast wave into motion,
a terrifyingly destructive, fully cresting wave – and it hammered him.
Just as a furious wind will scatter a heap of dry
chaff and send it off in every direction,
that's how Poseidon scattered the boat's long planks. Odysseus   5.370
made for one of them and rode it like a horse;
he then stripped off the clothes that Lady Calypso had given him,
and immediately stretched the veil across his chest.
He fell into the sea head first, spread his arms,
and struggled furiously to swim. Lord Earth-shaker saw him.   5.375

---

angry   again a wordplay on Odysseus' name (see **1.62**).

divine veil   a kind of talisman that fits more comfortably in the world of the *Odyssey*
and its traveller's tales than in that of the *Iliad* (see Page 1973 and Hansen 1997 for
general treatments of folktale in the epic); note too how a distinctly feminine object is so
vital to Odysseus' chances for survival (compare **1.334** and **6.100**).

He shook his head and addressed himself:
'Lost at sea! You've got more trouble like this ahead of you
before you can ever share company with the Zeus-sprung Phaeacians!
I suspect that even when you get there, however, you'll have more problems
                                                                    to find.'

    With these words Poseidon whipped his fair-haired horses   5.380
and went to Aegae, home to his famous palace.
Athena, meanwhile, daughter of Zeus, had something else in mind.
She stilled the course and path of the winds
by ordering them all to hush and stop.
She then stirred up swift Boreas alone and used it to beat down the waves   5.385
until Zeus-born Odysseus could escape death and destruction
and share company with the oar-loving Phaeacians.

---

1   Why do you think female figures come so frequently to Odysseus' rescue?

2   Does Odysseus have good reason to be wary of Leucothea's instructions?

5.388–493 (end)

Odysseus now spends two more days and nights out on the sea, but on the third morning he finds Scheria, land of the Phaeacians, within reach. With some help from Athena he finally secures a place to land, the mouth of a river. He is in terrible shape but still sufficiently alert enough to remember to throw Leucothea's veil back into the sea. He decides to head for the woods and finds shelter underneath a thicket of shrubbery and an olive tree (the latter will echo throughout the poem as a symbol of Athena's protective care (e.g. in Book 13), while the description of the thicket closely resembles the lair of the wild boar in Book 19). As the book closes, Odysseus is happily covering himself in leaves and Athena pours sleep over his eyes.

Book 6

6.1–84

And so much-suffering, noble Odysseus lay resting there,
overwhelmed by toil and sleep. Meanwhile Athena
went to the city of Phaeacia and its inhabitants.
Previously the **Phaeacians** had inhabited spacious Hyperia,
near the arrogant Cyclopes,   6.5

Phaeacians as Hainsworth 1988 notes: 'the element of fiction … in the Phaeacian episode is so strong that it would be unwise to see any shadow of historicity in these lines', yet the subject of colonization 'was topical from the mid-eighth century onwards'. The Phaeacians, like Calypso, are unknown elsewhere in Greek myth; some have compared them to the real-world sea-faring Phoenicians (who were also famous as traders of the purple cloth that the Phaeacian queen is spinning in line 53 below). The Cyclopes, whom we will meet in Book 9, form a neat foil to them.

who, because they were more powerful, used to raid Hyperia regularly.
Godlike **Nausithous** led his people out of Hyperia
and settled them in Scheria, far from mortal men,
where he built a walled city for them, constructed homes,
made temples for the gods and allotted fields. 6.10
When his day of doom came and he departed for the Underworld,
Alcinous then gained control, a man gifted with wisdom from the gods.
His palace was now Bright-eyed Athena's destination:
she was devising a plan to get Odysseus back home.
She made for the finely wrought bedchamber, where a girl 6.15
lay sleeping. **Nausicaa** was great-hearted Alcinous'
daughter, like a goddess in shape and beauty.
Two slaves were on hand – their beauty came from the Graces –
standing on each side of the door-posts. The resplendent doors were shut.
Like a gust of wind Athena made quickly for the girl's bed. 6.20
She then stood above her head and spoke to her,
looking like the daughter of one Dymas, who was famous for his ships.
This girl was Nausicaa's age and dear to her heart.
Bright-eyed Athena made herself look like her and said:
'Nausicaa, you are so lazy! How could you be your mother's daughter? 6.25
Your splendid clothes lie about neglected, you know,
but you've got a wedding coming and you've got to dress well
for it! And you've got to provide nice **clothes** for all the bridal retinue!
Don't disappoint your father and mother: you can win
a good reputation if you handle this in the right way. 6.30
Come on, let's go wash all of this at daybreak.
I'll come along and work with you so that you can have everything
ready as quickly as possible – you won't be a little girl much longer!
All the finest men from all over Phaeacia are already

Nausithous   his leadership in taking his fellow citizens from Hyperia (literally 'faraway land') is reminiscent of the colonizing expeditions sent by so many a Greek city-state (*polis*) during the Archaic period in which Homer lived: see Malkin 1998, Antonaccio 2007 and **9.116** ff. Contrast the themes of civilization here with the wildness of Calypso's Ogygia (Book 5) and the primitive existence on Polyphemus' island (Book 9).

Nausicaa   the name (like Nausithous) is based on the Greek word for ship, *naus* (see note on **1.62**), appropriate for the ship-loving Phaeacians. The girl forms a foil to Calypso in that any proposed union with Odysseus (see the end of Book 7) would naturally derail his plans for home. In later legend she marries Telemachus.

clothes   note the efficiency of the narrative: Odysseus requires clothes, so it makes sense for Nausicaa to be washing – the fact that it's her wedding clothes is a special touch (compare the note on Maron's wine at **9.348**). Athena uses speech again to rouse someone to action. The normal situation with the suitors here contrasts with the irregular situation back on Ithaca, where the suitors are courting a married woman.

vying for your hand, and Phaeacia is where you're from, your family is here. 6.35
Come on, when morning comes stir your famous father into action:
tell him to get some mules and a wagon ready for carrying
the girdles and robes and bright garments.
This will be much better for you than going
on foot anyway: the place for washing is far away from town.' 6.40
With these words Bright-eyed Athena left and made
for Olympus, where, so they say, the residence of the gods is always
safe and secure. The wind is gentle there, and it never sees rain
nor snow: the bright blue sky stretches
and spreads without a cloud and the sun's rays flash brilliant white. 6.45
This is where the gods pleasurably while away their time,
and this was Athena's destination after she had spoken to the girl.
　　　But as soon as Fair-throned Dawn came, Athena woke up
fair-robed Nausicaa. The girl quickly gave up dreaming
and went through the palace so that she could report 6.50
to her dear father and mother. She found them within.
Her mother sat at the hearth with her slave-women,
spinning sea-purple yarn. She met her father as he was making
for the door to attend a council meeting with the distinguished
elders – this was where the noble Phaeacians could ask the king for advice. 6.55
Nausicaa drew close and addressed her beloved father:
'Daddy dear, could you please equip a large, stout
cart for me so that I can take my fine clothes and garments
down to the river and wash them? All my clothes are too dirty for me.
It wouldn't hurt for you too to have some clean clothes on: 6.60
aren't you about to meet with our leaders to talk politics?
And you've got five beloved sons here in the palace:
two married husbands and three bachelors in the prime of youth;
they always insist on going to the dances with
fresh clean clothes on. I'm quite concerned about all this!' 6.65
　　　This is all she said: she was embarrassed to speak of weddings
to her beloved father; but he understood what was happening and replied:
'You are welcome, my child, to the mules and everything else.
Get going: the slaves will fit out the cart for you,
a large, stout one, fitted with a hood for cover.' 6.70
　　　With these words he summoned the slaves and they obeyed.
They worked outside to get the smooth-running, mule-drawn
wagon ready and yoked the mules to the cart.
Nausicaa brought the fine clothes from her bedchamber
and put them safely in the well-made cart. 6.75

Her mother placed all kinds of good things to eat
in a basket: she put in some cooked food and poured some wine
into a goatskin flask. The girl climbed into the cart.
She put some luscious olive oil into a golden oil-flask
so that she would have some for a bath along with her slave-women.   6.80
She took the whip and sleek reins and
whipped the mules into action. With a clatter they were off.
The mules ran at full stride without break as they carried her and her clothing,
and she wasn't alone: her slaves had joined her as well.

---

1   Why might Athena have chosen to disguise herself as a young girl here
    when in Part 1 she appeared to Telemachus as old men (Mentes, then
    Mentor)?

2   Which other characters in the epic can we compare with Nausicaa? How
    would you characterize her relationship with her parents?

6.85–185   Once they had reached the beautiful river-streams   6.85
            where there was plenty of space for washing and enough fresh water
            flowed in abundance for cleaning even the dirtiest items,
            the slave-women unyoked the mules from the cart
            and brought them quickly down to the swirling edges of the river
            to eat some sweet clover and grass. They then fetched the garments   6.90
            from the cart, brought them to the dark water
            and began rapidly stamping on them in the hollows, vying to see who
                                                    could do it best.
            But when they had washed and cleaned off all the dirt,
            they spread everything out along the seashore at a place where the sea
            had deposited the most pebbles on dry land.   6.95
            They bathed and anointed themselves with oil,
            then took a meal along the river bank
            while they waited for the sun's rays to dry the clothes.
            Once Nausicaa and her attendants had had enough of the food
            they took off their **veils** and started playing ball.   6.100
            White-armed Nausicaa was leader in the play.
            Just as Arrow-pouring **Artemis** comes down from the mountains,
            whether it's massive Taygetus or Erymanthus,
            delighting in boar and swift deer,

---

veils   commentators find erotic overtones in the girls' removal of their veils and ball-playing; we find ourselves (like Odysseus) in the position of voyeurs watching the unsuspecting maidens at play.

Artemis   the patron goddess of virgins who presided over their transformation into married women; she is also goddess of the hunt. Leto is her mother.

accompanied by her nymphs, daughters of **Aegis-holding** Zeus –   6.105
fields are their stomping grounds – all to the delight of Leto:
Artemis stands head and shoulders over them all
and is easily seen (though the others are beautiful too) –
that's how conspicuous the unwed girl Nausicaa was among her slaves.
Now when she was on the point of returning home   6.110
Nausicaa yoked the mules and folded all the fine clothes.
Bright-eyed goddess Athena, however, had something else in mind:
she intended to wake Odysseus and have him see the fair girl;
Nausicaa could then guide him to Phaeacia and its citizens.
The princess tossed the ball toward one of her slaves.   6.115
She missed her target and it landed in a deep river-eddy instead.
When all the girls shrieked and shouted at this, splendid Odysseus woke up.
As he sat there he debated deep in his heart what to do:
'Whoa! What's that? Have I finally come to a land where mortals live?
Are these people insolent, uncouth and unjust,   6.120
or are they kind to strangers? Have they any sense of piety?
That was a woman's cry – a girl's shout – that just reached my ears!
Surely they are nymphs: it's they who inhabit steep mountain-tops
and river-springs and water-meadows.
It's either that or – I am now possibly near human beings!   6.125
Come on: let me try and have a look.'
        With these words noble Odysseus sank behind some shrubbery
and snapped off a branch from the thicket with his strong hands.
He chose one full of leaves, so that he could keep his genitals from being
                                                            exposed.

He moved like a mountain-bred lion in its prime,   6.130
windswept and soaked in rain, but with fire
in its eyes: he attacks cows, sheep,
wild deer; his appetite drives him
to find a hidden lair and raid the flocks.
That's exactly how Odysseus was as he prepared to meet   6.135
these fair-haired girls, naked though he was: he had no choice.
All covered in foul brine he seemed terrifying to them:
they dispersed in every direction and made for the sand dunes.
Only the daughter of Alcinous remained: Athena
had put courage in her heart and kept her from trembling in fear.   6.140
She held her ground and stood in front of him. Odysseus didn't know
                                                            what to do:

Aegis-holding an epithet for Zeus and Athena; an aegis is a goatskin shield. Note the slow pace and scene-setting: something dramatic is about to happen. (Note too the emphatic use of similes here and below.)

Odysseus in supplication while Athena watches over him and the slave-girls run away; vase-painting, fifth century BC.

whether to **supplicate** this beautiful girl by taking her by the knees,
or supplicate her in some other way – by standing apart and using
kind words to see if she would show him her city and give him something
to wear.

On reflection it seemed preferable   6.145
to supplicate from a distance and speak kindly to her:
he didn't want to anger the young girl by seizing her knees.
Instantly he came up with something both clever and kind to say:
          'I cling to your knees, your majesty! Are you goddess or mortal?
If you are in fact one of the gods who hold wide heaven,   6.150
to judge from your physique and appearance I think you are
most like Artemis, daughter of mighty Zeus!
But if you are mortal, an earth-dweller,
your father and lady mother are quite lucky – yes, extremely lucky – to have you,
your siblings as well. What joy, what sheer delight   6.155

---

supplicate   supplication is a common and significant practice in ancient Greek culture: the person in need typically crouches before the other person and takes him by the knees (or chin: **19.473**), thereby hoping to win safety for himself. The act is ritualistic and has important religious elements: 'Zeus of Strangers' (Zeus Xeinios) is the protecting deity of supplicants – see **6.207–8** and **9.270–1**. Odysseus' choice of a metaphorical supplication at 6.145–7 is therefore exceptional and in a sense an oxymoron (since grasping the knees of the supplicated was an integral element of the gesture, indicating as it did that the supplicant was unarmed and in a subservient position), yet he clearly feels that it would be inappropriate for him, a naked stranger, to touch a young girl.

must be theirs – all on account of you –
as they watch such a beautiful flower make her way to a dance.
But the luckiest of all by far is the man
who will spoil you with the most bride-gifts and take you home.
I've never seen a mortal such as you in all my life,   6.160
neither man nor woman! I'm filled with awe as I look upon you.
Why, once long ago, on **Delos** at the altar of Apollo, I noticed something
similar to you: it was a young palm tree, shooting up.
I had gone to Delos with a number of men following me
on a trip that would come to mean a great deal of suffering for me.   6.165
Just as I do now, I looked at that tree and felt stunned
for a long time: no such tree had ever sprung from earth –
and that's exactly how I marvel at you right now, my lady! I shudder to think
of touching your knees. And now a wave of grief washes over me:
yesterday I escaped a twenty-day ordeal on the wine-dark sea.   6.170
For all of that time the waves and fierce storms carried me off,
away from the island of Ogygia, but now some god has beached me here
so that I can suffer some new misfortune in this country as well, I'm sure. I
have no reason
to think it's going to stop: the gods will do much more to me before that
can happen.
But have mercy, your majesty: amidst all these trials and miseries   6.175
you are the first human being I have encountered, and I know no one else
of those who inhabit this land and its capital.
Show me the city, give me something to wear;
perhaps if you were to go there you could find something I can throw on.
And may the gods give you all you want and nothing less: 6.180
a husband and a home, and may they grant the two of you the blessing
of **unanimity**. Nothing is better, nothing finer,
than when a husband and wife who think alike
share a home. Those who wish them ill will suffer,
those who wish them well will benefit, and the couple will enjoy a fine
reputation.'   6.185

Delos 'Brilliant' or 'Shining Isle' in Greek; a small and largely uninhabited island in the centre of the Cyclades archipelago; it is Artemis and Apollo's birthplace and from very early times was a centre for religious worship. Since we know nothing else of this episode in Odysseus' legend, it is not possible to tell whether Odysseus is telling a true story here or lying – as he will come to do so conspicuously with those he meets in the second half of the epic. There was a famous palm tree on Delos associated with Artemis and Apollo's birth: Leto was said to have leaned against it in giving birth to the twins.

unanimity the description of marital unanimity, or 'same-mindedness' (*homophrosunē*) prepares the way for us to think of the relationship between Odysseus and Penelope and the degree to which they can be said to share this quality. See further on **19.568–81**.

6.186–235   White-armed Nausicaa then replied:
'You, stranger, seem like a fine man and a very clever one at that.
But it's Olympian Zeus who decides whether the good or the wicked
end up happy – and Zeus does whatever he wants.
He's responsible for what's taken place and he has made it happen,
                                                                    I am sure.   6.190
And so now you're here: you've come to the land and city of Phaeacia,
and so that's why you will not want for clothes or anything of the sort that
a wretched supplicant would come here begging for.
I will show you our city and I will tell you who we are.
This land and its city belong to the Phaeacians,   6.195
and I am the daughter of great-hearted Alcinous;
his position and its powers are derived from the Phaeacians themselves.'
        She then ordered her fair-haired slave-girls:
'Stand your ground, slaves! So you saw a man. Why exactly did you run away?
Surely you don't think that this man is an enemy!   6.200
No such man exists nor has ever existed:
no one will ever bring war to the land
of the Phaeacians because we are so dear to the immortals.
We live far off, out on the turbulent sea,
at the very edge of the world, and we will never share company with
                                                another mortal.   6.205
But now this poor wandering creature has arrived on our shores
and we must look after him. All strangers and beggars are under
the protection of Zeus, and they welcome what we give them, even if it isn't
                                                very much.
So **give this stranger** something to eat and something to drink, girls,
and wash him in the river – somewhere with some cover from the wind.'   6.210
As she spoke her slaves took their places and began telling one another what to do;
they then brought Odysseus down to a sheltered spot, just as Nausicaa,
daughter of great-hearted Alcinous, had instructed.

---

give this stranger   Nausicaa's treatment of Odysseus contrasts strongly with that of the suitors and Polyphemus, as we shall see. Compare also Telemachus' behaviour at **1.113–35**.

They put a cloak, a tunic and other garments there for him,
and put some luscious oil in a golden oil-flask,   6.215
and told him to wash in the streams of the river.
         Divine Odysseus then addressed the slaves:
'Stand there just like that, keep some distance, so that
I can wash the brine from my shoulders and anoint
myself with this oil. It's been a long time since this skin of mine has seen
                                          any kind of oil!   6.220
But I won't stand in front of you doing this: I'm embarrassed
to be naked in the company of beautiful young girls!'
         At this they left him and went to speak with Nausicaa.
Divine Odysseus set to washing the brine off his skin
in the river. It coated his back and broad shoulders.   6.225
He rinsed flakes of dried salt from the barren sea out from his hair.
When he had finished bathing and anointing himself
he put on the clothes that the unwed girl had given him,
and Athena, born of Zeus, made him
larger and stronger in appearance, and made his curly   6.230
hair cascade down his head; it resembled a hyacinth.
Just as when a skilled craftsman gilds silver
with gold – someone whom Hephaestus and Pallas Athena have instructed
in every kind of craftsmanship, someone who can make delightful works of art –
that's exactly how Athena showered Odysseus with beauty on head and
                                          shoulders.   6.235

> **1** This simile is repeated verbatim when Odysseus is finally reunited with
> Penelope (**23.157–62**): what is the effect of the correspondence? Is it merely
> an example of the repetition of lines and groups of lines typical of oral epic,
> or is there something more subtle going on?
>
> **2** Note the emphasis on craft and skill: where else do we find art in the
> *Odyssey*? Might Odysseus be taken as Homer's 'work of art'? (It is the gods
> who inspire true skill: compare the invocation to the Muse in the prologue
> and Phemius' claims at **22.347–8**.)

6.236–331   He then approached the seashore and took his seat,
luminous in handsome beauty. The girl marvelled at him
and then addressed her fine-haired slaves:
'Listen to me, white-armed slaves: I have something to say.
It is clearly the will of the gods who inhabit Olympus   6.240
that this man meet the godlike Phaeacians.
Though he seemed ugly to me before,
he now resembles the gods who hold wide heaven.
How I wish someone like him lived here
and could be called my husband – and how I wish he would be content to
                                          stay here!   6.245

But come now, slaves, and give our guest some food and drink.'

They immediately obeyed Nausicaa's command
and put food and drink before Odysseus.
The long-suffering noble hero drank and ate
voraciously: he had gone for so long without eating.   6.250

Meanwhile white-armed Nausicaa devised her special plan.
She finished folding the clothes and put them in the fine cart,
yoked the strong-hoofed mules and then mounted the vehicle herself.
She then pressed Odysseus and addressed him with the following words:

'Now get ready to make for Phaeacia, stranger. I want to send you   6.255
to my shrewd father's palace, where I promise you will
meet the finest men of all Phaeacia.
This is how to do it – I think you can follow my instructions:
While we're walking out here among the fields and farms,
move quickly and keep up with the slaves   6.260
behind the mules and the cart – I'll lead the way.
But once we reach the city, there you'll see the huge
encircling towers, excellent harbours on each side,
and a narrow road that leads in. Ships and their curved hulls will be drawn up
along the path – each citizen of Phaeacia has his own mooring point.   6.265
You'll also see the place of assembly that surrounds a fine shrine to Poseidon;
it's firmly built with deeply embedded paving stones.
That's where they take care of ship tackle,
the cables and sails, and keep the oars cut fresh.
Phaeacians don't use bows and arrows, you see;   6.270
they only know the masts, oars and ships
they use to sail so proudly over the white-flecked sea.
I'm going to avoid the unkind gossip Phaeacians are capable of so that
no one will find fault with me – some of our people are quite arrogant!
In fact if we were to encounter one of the worse sort now he might say: 6.275
"Who's this good-looking, well-built stranger accompanying
Nausicaa? Where did she find him? He must be her husband
or else she has managed to bring in someone who's lost his way on the sea.
He must have come from far away, seeing as no one lives near us.
Or else some god has descended from heaven and come to her   6.280
in response to her fervent prayers, and he'll make her his for ever.
It would in fact be better for her anyway to go and find a husband of her own
from some other country – she's bringing dishonour on these
many fine men from every quarter of Phaeacia who are currently seeking
her hand!"

That's what they will say, and it would give me a bad reputation.   6.285
I too would be upset with a girl who did something like this,
getting intimate with men before marrying,
against the will of her dear father and mother.

You must understand what I'm saying, stranger. I want to make sure
you can get a swift send-off home from my father.   6.290
We are about to come to a sunlit grove dedicated to Athena; it's near the path
and full of poplars. There's a spring that flows there and a field surrounds it.
My father built a shrine there and there's a luxuriant garden;
it's just within a shout of the city.
Find a place to sit in this grove and wait a bit until   6.295
we reach town and get to my father's palace.
The moment you think we've reached the palace,
come to Phaeacia and ask after
my great-hearted father Alcinous' palace.
It will be easy to spot: even an infant could lead you   6.300
there! No other residence in Phaeacia has ever been made
to compare with Lord Alcinous'
house. Once you're there and find yourself in the courtyard,
head straight for the main hall so that you can find
my mother. She'll be sitting at the hearth in the light of the fire,   6.305
spinning her fantastically beautiful sea-purple yarn
as she leans against one of the columns. Her slaves will be sitting behind her.
My father's throne sits there near hers –
he'll be sitting there sipping his wine like an immortal god.
Pass him by and throw your hands around   6.310
my mother's knees: *that's* how you'll get to see the joyous day of your return
all the more quickly – if you are, as you say, from quite far away.
If she's well-disposed towards you
then you can expect to see your loved ones and reach
your well-founded home and fatherland.'   6.315
With these words Nausicaa whipped the mules with her shining
whip. They quickly left the flowing river.
They pranced and ran at a good pace
but Nausicaa drove them so that her slaves and Odysseus
could follow behind on foot; she was careful with the whip and reins.   6.320
The sun sank and they arrived at the famous sacred grove
of Athena, where divine Odysseus took a seat
and prayed to the daughter of great Zeus.
'Listen to me, offspring of Aegis-holding Zeus, **Atrytone**.
Listen to me now: earlier on you did *not* listen to me   6.325
during my ordeal at sea, when famous Earth-shaker broke me down!

---

my mother's Nausicaa's advice for Odysseus to seek out her *mother* first has long
puzzled commentators; at the least we can compare Helen's prominence in Sparta and
Penelope's in Ithaca; some have seen signs of a matriarchal society in Phaeacia.

Atrytone the real meaning of the epithet Atrytone, like many epithets, is unknown to
us.

Grant that I have come among friendly people, or at least ones who can show
me some pity.'

Pallas Athena heard his prayer
but she did not reveal herself to him out of respect for
her father's brother. Poseidon meanwhile was bursting with rage   6.330
at godlike Odysseus – and would do so until he reached home.

> 1 The Phaeacians are a powerful sea-faring people who worship Poseidon
>   (line 266). At the close of this book we are reminded that Poseidon is
>   'bursting with rage' at Odysseus. Is it clear that Odysseus' encounter with
>   Nausicaa is going to speed him on his way? What arguments would you
>   bring to this question?
> 2 How is Nausicaa characterized in this book? What qualities does she possess,
>   and at what points in the narrative are they shown?
> 3 Does everything seem to be going to plan at this point in the narrative?
>   Or does the attraction that Nausicaa feels towards Odysseus seem likely to
>   derail our hero's *nostos*? It is worth comparing the disastrous consequences
>   of Aeneas' dalliance with Dido in Virgil's *Aeneid* (see note on **10.472–4**).

Book 7

As Book 7 opens, Nausicaa now returns to the palace and Athena contrives to get
Odysseus there safely. He enters the sumptuous palace enshrouded in a magic
mist and finds the Phaeacians feasting and pouring a libation to Hermes. It is
near bedtime. Odysseus' mist dissolves as he clasps Queen Arete's knees and begs
her for safe passage home, praying for her prosperity. All are shocked but King
Alcinous treats Odysseus to his hospitality and promises to get him home safely.
Without yet disclosing his full identity, Odysseus briefly narrates his passage
from Ogygia to Scheria. Alcinous is so impressed with Odysseus that he offers his
daughter's hand in marriage to the hero, but does not press the point. The book
closes with nightfall and sleep.

Book 8

Book 8 opens with sunrise; the Phaeacians wake and make for their place
of assembly. Athena disguises herself as one of Alcinous' heralds, and goes
throughout Phaeacia summoning everyone to the meeting to find out about
Odysseus – all the delicate ruses at work here seem to prefigure those that will
take place when Odysseus returns to Ithaca. Athena showers 'a divine grace' on
Odysseus so that all admire him. Alcinous urges his countrymen to give Odysseus
(still unknown) a proper feast, accompanied by singing from the blind poet
Demodocus (lines 44 ff.; his name means 'pleasing to the people'), followed by
a send-off. The Phaeacians duly prepare the ship and the feast. At the banquet,
Demodocus sings of an (otherwise unknown) episode from the Trojan War, a
quarrel between Achilles and Odysseus. The singing drives Odysseus to tears,

and Alcinous, wishing to spare his guest, calls for an end to it and urges the company to start some athletic games so that their guest will know and tell of the Phaeacians' strength. Odysseus endures some verbal abuse at the hands of one of the Phaeacians (who later apologizes), but proves his might in the discus-throwing and challenges the men to a contest of archery; a taste of things to come. Alcinous then again tactfully changes gear and suggests that they engage in music and dancing. Demodocus sings the story of the adulterous love of Ares and Aphrodite, and how the cuckolded but clever Hephaestus trapped the couple in a net – the story resonates powerfully with the themes of love, adultery, cleverness and revenge across the epic. Alcinous now urges his fellow chieftains to give Odysseus special guest-gifts. Arete gives Odysseus a fine cloak and tunic for the journey back, echoing Calypso's last gift to Odysseus. Odysseus bathes and has a short conversation with Nausicaa, in which they exchange brief but touching farewells: Nausicaa asks Odysseus to remember her for saving his life, and Odysseus says he will pray to her as to a goddess. Another feast then follows, and Odysseus sends a special piece of pork to Demodocus as a sign of respect and requests the song of the Trojan Horse – which only brings the hero to tears once again. Alcinous then again stops the singing and asks Odysseus directly to identify himself.

This nineteenth-century cameo by Domenico Calabresi perfectly captures Hephaestus' anger at Ares and Aphrodite.

Part Three (Books 9–12): Much-travelled Odysseus

Book 9

9.1–36   In reply clever Odysseus said:
'Lord Alcinous, distinguished among all peoples,
this is truly a good thing, this chance to hear a poet
of this calibre, one whose voice approaches divinity itself.
For my own part I believe that there is no greater culmination of happiness   9.5
than when everyone in a group feels cheerful,
sitting at a feast in a palace and listening
to the voice of a poet. The guests sit close, their tables laden
with bread and meat, while a steward brings wine,
ladles it from the mixing-bowl, and pours it into each cup.   9.10
What a supremely good thing this is, to my thinking!
But you are inclined to ask about my pitiable
sorrows – and as a result I can only groan more with grief.
Where am I to start? And what should I save till the end?
So many sorrows – and they've all come from the hands of the gods
                 themselves.   9.15

But first let me tell you my name – you needn't be
in the dark – and if in fact I escape the day of doom I could
be your host one day, though I live far away.
I am Odysseus, son of Laertes. My fame is exalted,
and when it comes to trickery, everyone knows that I'm the best.   9.20
Bright Ithaca is my home. The island has a mountain,
Mount Neritus – it's covered in trees and easy to see for miles around. Many
other islands lie nearby, all quite close to one another;
Dulichium, Samé and woody Zacynthus.

I am Odysseus   Odysseus finally reveals his name to the Phaeacians as he begins what will be a very long narrative, lasting all the way to 11.332, and then resuming for all of Book 12 – even in antiquity Odysseus was held to be talkative. Odysseus is basing his proud claim here on what the poet Demodocus had just sung about at the end of Book 8: Odysseus' invention of the Trojan Horse, the final means by which the Greeks took Troy (see also **4.272**).

But Ithaca lies furthest of these out in the sea, **towards sunset,**   9.25
and its coasts slope low, while these others face the morning sun.
The island is rocky but it's a good place for raising families: I've never
seen anything sweeter than Ithaca.
And yet Calypso, resplendent goddess, kept me in her domain
among the hollow caves, longing for me to be her husband.   9.30
And similarly, tricky Circe, of the island Aeaea,
kept me back in her palace out of exactly the same longing –
and yet she couldn't manage to persuade my heart.
There's simply nothing sweeter than home
and children, even if you live in a wealthy palace   9.35
in some distant foreign land, apart from your children.

1   With Odysseus' emphatic reflections on home, Heubeck 1989 points out
    that such words will persuade the Phaeacians 'to think of him not as an
    adventurer for the sake of adventure, but as one whose sole aim is to see
    his home again'. Can you think of other such uses of persuasion in the epic,
    instances where characters carefully choose their words in order to motivate
    and convince?

2   Homer's method of giving his protagonist so much narrative space of course
    means that the poem can cover many years without becoming a tedious,
    linear catalogue of events, but it creates special problems too. As you read
    Odysseus' narrative, can you find ways in which his presentation varies
    from what Homer might have done if he had narrated the story in the third
    person? What do you make of Odysseus' self-presentation and tone? What
    about his selection of events? Do you always believe what he has to say? Bear
    in mind that his narrative will cover almost nine years, seven of which were
    spent with Calypso (see p. 123 on the end of Book 12). Is it useful to think of
    Odysseus himself as a kind of poet? What about his audience, the Phaeacians,
    and his relationship with them?

3   What do you make of the *world* of Odysseus' narrative? Many commentators
    have observed that it differs from the world of the rest of the epic: there are
    monsters and magic from the world of folklore (see especially Page 1973 and
    Hansen 1997), and the geography is that of a fantasy land. Athena, too, is
    absent here. What might be the reasons for this difference, and what are its
    potential effects?

4   By contrast, what (sometimes gritty) realities have you seen reflected in the
    poem – even if elements of the fantastic are blended in?

5   Why does Odysseus delay revealing his identity to the Phaeacians for so long?

towards sunset Odysseus' words have long caused confusion: it is not modern-day
Ithaca but the larger neighbouring island of Cephalonia that lies furthest out, 'towards
sunset'. Different scholars have posited a variety of solutions to the problem (see Graziosi
2008); what's important is that we see the function of space and locale within the poem.
For a survey of early archaeological finds among the Ionian islands see Souyoudzoglou-
Haywood 1999: unlike the mainland and Cretan finds there has been relatively little
found to date here; the overall picture suggests the peripheral status of the Ionian islands
and raises the possibility of large-scale invention on Homer's part.

9.37–141 But come now, let me tell you about the troubles I've had on this journey home –
troubles which Zeus has sent my way since I left Troy.
The wind took me from Ilium to the land of the **Cicones**,
Ismarus. I sacked the city there and killed the inhabitants.   9.40
We took many women and possessions from the city
and split them up fairly, so that no one could go deprived of his fair share.
Of course I then instructed my men to make haste
and leave, but they, the **fools**, didn't listen.
Vast quantities of wine had been drunk and sheep   9.45
slaughtered along the beach there, as well as great, lumbering, horned oxen.
Meanwhile some neighbouring Cicones then came and screamed
bloody murder – these Cicones were more numerous and stronger than the
                                                                            first ones;
they inhabited the mainland and could fight
on horseback and on foot as well, when necessary.   9.50
They came in huge numbers, like budding flowers in the spring,
and launched a raid at dawn. Dread doom fell upon us there, sent
by Zeus: we had been fated to suffer miserably.
We took up positions alongside the swift ships and joined battle,
striking one another with our bronze lances.   9.55
As dawn rose and the day stretched before us
we tried to stand our ground and fight them off, despite their numbers.
But when the sun passed off into early evening,
the Cicones defeated the Achaeans and put them to flight.
Six well-greaved men from each of the ships   9.60
had perished, but the others escaped doom and death.
We set sail from there with heavy hearts;
relieved to be alive but sad at the loss of our friends.
My good ships sailed no further
until one of my wretched men had called out three times the names of those 9.65
who had been defeated and killed on the plain by the Cicones.

Cicones allies of the Trojans and mentioned in the *Iliad*.

Ismarus in Thrace, in northern Greece. Note how Odysseus starts his narrative in the real (epic) world before slipping away into fantasy land after rounding Cape Malea (line 81).

fools see **1.8**; Odysseus' relations with his men will gradually deteriorate throughout Books 9–12; by the end of the narrative he has lost them all. Odysseus' long speech can be taken as an *explanation* to the Phaeacians as to how this happened; there were, after all, 12 ships and hundreds of men lost (perhaps as many as 600: we can assume there were 50 rowers per ship from passages such as *Iliad* 2.719–20 and *Odyssey* 8.35). Homer's Odysseus is rather individualistic: he survives because he is clever and Athena protects him; we may compare and contrast Virgil's Aeneas, who takes great care to ensure the survival of his companions in the *Aeneid* (they will be needed to start a new settlement in Italy).

Cloud-gathering Zeus set the wind Boreas on our ships
with a rushing storm and covered both land and sea
with clouds. Night fell from the sky.
The ships were carried off sideways as the force   9.70
of the wind tore their sails to shreds.
In fear of being wiped out we bundled the sails into the ships
and rowed with all our might towards dry land.
There we lay for two whole nights
and days, gnawing at our hearts with exhaustion and grief.   9.75
      When Fair-haired Dawn brought round the third day,
we fixed the masts in place, hoisted the white sails,
and embarked. The wind and pilots steered the ships.
At this point I would have reached my fatherland unscathed,
but the waves, the current and Boreas pushed me away   9.80
as I was rounding **Cape Malea**, and drove me back from Cythera.
For nine days deadly winds drove me
over the teeming sea, but on the tenth we came
upon the land of the Lotus-eaters, who take only the lotus flower as their food.
There we set foot on dry land and gathered fresh water;   9.85
we soon had a meal alongside the swift ships all together.
Once we'd fed on food and drink
I then sent some of my men to find out
what sort of mortals inhabited this land.
I chose two of them and provided a herald as a third.   9.90
They soon encountered the Lotus-eaters,
people who had no intention to destroy
our men, but they gave them lotus to eat,
and whoever ate the honey-sweet fruit of that plant
lost interest in communicating with us and even returning –   9.95
they merely wanted to remain there, munching lotus
among the Lotus-eaters, and to forget about coming home!
Despite their tears I forced these men back to the ships;
I hauled them on board and tied them underneath the benches.
Meanwhile I ordered the remaining trustworthy men   9.100
to hurry back and board our swift ships,

Cape Malea a promontory on the southern coast of the Peloponnese that was famous
for its dangerous crosswinds (see also 4.515); an ancient saying, preserved in Strabo,
Geography 8.6.20 stated: 'When you round Cape Malea, forget the folks at home.' Cape
Malea and the nearby island of Cythera are real places, but after this we enter a fantasy
land envisioned on the extreme edges of the world where, appropriately enough, we
encounter a people (unknown otherwise before Homer) who make others forget about
going home (*nostos*). The land of the Lotus-eaters has traditionally been set in North
Africa, yet attempts to locate a fantasy land in the real world are by definition misguided
(see Eratosthenes' quotation on p. 1).

in fear that one of them might eat the lotus and forget about our journey.
They got on board immediately and sat at the oar-locks;
once they were all in order they began to strike the white-flecked sea with
their oars.

We sailed further on with heavy hearts. 9.105
        We now reached the land of the reckless and lawless
Cyclopes. These creatures simply trust in the immortal gods
and do not plant or plough anything by hand;
everything there springs up **without any cultivation**,
wheat and barley and vines for producing 9.110
good wine – Zeus sends them rain so that these things can grow.

---

without any cultivation in the Greek myth of the Golden Age the land produced crops spontaneously; the Cyclopes are a hold-over from such a primitive age. Contrast Nausithous' deliberate cultivation of Scheria at **6.7–12**. See Vivante 1985, chapter 4 for a stimulating study of nature in Homer.

These creatures have no assemblies for political discussion, nor laws –
they simply live on the mountain-tops
in hollow caves, and each one rules over his own
wife and children, without a single care for one another.   9.115
An overgrown island lies across from the harbour
of the Cyclopes' land, not too far and not too close,
covered in trees – and there are countless wild goats
there. No human presence scares them off
and there are no hunters there roughing it out   9.120
in the woods and on the mountain-tops.
The island has no flocks or fields
but it lies completely uncultivated
and uninhabited; it just feeds these noisy goats!
The Cyclopes, furthermore, have no ships   9.125
nor builders who could make
any for them and enable them to trade
at large – the kind of exchange that
normally occurs when men cross the sea – this is what
could have made that island inhabitable.   9.130
It's a perfectly good place, one that could yield a regular crop.
There are some grassy, well-watered
meadows running right along the sea-coast. Vines would really prosper there;
ploughing would be easy, and they could reap tall-standing
wheat in season – the soil is particularly rich.   9.135
There's a calm harbour where you've no need for ropes,
no need to cast anchor or tie down stern cables.
Just beach your ship! Then push off whenever your
sailors want to and the breezes are blowing.
Crystal-clear water flows from the head of the harbour;   9.140
there's a spring underneath a cave, surrounded by poplars.

---

1   A pace-slowing description (*ekphrasis*) is a common convention of the epic
    style; where the narrative lavishes descriptive detail on a beautiful natural
    setting, we call this a *locus amoenus*, Latin for 'beautiful place'. In Homer
    such descriptions are usually followed by some exciting event. How does
    Odysseus handle this description? Odysseus seems to be eyeing up this
    island just as a prospective Greek colonizer of the eighth or seventh century
    might (see note on **6.7**). Note that Homer both achieves characterization of
    his protagonist and maintains control of the narrative pace all at the same
    time.

2   How does Homer use landscape in the *Odyssey*? Is there a relationship
    between the way he describes a given location and the type of people we
    find there?

3   How are the Cyclopes characterized in their initial presentation? Is the
    comment that they 'simply trust in the immortal gods' (line 107) meant to
    showcase their piety, or is the poet making some other point?

This was the harbour we were making for – some god must have led us
through the murky night; there was no light for seeing anything.
It was pitch black around the ships: no moonlight
was in evidence because it had been covered by cloud. 9.145
No one even caught sight of the island
nor did we see the large waves rolling in
to the shore before we had actually beached our good ships.
Once situated, we pulled down all the sails
and disembarked onto the beach, where 9.150
we fell asleep and awaited noble Dawn.
　　　When Early-born Rosy-fingered Dawn appeared
we roved and roamed over the island in wonder.
And then the nymphs, daughters of Aegis-holding Zeus,
stirred up some mountain goats so that my men could have a meal. 9.155
We immediately took our curved bows and long-socketed
spears from the ships, divided into three groups,
and started killing the animals: the gods had given us quarry in abundance.
Twelve ships had followed me and nine goats
were apportioned to each ship; but for me alone my men picked out ten! 9.160
We sat there feasting on vast quantities of meat and sweet wine
the whole day long until sunset.
Red **wine** was still on board the ships – it hadn't yet
run out because we had all taken and put so much wine
into storage jars when we sacked the holy city of the Cicones. 9.165
We could see across to the land of the Cyclopes: they were close;
we saw their smoke and heard the sound of their **sheep and goats**.
When the sun set and sank into the gloom
there we slept, on the seashore of the island of goats.
When Early-born, Rosy-fingered Dawn appeared, 9.170
I called an assembly and spoke to all my men:
"I'm going with some shipmates
to find out about the men who live over there
and I want the rest of you, my trusty companions, to stay here.
We will see who these people are: are they piously minded and kind to
　　　　　　　　　　　　　　　　　　　strangers, 9.175
or are they reckless, abusive and unjust?"
　　　With these words I climbed on board and ordered my men
to embark and loosen the mooring cables from the prow.
They quickly got in and sat at the oar-locks;
once they were all in order they began to strike the white-flecked sea with
　　　　　　　　　　　　　　　　　　　their oars. 9.180

---

wine, sheep and goats　these details will be of vital importance in the narrative to come
(see note on line 347).

Once we reached the land – it lay close –
we spotted a cave there on the edge, near the sea;
it was very high and covered with laurel trees. There were great
flocks of sheep and goats there, lying about and sleeping. A very tall,
enclosing penfold
had been built for them out of stones dug in deep,   9.185
long pines, and leafy oaks.
This is where a monster of a man had made his bed – he shepherded
his flocks all alone, out in the distance; he kept company
with no one but lived off on his own, alone with his wickedness.
He was an astounding creature: he didn't look like   9.190
a normal, bread-eating human being, but the woody
peak of a lofty mountain, set off from any others.
It was then that I ordered my men
to wait there by the ship and protect it
while I selected twelve of the best of them   9.195
and went. I had a goatskin of dark, sweet
wine with me. It was a gift from Maron, the son of Euanthes.
He was a priest of Apollo, guardian god and protector of **Ismarus**.
He gave it to me because we had respected his role as priest
and saved him, along with his wife and son. He lived in a tree-lined grove   9.200
sacred to Phoebus Apollo, after all. And he gave me outstanding gifts:
seven talents of beautifully worked gold,
a mixing bowl made completely out of silver; then
he filled twelve storage jars with wine,
sweet and unmixed, a divine drink! None of the slaves   9.205
or attendants there in the house knew of the wine,
only he and his wife and one housekeeper.
Whenever they would drink this honey-sweet red wine,
he would fill up one cup with **twenty parts of water to one**
part wine, and a sweet, godlike scent would rise   9.210
from the mixing bowl – not the sort of thing anyone could resist!
I filled a large goatskin with this wine and also put some provisions
in a bag. I had a premonition in my sharp mind that
I was going to encounter a man endowed with vast strength –
a savage, someone with no sense of justice or decency.   9.215
We reached the cave quickly and found no one
inside; the Cyclops was shepherding his fat flocks out in the pasture.

Ismarus   the land of the Cicones, mentioned at line 40.

twenty parts of water to one   the Greeks always drank their wine diluted – drinking unmixed wine was a token of barbarism (note especially line 297). The normal ratio of water to wine was three to one; this special wine is therefore particularly potent: an important detail in the narrative to come (see note on line 348).

We entered the cave and marvelled at everything we saw:
baskets brimmed full of cheese and pens were stuffed full
of lambs and kids. Each kind of animal had been penned 9.220
separately: there were separate places for the older,
the middle and youngest creatures. Each and every bucket
stood full of whey, the pails and bowls he had made for milking as well.
My men then appealed and begged me to let
them first take some cheese and return, then later 9.225
quickly drive some lambs and kids from the pens
back to the swift ship and set sail again on the briny ocean.
But I didn't listen to them, refusing to leave until I had seen the Cyclops
                                    and had found out whether
he would give me guest-gifts – though it would have been much better
                                                otherwise:
as we were to discover, once he made his appearance it wasn't going to be
                                    pretty for my men. 9.230
        We kindled a fire there, made sacrifice to the gods, and helped
ourselves to the cheese. We sat waiting for him
inside until he came back from shepherding. He was carrying a massive load
of dry wood for making his supper,
which he threw down, raising a huge din within the cave. 9.235
In terror we fled to a corner.
He then drove his fat flocks into the cave's wide mouth –
all of the females, that is, for milking – and he left
the rams and billy goats outside, in the deep-set pen.
He then lifted up the huge, massive door-stone and put it 9.240
in its place. Twenty-two four-wheeled wagons, even the best ones,
could not have budged it from the ground –
that was the size of this towering rock that he placed at the door.
He took his seat and began milking the sheep and bleating goats,
all of them in due order, putting babies underneath their mothers. 9.245
He curdled half of the white milk
then collected it in and put it into woven baskets;
the other half he put in buckets so that he could
have it for drinking and for making his supper.
Once he had made quick work of these jobs 9.250
he then lit up a fire and saw us. He asked us:
"Who are you, strangers? Where have you come from on your way across
                                                the sea?
Are you here on some mission? Or have you wandered here randomly,
like pirates on the sea, roving
at risk of life and bringing misfortune to people they don't know?" 9.255

Our hearts broke at the sound of his words:
we were terrified by this deep voice and the sight of such a monster.
Nevertheless I spoke up and replied to him:
"We are Achaeans from Troy who have been driven off course
by the winds across the great expanse of the sea.   9.260
We are aiming for home but we've now reached you
by an altogether different path – but perhaps Zeus wanted things to work
                                     out like this.
And we declare that we are the warriors of Agamemnon, the son of Atreus –
the most famous person alive today;
he sacked a very important city and wiped out many   9.265
men. We fall at your knees then,
looking for mercy: might you give us a guest-gift or perhaps
show us some other kindness? It is customary to do this for strangers.
Have a thought for the gods, my good man: we are your suppliants.
It is **Zeus of Strangers** who protects suppliants   9.270
and strangers; he looks after those who revere him."

---

1   What do you make of the description of Polyphemus' living arrangements as seen through the eyes of Odysseus and his men at lines 219–23?

2   Has Odysseus violated *xeinia* by entering the cave uninvited and helping himself to the Cyclops' cheese?

3   How would you characterize Odysseus' tone and handling of this conversation?

9.272–352   He replied at once to my words with a cruel heart:
"You are either an idiot, stranger, or you've come from a great distance!
You are telling me to fear the gods and keep clear of them?
But Cyclopes don't care about 'Aegis-holding' Zeus   9.275
or the 'blessed' gods! We're much mightier than they.
Unless I really wanted to, I wouldn't spare you
or your men here just to appease Zeus!
But tell me: where did you moor your good ship when you got here?
Out on the edge of the island somewhere, or close by? I want to know." 9.280
    He was testing me with these words but experience had taught me
                           to know where he was going
and my reply was designed to deceive:
"Earth-shaker Poseidon destroyed my ship:

Zeus of Strangers one of Zeus' roles in Greek theology is to look after strangers and to preserve the guest–host relationship (*xeinia*: see **1.123** and note on **6.142**). Odysseus' boasting tone and his plea here fall on deaf ears outside the world of normal heroic values and experience. His appeal to Zeus for protection echoes Telemachus' appeals to the suitors in Book 2.

he drove us right into the headland and smashed it against some rocks –
it was out on the very edges of your land. A wind then came from the sea
and took it away.   9.285
But my men here and I managed to escape complete destruction."
            So I spoke but the pitiless monster made no reply;
he simply sprang up and thrust his hands out towards my men;
he grabbed two of them and smashed them on the ground as if they were
puppies. Their brains flowed out onto the ground and soaked the earth;   9.290
he then sliced their arms and legs off and made his supper of them.
He ate them like a mountain-born **lion** might: he left nothing behind
as he gobbled down their innards, flesh and bones – marrow and all.
In tears we lifted our hands to Zeus,
witnesses to such cruelty; a sense of helplessness overwhelmed us!   9.295
But once the Cyclops had filled his vast belly
with this feast of human meat and his drink of unmixed milk,
he lay down in the cave, stretched out among his flocks.
            I felt brave and drew close to him, seriously
thinking of stabbing him in the chest as I drew   9.300
my sharp sword from my belt. I felt for the fatal spot
on his body, where the midriff surrounds the liver, but a second thought
held me back:
we would have perished completely there in the cave
because we wouldn't have been able to push away the vast rock
that he had put in front of the sky-high door!   9.305
We groaned as we waited for noble Dawn to come.
            When Early-born Rosy-fingered Dawn appeared,
he kindled a fire and began to milk his fine flocks,
all of them in due order, putting babies underneath their mothers.
Once he had made quick work of these jobs   9.310
he grabbed two of my men again and made a meal of them.
After eating he drove his fat flocks out of the cave,
removing the massive door-stone with ease. He then returned it
back to its original position as if he were putting a lid on a quiver.
The Cyclops whistled loudly at his fat flocks as he drove them   9.315
towards the mountain. Meanwhile I was left to contemplate his destruction:
how could I punish him? How could Athena give me that victory?
This is the plan that seemed best to my mind:
the Cyclops had a huge walking-stick made out of fresh green olive wood
and it lay there, next to the penfold. He had cut it so that he could use it   9.320
once it dried. As we gazed at it, we reckoned
it was as big as the mast of a twenty-oared black ship,
one of those wide barges that can cross the whole width of the sea.

---

lion   note that Odysseus is compared to a lion at 4.336, **6.130** and **23.48**.

That's how long and wide it seemed, in our eyes.
I stood next to it and cut off two yards of it   9.325
which I then gave to my men with an order to shave it down.
They made it smooth, then I stood beside them and sharpened
the tip, then took it and hardened it in the blazing fire.
I then hid it carefully under some manure –
there was a very great deal of it about in that cave!   9.330
I next ordered the others to cast lots
as to who would dare lift this beam with me
and twist it into the Cyclops' **eye** in the moment that sweet sleep came upon him.
The men who drew the winning lots were the ones I would have selected myself;
there were four of them and I was added to them as a fifth.   9.335
He came back that evening from pasturing his fine-haired flocks.
He drove his fat flocks into the cave's wide mouth,
many of them this time; he didn't leave any outside in the deep-set pen,
either intentionally or because the gods had impelled him.
He then lifted up the huge door-stone and put it in its place.   9.340
He took his seat and began milking the sheep and bleating goats,
all of them in due order, putting babies underneath their mothers.
        Once he had made quick work of these jobs
he grabbed two of my men again and made his supper of them.
I then stood myself near and addressed him,   9.345
holding a wooden bowl of dark wine in my hands:
"Here, Cyclops, have some wine. After all, you've just had some ... **meat** ...
                                        some *human* meat ...
try the **wine**: I want you to know what kind of stuff our ship had
on board! I would have used it as a drink-offering here, so that you could
                                        have pitied me

---

eye   clearly the Cyclops (literally 'roundface') has only one eye here in Homer, but in some traditions the Cyclopes had two or even three eyes.

meat   Odysseus' word for meat is very common in traditional heroic feast scenes but here it appears with the gruesome epithet 'human'; the phrase serves to emphasize just how much Polyphemus has perverted the normal human pattern: instead of offering his guests meat to eat, he is eating his guests as meat! There is a similarly unexpected word when the crazed suitors ominously feast on 'meat exuding blood' (20.348) prior to their slaughter; they too have of course violated civilized norms. In the celebrated distinction made by anthropologist Claude Lévi-Strauss, *raw* food has long been associated with a lack of civilization in comparison with *cooked* food. And yet Polyphemus does not live amid total chaos: note the orderly care he takes over his animals.

wine   we observe how Homer has planted a 'seed', in narratological terms (see above all De Jong 2001), with the story of Maron (lines 196–211) that now takes root. Polyphemus is taking the wine unmixed and from the unusually low proportion of wine to water mentioned at line 209, this must be very strong stuff.

and sent me home. But as it is, I cannot endure your rage any longer!   9.350
You cruel creature, how do you expect any other human being
would countenance coming here, seeing that you've done so much wrong?"

> 1   As he did to the Phaeacians, so here Odysseus tells a story of shipwreck to
>   Polyphemus (though in this case it is a lie). What other points of comparison
>   do you see between the two episodes?
>
> 2   Think carefully about the presentation of Polyphemus: is it all black-and-
>   white or are there some subtleties here?
>
> 3   How does Homer create suspense in this episode?

9.353–566   That's what I said – he then took the wine and drank it. He loved that
sweet stuff so much that he asked me for a second helping:
"Give me some more, since you're being so kind, and tell me your name –   9.355
right now! – and I'll give you a guest-gift, one that you'll like.
The soil around here is rich, actually, and yields some very fine wine indeed
for us Cyclopes, and of course Zeus sends us his rain to make it all grow –
but this here stuff has something of ambrosia about it!"
    I gave him more of the luscious red wine, just as he asked.   9.360
In fact I gave it to him three times, and thrice he drank it up – the fool!
After it had overwhelmed his senses
I chose that very moment to address him and butter him up:
"Ah, was it my famous name you were after, Cyclops?
I'll tell you, but you must give me that guest-gift, just as you promised.   9.365
My name is **Noman**. My mother, my father,
and all my friends call me Noman."
He then cruelly replied to my words:
"Then I shall eat this Noman last of his friends –
the others will come first! *That's* the guest-gift you're going to get!"   9.370
    With these words he sank to the earth, reclining;
he then lay down with his fat neck at an angle, and all-conquering

Noman   this is perhaps as close as we can get to the effect of the Greek: editors place
the accentuation marks on the word in the original to show us that Odysseus has actually
pronounced the word for 'no one' in such a way as to suggest to the Greek ear that this
is a legitimate name (*Oûtis*), rather than the word 'no one' (*ou tis*). The trick is more
subtle and credible than it may seem at first, and it is not a matter of Polyphemus being
a simpleton: imagine, perhaps, the name 'Norman' pronounced in a strong regional US
Boston or UK Newcastle accent, where the *r* would be dropped; we must also bear in
mind that Polyphemus is drunk. Commentators (especially Goldhill 1991, chapter 1 and
Segal 1994, chapters 5 and 10) have also drawn attention to the irony of Odysseus' word
choice: he is the great epic hero, sunk to a desperate fate, and in fantasy land he really
is 'no one'. At the same time, he owes his very life to a trick that will allow him to escape
dying an obscure death: by denying his famous name, he lives to tell it.

sleep then mastered him. Out of his throat dribbled the wine
and bits of human flesh; and in a drunken stupor he vomited.
Meanwhile I shoved the beam into a large heap of hot ashes and   9.375
held it there, waiting for it to get hot. I turned to my men and roused them all
with my words, lest any fail me through fear.
And when the olive-wood beam was about to catch
fire – it was still fresh and woody but it glowed magnificently! –
then I took it from the flame and my men   9.380
gathered round. A god breathed supernatural confidence into us as
they took the olive-wood beam, so sharp at the tip,
and drove it into his eye! I was leaning heavily on it from above
and I began to twist it – as a carpenter might drill a **ship's mast**
with a bore, and his assistants would work it round and round with a leather
strap   9.385
from underneath, grasping it on both sides, and the thing would be
constantly whirling round –
that's how we took that flaming sharp beam
and spun it in the Cyclops' eye! Blood encircled the hot eye,
and the blast of heat singed his eyelid and eyebrow completely;
the pupil itself was on fire and the roots of the eye sizzled and hissed.   9.390

The blinding of Polyphemus was a popular theme in antiquity; note how this mid-sixth century BC artist has summarized three separate actions from the narrative into one scene: Polyphemus holds the legs of a just-eaten victim, Odysseus gives him wine, and the men stab him in the eye (on this 'synoptic' style, see Snodgrass 1998). What is the function of the snake above, or the fish below?

ship's mast Odysseus' choice of drilling a ship's mast as a simile is not only vivid but poignant: it reminds us of how he chides the Cyclopes for not having the art of shipbuilding at lines 125–30. Odysseus seems here like a kind of master craftsman instructing his cooperative assistants – yet their work is not creative, but destructive. See also **5.248**, where Odysseus builds his own ship.

It was just as when a blacksmith dips an axe or a hatchet
into cold water: he tempers it and it makes
a great noise – that's where **iron** gets its strength, isn't it? –
and *that's* how his eye hissed when we put that olive-wood beam in it.
With a piercing shriek he screamed in pain and the rocks around echoed
his cry;   9.395
we rushed away from him in fear. Then he plucked
the beam from his eye; it was stained bright red with all that blood!
He hurled it away, beside himself in pain.
      He then shouted out to his fellow Cyclopes who lived
nearby in caves among the windswept mountain-tops.   9.400
They heard his shout and came from their homes;
they stood at the mouth of the cave and asked what was upsetting him:
"Polyphemus, what's wrong? Why have you been shouting so much?
You're keeping us awake on this pleasant and fragrant evening!
Surely no man is making off with your flocks against your will?   9.405
Surely no man is trying to kill you through trickery and violence?"
      Mighty Polyphemus addressed them in reply from the cave:
"My friends, **Noman** is trying to kill me through trickery and violence!"
      They then spoke their reply in vigorous language:
"Well, if in fact **no man** is hurting you all on your own in there,   9.410
there's nothing we can do: it's impossible to escape an illness that comes
from Zeus.
You should pray to our father King Poseidon."
With these words they left. My heart laughed within me,
since the perfect **cunning** of my name had tricked him!

---

iron   with the mention here of iron, we are reminded that many elements in the *Odyssey* describe life in the Iron Age, when Homer was living, while others go back to the Bronze Age during the Mycenaean civilization when the Trojan War took place. While iron smelting didn't occur until the Iron Age, craftsmen during the Iron Age continued to work with bronze to produce objects of ceremonial function or high value, especially for decoration, whereas utilitarian tools such as swords and arrow-heads were now made of the tougher iron.

Noman, no man   the Greek makes it clear that the Cyclopes have taken Polyphemus' pronunciation of this word at line 408 not as a name ('Noman') but as the negative pronoun ('no man'; see note at line 366) and reasonably conclude that he is showing signs of insanity ('the illness from Zeus'). We could infer that Polyphemus hasn't enunciated the word as a name clearly because he is shouting in pain and quite drunk, and indeed the difference is subtle in Greek.

cunning   the particular form of the word 'no man' at line 410 (*me tis*) quite clearly resembles the Greek word for cleverness or cunning (*metis*) – it is what Odysseus was renowned for (see also **5.248** and **9.20**). But is he so clever? If Odysseus' only means of escaping the island is via ship, it seems he would be alarmed to learn that Polyphemus is son of the god of the sea.

The Cyclops continued shouting and reeling with pain;   9.415
he started to grope about with his hands and finally took the door-stone
                                                    from the door.
He sat himself there and spread out his hands
so that he could lay hold of anyone making for the door with his sheep.
That's how stupid he was expecting me to be!
But I began to develop a plan for finding the best way forward,   9.420
some way to deliver my men and myself
from death. I **mulled carefully** over every possible way to trick him:
our lives were at stake and terrific danger lay right at hand.
In the end this plan seemed best to my mind:
there were some very well-nourished and thick-woolled sheep in the cave, 9.425
fine big beasts they were, with wool of dark violet.
In silence I set about tying these sheep together with the pliant twigs
on which the monster Cyclops slept, lying there in all his godlessness.
I took the sheep in threes: the one in the middle would carry someone
while the two on either side would go and deliver my men to safety,   9.430
three sheep for each man. As for me,
well, there was a full-grown ram in there, by far the best out of the entire flock;
I took him by the back and curled myself up underneath his shaggy belly
and lay there, clinging to that divine wool
continually, patiently – and upside-down.   9.435
That's how we spent the night, grieving and waiting for the morning sun
                                                    to shine.

        When Early-born Rosy-fingered Dawn appeared
the male sheep made a rush for the pasture
while the females began to bleat, hanging about their pens **unmilked**;
their teats were full to bursting. Though exhausted with pain   9.440
their master began to feel along the backs of all the sheep
as they stood there before him. But the fool didn't realize
that my men had been tied up underneath the chests of his very own
                                                    woolly-fleeced sheep!
Last of all the flock my ram approached the door,
heavily encumbered with all that wool – and me and my fast-thinking
                                                    as well.   9.445
Mighty Polyphemus felt with his hands along his back and addressed him:

---

mulled carefully   the Greek here for 'mulled carefully' is actually 'wove a plan', linking
Odysseus with the great theme of weaving in the epic (see **1.238** and box on p. 142);
Odysseus is particularly proud of his cunning here and uses just these words when he
comes to a moment of crisis with the suitors in Book 20 (lines 18–21): he looks back to this
escape from Polyphemus' cave for inspiration (compare **12.209**).

unmilked   Polyphemus' blindness prevents him from milking the ewes.

Odysseus' escape from Polyphemus, in its celebration of wit versus brutality, was frequently represented in ancient art.

"**My sweet ram**, why are you the last of the flock to leave the cave
like this? In the past you've never been left behind by the sheep;
you've always been the first to graze on the fresh grass,
taking those huge strides of yours, first to reach the flowing streams,   9.450
first to want to come home to the fold
in the evening, but this time you're by far the last. Do you miss
your master's eye? A wicked man, along with his wicked men,
blinded me by subduing my wits with wine.
Noman is his name, and I tell you he hasn't yet escaped destruction.   9.455
How I wish you could think like me and could also talk
and tell me how this creature escaped my might!
I will crush him and smash his brains on the ground and spread them
everywhere throughout this cave, and my heart
will find relief from these woes that this good-for-nothing Noman gave me!"9.460
With these words he released the ram and sent him outside.
When we had come a little away from the cave and the yard
I was the first to untie myself from my ram; I then did the same for my men.
In haste we quickly rounded up the long-striding sheep,
rich in fat, and drove them until we reached   9.465
the ship. We were a welcome sight to our beloved men there –
we, the ones who had escaped death. But they mourned for the others, wailing.

My sweet ram   here we find an echo of those moments in the *Iliad* when the great heroes Hector, Achilles and Antilochus each address their own horses; another echo is found in the phrase 'huge strides' (line 450), a common term for heroes advancing into war. Commentators note that animals in epic can indeed sympathize with and miss their masters: Achilles' horses weep for Patroclus in *Iliad* 17.

The *Odyssey* and later literature: Theocritus' *Idylls*

This excerpt from the Hellenistic poet Theocritus (third century BC) shows us a very different Polyphemus indeed; here the Cyclops is a gentle shepherd, pining for the love of the nymph Galatea.

Galatea, why do you treat your lover harshly?
You are whiter than ricotta, gentler than a lamb,
Livelier than a calf, firmer than an unripe grape.
You wait until sleep takes hold of me to come here
And when sleep lets me go, then you slip away
As if you were a sheep and I the great grey wolf.
I fell in love with you, girl, on your first visit.
You came with my mother, wanting to gather orchids
In the hill-meadows. It was I who showed the way.
To you it meant nothing at all. But to me the moment
When I set eyes on you lasts from that day to this.
You slip away from me, girl, unreachably graceful.
No need to say the reason: this shaggy eyebrow
Which stretches from ear to ear across my forehead;
This single eye and flattened nose, these lips.
But fine looks could not buy me the flock I graze,
A thousand strong, nor the milk I draw and drink
Nor the cheese which lasts through summer into autumn
And loads the racks down even to winter's end.
No other Cyclops plays the pipe as I can,
Singing far into the night, my silver pippin,
Of you and me. For your amusement I rear
Four bear-cubs and eleven fawns with dappled coats.
Come to me then.

Theocritus, *Idyll* 11 (tr. R. Wells 1988)

Polyphemus appears similarly cultured (relatively speaking) in Euripides' *Cyclops* and Ovid's *Metamorphoses* Book 13; this gentler Polyphemus was popular in post-Renaissance art. He makes a neat cameo in Virgil's *Aeneid* Book 3: one of Odysseus' men, Achaemenides (unnamed in the *Odyssey*), gets separated from his leader and now stumbles upon Aeneas in *his* wanderings. Achaemenides tells Aeneas what took place in the cave and then Polyphemus himself appears, blinded and moaning; Aeneas and his men escape without harm.

I wouldn't have it at all, however, and I glared at each of them and forbade them from crying. I ordered them to put the fine-woolled sheep into the ship in haste and set sail on the briny sea. 9.470
They quickly got on board and took their seats,

and sitting in their rows began to beat the white-flecked sea with their oars.
      But when I was just within a shout of him
I turned to mock the Cyclops with these words:
"It wasn't the comrades of some weakling who you planned   9.475
to use such violence on and feast upon, was it, Cyclops, back there in your
                                                              hollow cave?
Such evil deeds were bound to catch up to you,
you cruel creature: you had no scruple over eating guests
in your house! This is why Zeus and the other gods have punished you."
      In a flying rage at my words   9.480
he tore off a peak from the huge mountain and hurled it;
it crashed down just in front of our dark-prowed ship
and almost struck the tip of the rudder.
The force of the rock as it went down made the sea swell
and a heaving wave from the ocean propelled the ship   9.485
back to the mainland, forcing it onshore.
I then grabbed a very long pole
and pushed us off, urging and gesticulating to my men
to throw themselves at the oars so that we could
escape destruction. They lurched forward and rowed.   9.490
      When we had managed to get twice as far away out on the sea,
I called to the Cyclops again this time. My men surrounded me and
tried variously to persuade me not to:
"You obstinate creature! Why do you want to anger this savage?
He just threw a rock at us and brought the ship   9.495
back to land again: we thought we were dead!
He can throw so far, in fact, that if he had heard any one of us
utter so much as a single word he would have bashed our heads together
and smashed our ship's timbers with a jagged stone!"
      Their words failed to persuade my stout heart   9.500
and so I called out to him again, very angrily:
"If any mortal were to ask you, Cyclops, how you
came to be so blind and disfigured,
tell them **it was Odysseus**, sacker of cities, son of Laertes,
and citizen of Ithaca who blinded you!"   9.505
At these words he shouted in pain and replied:
"Woe is me! That old prophecy has actually reached me now!

---

it was Odysseus   Odysseus cannot resist this boast and yet it can be taken to guarantee
his forthcoming difficulties: now that Polyphemus knows his name he can curse him –
a prayer or curse can only be effective if an individual is named. Why does Odysseus
reveal his identity to Polyphemus after having gone to the trouble of devising the trick
of calling himself 'Noman'?

There used to be living here a good and mighty seer,
Telemus, son of Eurymus. He was an excellent prophet
and he grew old among us Cyclopes, practising his craft.   9.510
He told me that all these things would happen to me one day,
that I would be robbed of sight at the hands of one Odysseus.
I had always supposed that some huge, handsome fellow
would come here, a man endowed with vast strength.
But as it is some puny, small and worthless creature   9.515
has deprived me of my eye – and that only because he conquered me with wine!
Come here, Odysseus, let me give you a proper guest-gift:
I'll stir up glorious Earth-shaker to give you a send-off!
I'm his son and he's proud to say he's my father.
He will heal me, if he wants to, and no other   9.520
blessed god or mortal man can do this."
        In reply to these words I said:
"If only I could strip you of life and spirit
as well, and send you down to the house of Hades –
not even Earth-shaker could then heal your eye!"   9.525
        After I spoke he then prayed to King
Poseidon as he stretched out his hands to the starry sky:
"Hear me Poseidon, Earth-possessor, Dark-hair:
if it's true that I am your son and that you are proud to say you're my father,
grant that this Odysseus, sacker of cities, son of Laertes,   9.530
and citizen of Ithaca, does not reach home!
But if he is destined to make it back to his homeland
and well-founded home and see his loved ones,
let him find the journey slow and hellish, let him lose all his men,
let him make the journey on some other man's ship, and let him find
                                        hardship at home!"   9.535
This was his prayer, and Dark-hair heard him.
        Now the Cyclops yet again took a stone, much larger this time,
whirled about and hurled it, leaning in with all his vast might.
It crashed down just in front of the dark-prowed ship
and almost struck the tip of the rudder.   9.540
The force of the rock as it went down made the sea swell
and a wave propelled the ship forward, forcing it ashore the nearby island
                                        of goats.

The moment we hit the island, where the other
well-benched ships had gathered, waiting – the men were sitting
there, crying and wailing, constantly looking for us –   9.545
we found them and beached our ship in the sand,
disembarking onto the seashore.
We took the Cyclops' flocks from our hollow ship
and distributed them fairly, so that no one would go off without his due share.

In the process my well-greaved men gave   9.550
the splendid ram to me alone; I then sacrificed it
on the beach and burned the thighs for Zeus, Black-cloud, son of Cronus,
who rules over all. But he didn't accept this sacrifice:
he rather was contemplating how best to destroy all
the well-benched ships and my trusty men.   9.555
We sat there feasting on vast quantities of meat and sweet wine
the whole day long, until sunset.
When the sun set and sank into the gloom
there we slept, on the seashore.
         When Early-born, Rosy-fingered Dawn appeared,   9.560
I roused my men and ordered them
to embark and loosen the mooring cables from the prow.
They quickly got in and sat at the oar-locks;
once they were all in order they began to strike the white-flecked sea with
                                                                         their oars.
We set sail from there with heavy hearts;   9.565
relieved to be alive but sad at the loss of our friends.'

> 1   What are Odysseus' strengths and weaknesses as a leader? How does he go
>   about making decisions?
>
> 2   At lines 227–8 Odysseus admits that it would have been better if he had
>   listened to his men's urgings to leave quickly, but he didn't do so. Why?
>
> 3   Is the story of the encounter with Polyphemus affected by the fact that it is
>   told by Odysseus himself?
>
> 4   Is the persona presented in the first-person narrative different from the
>   Odysseus we encounter in earlier books?

Book 10

10.1–134   'We reached the island of Aeolia, home of
           Aeolus, son of Hippotes. He is loved by the immortals
           there on that floating island. The smooth stone rises from the sea
           and he's crowned it with a wall of unbreakable bronze.
           Twelve children live with him there in his palace –   10.5
           six sons and six daughters, all in the prime of youth –
           and so he's given his daughters in marriage to his sons.

Twelve children   the number 12 in a number system based on 12, as were many early
Mediterranean numbering systems, is a symbol of completeness. Such intermarriage was
forbidden in ancient Greece yet common among the Egyptians of antiquity – and of
course among the gods: Zeus and Hera are siblings.

They are constantly feasting there with their dear father
and good mother and they've an abundance of food on hand.
By day the palace is redolent with the smoke of sacrifice and resonant   10.10
with the music of pipes; at night the menfolk sleep beside their faithful
wives in their blankets and cabled beds.
This was the admirable palace-community we found there.

   Aeolus entertained me for an entire month and asked for every detail
about Ilium, the Argive fleet, and the homeward journey of the Achaeans;   10.15
I narrated everything to him in due order.
When I asked him how I should make my way home and requested
a send-off he kindly complied and made preparations.
He took some fine cowhide, made a leather bag for me,
and put the currents of the howling winds inside –   10.20
Zeus had made Aeolus **keeper of the winds**
and he could start or settle any wind he wanted.
As we stood in the hollow ship he tied it shut with a bright silver
cord so that not even the tiniest breeze could escape.
It was the breath of the Zephyr that he stirred up for me;   10.25
that's what would carry us and the ships along. And yet this is not
what was to transpire: instead we were annihilated as the result of our
                                                            own witlessness.

   We did manage to sail for nine full days and nights altogether –
and by the tenth our fatherland was in sight.
We were so close that we could even see people in the firelight.   10.30
But at that very moment I felt overwhelmed with exhaustion and sweet
                                                            sleep took hold –
I had been constantly manning the ropes of the sails myself and had refused
                                                            to give them
to any of my men so that we could reach our homeland more quickly.
Meanwhile they began to talk and spread
word that I was ferrying home gold and silver,   10.35

---

keeper of the winds   the incident with Aeolus and his magical bag of winds and the
encounter with the Laestrygonians (lines 80–134) retain the hallmarks of having originally
been folktales. (The name Aeolus literally suggests fleeting movement; it is consistent,
perhaps, with his floating island and his change of heart towards Odysseus at lines 72–5.)
Here, for example, the woman is as tall as a mountain (line 113) and Odysseus' men are
then speared like fish (line 124). The German scholar Hackman identified 221 versions of
the one-eyed, man-eating giant story originating in 25 different countries. Such world
myths (or *Weltmärchen* as he called them) may have provided the kernel of the tale
of the one-eyed Cyclops that Homer may then have embellished into a fully-developed
narrative, shaped to reflect the themes of the poem, showcasing Odysseus' craftiness,
highlighting the theme of hospitality that runs through the whole poem, and giving the
giant a fully rounded characterization.

gifts of great-hearted Aeolus, son of Hippotes.
They huddled close with earnest looks and spoke words to this effect:
     "By the gods we are fools! Wherever he goes, city or land,
Odysseus here has found friendship and respect!
While *he's* ferrying heaps of treasure that he plundered   10.40
from Troy, *we* in turn have now come to the end of the exact same journey,
and yet we've come home **empty-handed**!
And now it's Aeolus who has lavished friendship on him
and given him these gifts. Come on, let's see just what we've got here:
let's see just how much silver and gold there actually is in this leather bag!"   10.45
With these words my men's disastrous idea gained the upper hand:
they opened the bag and all the winds leapt out!
A sudden gust grabbed them as they wept aloud; it carried them out
towards the sea, away from our fatherland. Meanwhile I woke up
and deliberated in my own good heart   10.50
whether I should jump overboard and perish in the sea
or just suffer in silence and remain among the living.
I persevered and stayed on board; I hid myself and lay down
in the ship. The baleful gust of wind then drove all the ships
back again to the island of Aeolia, and my men groaned with heartache.   10.55
     We stepped out onto the dry land and collected fresh water.
The men then immediately took supper beside the swift ships,
and once we had fed on food and drink
I summoned one herald and one of my men
to go with me to the glorious palace of Aeolus. I found him   10.60
feasting alongside his wife and children.
We entered the palace and sat ourselves on the threshold,
at the doorposts. In astonishment they asked us:
"How have you managed to get here, Odysseus? What god has treated you
                                    so wickedly?
We sent you off dutifully enough so that you could reach   10.65
your fatherland, your home and all you hold dear!"

---

empty-handed   note the mutual distrust between Odysseus and his men here: he won't let any of them navigate and they are jealous of his possessions. The notion of a fair share is fundamental among Homer's heroes. Getting one's due portion (*moira* – the same word can mean 'Fate') is what confirms status and indeed order: when Agamemnon overreaches and takes Achilles' slave-girl Briseis in Book 1 of the *Iliad*, he initiates a disastrous sequence of events for the Greeks at Troy. We might also usefully compare the insubordination here to Eurylochus' actions later in this book and in Book 12, as well as to the notorious Thersites (and Odysseus!) in *Iliad* 2. In a hierarchical society such as the Homeric one, subordinates could expect to receive their fair share of the rewards, but should not expect a share equal to that of their leader.

I answered their query with a heavy heart:
"It was cruel sleep – and my wicked men – that
confounded me! Help me, friends: only you can."
My reply was gentle, aimed to persuade,   10.70
but they fell silent. Then father Aeolus spoke:
"Be gone from my island right now, you despicable creature!
It cannot be right for me to host or send off
a man whom the blessed gods hate!
Be gone! You could only be back here because the gods **hate** you!"   10.75
With these words he dismissed me from his palace. I was miserable.
We then sailed further on from Aeolia, our hearts afflicted.
My men's courage was beginning to break down in the face of the difficult
and futile job of rowing: we had obtained no send-off from Aeolus this time.
We sailed for a full six days and nights altogether,   10.80
and on the seventh we reached the city of Lamus, perched high.
It's also called Telepylus and it belongs to **the Laestrygonians**. There a
                                herdsman driving his flock *home*
could call out to another who's driving his out to *pasture* – and get a reply!
It's a place where a man who needs no sleep could earn double wages:
one for herding cows and another for herding sheep: 10.85
that's how close the paths of night and day are there.
We put in to a glorious harbour there, surrounded by
steep rock continuously on both sides.
At the mouth of this harbour two promontories jut out,
opposite one another, making the entrance narrow,   10.90
and that's where my men all put our curved ships.
They were all moored close together within the deep
harbour because there's never a single wave inside,
neither big nor small: the water stands calm and clear.
But I alone kept my black ship outside the harbour,   10.95
just on the edge, and moored it to a rock.
I mounted a rocky look-out post and stood:
I could see no evidence of man nor beast;
we could only see some smoke rising from the land.

---

hate   there is no pun with Odysseus' name in the Greek here, as at **19.407** (see note there) but the thematic link is clear. For the connection between wrong-doing and punishment by the gods, see box on p. 43.

the Laestrygonians   some commentators have thought that the Laestrygonians live in the extreme north, yet as Heubeck 1989 demonstrates, Odysseus' point is that they have now travelled from the far western edge of the world to the far eastern edge of the world (see note on **5.275**), near the home of Dawn herself, where naturally the days are long and the nights are short. Odysseus' interest in financial matters here is noteworthy.

I sent some men ahead to determine 10.100
just who these men were who were living here.
I chose two, and sent along a herald as a third.
They made their way along a smooth path, one that wagons
could follow to carry wood from mountain to town.
On the way they met a young girl; she was fetching water just in front of the
city. 10.105

It was the mighty daughter of Laestrygonian Antiphates.
She was coming down from the fair-flowing spring called
Artacia – it was the city's source of fresh water.
As they stood and talked they asked her
who was the local king and who were his subjects. 10.110
She immediately pointed out her father's lofty palace.
They accordingly entered the magnificent home, only to find
his wife, a woman as tall as a mountain! They shuddered in revulsion at
the sight.
She then quickly summoned her husband, famous Antiphates,
from an assembly, and he of course devised a wretched way to kill them: 10.115
he instantly grabbed one of them and made supper out of him!
The other two sped away in flight and made it back to the ships.
Meanwhile Antiphates raised the alarm throughout his city,
and the mighty

This haunting Roman wall-painting (first century BC), one of a series depicting Odysseus'
adventures, captures effectively the violence and chaos of the Laestrygonian attack.

Laestrygonians heard and came from all directions,
thousands of them. They aren't like humans: they look like Giants.   10.120
Next they started to throw impossibly heavy stones
from the cliffs, pelting my men. An evil din immediately rose up around
            the ships:
it was the sound of the men dying and the ships breaking up.
They speared them like fish and won a gruesome meal indeed.
      While they busied themselves with slaughter inside the deep harbour   10.125
I drew my sharp sword from my belt
and used it to cut free the ropes of my dark-prowed ship.
I immediately stirred up my men and ordered them
to throw themselves at the oars so that we could escape the evil at hand.
To a man they tore at the work in utter fear of death   10.130
and my ship – what a relief! – made it out into the sea, away
from the steep cliffs. But the others, all of them, were lost then and there.
We then sailed further on from there, our hearts afflicted.
We were happy to have escaped death but we had lost friends.

> 1 In one fell swoop Odysseus has lost eleven ships and hundreds of men. Some
>   commentators have found Odysseus' behaviour unscrupulous and unheroic
>   here. What do you think?
>
> 2 Does Odysseus appear to learn from his mistakes?
>
> 3 It is typical of Homeric technique to include shorter episodes that
>   function as pendants to others (see p. 5). Look closely at the details of the
>   Laestrygonian episode: what points of intersection are there here with
>   Odysseus' experience with (i) the Phaeacians and (ii) the Cyclopes?

10.135–221   We reached the island of Aeaea, where fair-tressed   10.135
Circe dwelt; a formidable goddess who can speak with human voice,
and the sister of savage Aeëtes;
the two of them were the children of the Sun God Helios
by their mother Perse, whose father was Oceanus.
It was there, then, that we pulled up and silently beached our ship   10.140
in the sheltering harbour – some god must have been at the helm.
We disembarked and spent two full days and nights lying there
on the beach, wasting away out of physical exhaustion and grief.
But by the time Fair-haired Dawn brought day three

Circe   her name seems to trace back to the Greek word for 'hawk'; she and her brother
Aeëtes are relatives of Medea (see **12.70**), made famous in Euripides' *Medea* and
Apollonius of Rhodes' *Argonautica*. Homer seems to be drawing on earlier legends of
the great hero Jason, who belonged to the previous generation of heroes, and his quest
for the golden fleece, and audiences would have drawn a comparison between him and
Odysseus (see also note on **12.60** ff.).

I was ready to take my lance and sharp sword   10.145
and leave the ship, making a quick move for a look-out position:
I wanted to see and hear traces of human activity.
I mounted a rocky look-out post and stood:
I saw what seemed like smoke rising from the wide-open earth
in the palace of Circe, hidden in the dense thicket and wood.   10.150
I was then deeply conflicted as to what to do:
should I go and find out what I could, since I had seen the fiery smoke?
As I thought it through this seemed to me the better course of action:
go back to the beach and the ship,
give a meal to my men and send some of them out to enquire further.   10.155
Now just when I was getting close to my curved ship
one of the gods pitied me, all alone as I was,
and sent me a huge stag with big antlers,
right into my path. He had come from his woodland haunts and was
                                                        making for the river
to get water, parched by the heat of the sun.   10.160
Just as he was moving off the path I struck him right in the middle of his back,
by the spine, and my bronze spear went clean through him.
He fell to the earth with a groan as his spirit flew from his body.
With one foot on his body I pulled my bronze spear
out of the wound, then put the spear on the ground   10.165
and left it; I then pulled together some twigs and willow branches and wove,
left over right and right over left, a good strong rope,
about two yards long. Next I tied together the feet of this terrific beast,
and made my way to my black ship, carrying him on the back of my neck.
Because he was such a huge animal I had to prop myself up with my lance – 10.170
it was impossible to carry him on my shoulders with my hands alone.
I threw him down right in front of the ship and then approached each
of my men individually and tried to encourage them with these kind words:
"**I know you are suffering**, friends, but we are not yet due to descend
to the house of Hades; our day of doom is still yet to come.   10.175
Come on, let's not waste away out of hunger – let's remind ourselves what
                                                        food is
while we've something to eat and drink here in our swift ship!"
Easily persuaded by these words,
my men stopped their sobbing and spilled out along the coast of the barren sea;
they marvelled at the size of my magnificent, huge stag.   10.180

I know you are suffering   Odysseus' leadership skills are on display here: think carefully about his actions here and below. Killing the stag and feeding the men is prudent, but there are unsettling undertones here: the stag falls precisely like a hero on the Iliadic battlefield, and given the animals we are about to encounter (lines 212–19 below), the gruesome possibility emerges that they may be feasting on a human being!

After they had indulged their eyes with the sight of him
they washed their hands and made a glorious meal.
We sat there feasting on vast quantities of meat and sweet drink
the whole day long, until sunset,
and when the sun finally did set and sank into the gloom   10.185
there we slept, on the seashore.
      When Early-born Rosy-fingered Dawn appeared,
I called for an assembly and spoke to all my men:
"You have suffered, men, but hear my words:
we do not know, friends, where dawn or dusk comes in this country;   10.190
we don't know where the light-giving sun will sink
nor where it will rise, but let us be quick and think about
whether we can still devise some plan here. We may not be able to:
I mounted a rocky look-out post to see the whole
island and I could see that it's completely surrounded by endless ocean,   10.195
lying low. But in the middle I spotted
some smoke through a dense thicket and wood."
      At these words my men's hearts broke:
they were reminded of what the Laestrygonian Antiphates
had done, and the violence of the great-hearted cannibal Cyclops.   10.200
Their crying was shrill, and they shed warm tears –
but the weeping was of no effect.
I split up my well-greaved men into two
groups and assigned a leader to each.
I led one and godlike Eurylochus took the other.   10.205
We then shook lots in a bronze helmet, quickly,
and out leapt the lot of great-hearted Eurylochus.
He set out, taking with him his twenty-two
weeping men, and they left us behind in tears as well.
They were to discover the palace of Circe, made out of smooth stones,   10.210
tucked away in a clearing within a dell.
All round the palace were mountain-born wolves and lions –
these were men she had enchanted by giving them evil potions!
The creatures didn't attack the men; in fact they
reared up on their hind legs, wagging their long tails.   10.215
The strong-clawed wolves and lions merely fawned
upon them, like a dog greeting its master who's just
had a meal – they've always got some morsel on hand
to make them happy. But the men were terrified when they saw the dread
                                           creatures!

They came to stand at the forecourt gate of Fair-haired Circe's palace,   10.220
where they could hear the goddess **singing with her beautiful voice** from
within.

> 1   How does the description of Circe's island compare with that of Calypso's in
> Book 5 (**5.55–74**). Is one description more sinister than the other?
>
> 2   What other encounters have threatened to derail the *nostos* of Odysseus
> and his men by making them forget about their fatherland?

10.222–73   She was working at a huge loom, one fit for a goddess, one that could make
those fine, splendid and glorious pieces that goddesses make.
Polites, a true leader, was the first to speak;
he was my best friend and quite close to me: 10.225
    "There is someone inside, my friends, singing beautifully
and working at a huge loom: the whole courtyard resounds with her voice.
It's either a goddess or a woman – let's be quick and talk to her."
    At these words they spoke up and called out to Circe.
She immediately opened the magnificent palace doors and came out,   10.230
inviting them in. They all ignorantly followed her in
except for Eurylochus, who resisted. He thought it was a trick.
She led them in and sat them down on her chairs and couches,
then stirred up a drink made out of cheese, barley, fresh
honey and Pramneian wine. But she also mixed   10.235
her baneful potions into the concoction: she wanted them to forget all
about their fatherland.
Once they had drunk what she had given them she then
immediately struck them with a wand and herded them into her pigsties.
My men had the bodies, the heads, the voice and the hair
of pigs – but their minds remained just as they were before.   10.240
They wept as she penned them in. Circe tossed them
some holly berries, acorns and cornel berries
to eat, the kinds of things wallowing pigs normally eat.
    Eurylochus managed to make his way back to our swift black ship
with his report of the cruel fate of my men.   10.245
Though he wanted to he couldn't get out a single word:
he was deeply grief-stricken in his heart. His eyes
were full of tears and his mind was beset with grief.

---

singing with her beautiful voice   Circe's singing is perhaps the first indication of her
dangerous allure (in Greek, the words for singing and incantation are etymologically
related, and the effect of song is often described as being akin to enchantment). The
powerful effect of song is most vividly portrayed in the encounter with the Sirens in Book
12, but we also witness the effect of Phemius' singing on Penelope and of Demodocus
on Odysseus.

On this cup from the mid-sixth century BC, Circe, in the centre, stirs her potion, while Eurylochus (?) runs away on the right and Odysseus enters, sword drawn, on the left. The artist uses the 'synoptic' technique discussed on p. 78, on the blinding of Polyphemus.

Photograph © 2012 Museum of Fine Arts, Boston.

Each of us was stunned and kept putting questions to him
as he tried to explain how we had lost even more men: 10.250
"We made our way through the thicket, as you told us to, Lord Odysseus,
and we found the palace of Circe, made out of smooth stones,
tucked away in a clearing within a dell.
There was someone inside singing beautifully and working at a huge loom:
it was either a goddess or a woman – the men spoke up and called out to her. 10.255
She immediately opened her magnificent palace doors and came out,
inviting them in. They all ignorantly followed her in
except for me: I resisted because I thought it was a trick.
To a man, all at once, they vanished and I couldn't see
a single one – and I sat watching from my post for a long time."   10.260
        My reaction was to sling my silver-studded sword,
the great bronze thing, around my shoulders, and my bow as well.
I ordered Eurylochus to lead us all down the same path
but he grabbed me by the knees in supplication
and tearfully begged me in vigorous language: 10.265
"Don't make me go back there, Lord Odysseus: leave me here!
I am sure you won't come back, and you won't bring back
a single one of your men! Let's get out of here now
with the men we have right here: there's still time to escape the day of doom!"
        I then said in reply to these words: 10.270
"Stay right here, then, Eurylochus!
Take all the food and drink you want from our hollow black ship –
but I'm going: I simply must."

---

1   Why does Odysseus decide to visit Circe, despite Eurylochus' warning? Does he feel guilty about what happened with the Laestrygonians?

2   Does Odysseus come across as astute and quick-witted, or foolhardy and gullible?

3   Eurylochus' report repeats many of the details told in the narrative. How can we account for such repetitions?

With these words I left the ship by the shore,
made my way through the mystic glens,   10.275
and approached the great palace of Circe, mistress of potions.
As I neared it Golden-staffed Hermes
came to meet me, in the guise of a young man
sprouting his first beard in the very prime of youth.
He took me by the hand and spoke: 10.280
"Where exactly are you going, poor creature, wandering through this hill
                                        country all alone?
You have no idea where you are, do you? The men you're looking for
have been trapped and penned inside like pigs, locked up in little pigsties!
Did you really think you could come and free them? I assure you,
you won't make it back on your own: you'll get stuck here, just like
                                        the others.   10.285
But come now: I can save you and rescue you from evil:
take this good strong potion and make your way
into Circe's palace: it's got the power to keep the day of doom away.
And let me explain to you all the wily – and deadly – ways of Circe.
She'll make a concoction for you and put some potions in it,   10.290
but she won't be able to enchant you with it because the strong potion
that I'm about to give you won't let her. Let me explain the details:
once you have taken the potion and Circe sets to driving you with her long wand,
right then you must draw your sharp sword from your belt
and attack Circe as though you really mean to kill her.   10.295
In a fright she'll ask you to sleep with her
and you mustn't reject this offer of bedding a goddess:
this is how she will free your men and look after you as well.
But you must insist that she swear the great oath of the blessed gods
and promise not to hatch any plan of misfortune for you   10.300
or make a weak little wretch of you once she's got you naked."
        With these words the Slayer of Argus gave me the potion:
he dug it out of the ground and showed me what it was like.
It was black at the root and its blossom was milky-white.
The gods call it moly, and it's dangerous for mortal men   10.305
to dig it up – but the gods can do anything.

The gods call it moly   the gods call some things by different names than humans do;
they are occasionally said to have their own language in Homer; hence the epithet
for the goddess Circe at line 136 above. We don't know what plant moly ('mow-ly') is
meant to be, and since it's a magic plant the search seems pointless. If the moly protects
Odysseus, then why the need for an oath? It seems that Homer is combining elements
from folktale (see note on **5.346**), and we need not press too hard for consistency or logic
here, especially since all of this is actually put in the mouth of Odysseus.

- Compare Hermes' interaction with Calypso in Book 5. How might you characterize this god and his role in the epic? (See also **19.395–466**.)

10.307–35

Hermes then went off through the woods of the island
in the direction of great Mount Olympus while I went into
Circe's palace. My heart darkened with fear as I went.
I stood at the threshold of the beautiful goddess's house   10.310
and called for her. She heard my voice
and immediately opened the magnificent palace doors. She came out
and invited me in; I followed anxiously.
She led me in and sat me down on a chair studded with silver nails,
a beautifully made piece, and there was a stool underneath for my feet.   10.315
She made the concoction for me to drink in a golden goblet
and put her potion inside it, all according to her malicious plan.
But after I drank what she had given me she found that she couldn't enchant me:
she struck me with that wand and said:
"Off to the pigsty with you! Lie down with the others."   10.320
My response was to draw my sharp sword from my belt
and attack Circe as though I really meant to kill her.
She shouted loudly and threw herself down, grabbing my knees.
She wept and spoke in vigorous language:
"Who are you and where are you from?! Who are your parents? What city?   10.325
I'm stunned: you've drunk my potions but I can't enchant you at all!
No other human being has ever survived my potions –
not anyone who has ever let them get through the barrier of his teeth!
But you, your mind remains unaffected by my potions.
You are the ingenious and much-travelled Odysseus, the one that   10.330
the Golden-staffed Slayer of Argus has always told me would come
on his way from Troy in a swift black ship!
Come now, put your sword back in its sheath and let
the two of us make for our bed – let's
make love and come to some kind of mutual understanding."   10.335

1   Why does Circe grab Odysseus' knees in line 323? (See note on **6.141–4** on supplication.)

2   Note how Circe recognizes Odysseus: see **19.213** ff. In line 330 she uses the epithet *polutropos* ('ingenious and much-travelled'); it occurs only once elsewhere, in the first line of the poem (see note on **1.1**). What might be the significance of its use here?

3   As in the case of Calypso (**5.227**), so here love-making brings an end to conflict. Commentators have seen a phallic element to Odysseus' drawn sword. What do you make of the sexual dimension of this encounter? (Compare Odysseus' encounter with Nausicaa in Book 6.)

10.336–74 I spoke in reply to her words:
"How can you tell me to be gentle with you, Circe,
when you've changed my men into pigs here in your palace,
and now that you've got me you are crafty enough to invite me
into your bedroom and climb into bed with you –   10.340
all so that you can make a weak little wretch of me once you've got me naked.
I refuse to climb into bed with you
unless you, goddess, are prepared to swear the great oath of the gods
and promise not to hatch any plan of misfortune for me."
        In response she immediately took the oath, just as I asked.   10.345
Once she had finished swearing
I then climbed into **Circe's very beautiful bed**.
In the meantime her four attendants set about their work
in the palace: she keeps them there for household work.
They are nymphs, born from the island's springs and groves   10.350
and sacred rivers that flow towards the sea.
One of them was putting beautiful purple
spreads over the chairs, and putting fine linen cloth over the seats.
Another was putting out silver tables in front of the
chairs and putting golden baskets on them.   10.355
A third was stirring sweet, delicious wine in a
silver mixing bowl and ladling it into golden cups.
A fourth was bringing in some water and kindling a large
fire beneath an impressive tripod; the water began to warm.
Once the water had started to boil within the gleaming bronze,   10.360
she sat me down in a bath, mixed in water from the tripod
at just the right temperature, and began to bathe me, starting with my head
                                        and shoulders,
until she had managed to take all anxiety and exhaustion from my limbs.
After she had bathed me and spread rich olive oil over my body,
she put a beautiful tunic and robe over me,   10.365
led me in and sat me down on a chair studded with silver nails,
a beautifully made piece, and there was a stool underneath for my feet.
One of the attendants brought a water jug made out of beautiful gold
and poured water over my hands, holding a silver basin below
so I could wash my hands. Nearby she laid out a table of carved wood.   10.370

Circe's very beautiful bed Circe is said to have given birth to a son or two as the result of this union: Agrius and Latinus – or, in a different version of the myth, Telegonus; these later go on to found races in Italy (hence one tradition that her island is not in the east at all but in the Capo Circeo, just north of Naples). In yet another tradition Telegonus, much in the manner of Oedipus, then goes on to kill his father unwittingly and marry Penelope!

A dutiful steward then brought in some food and put it before me;
there was a good deal of it and she gave generously of what she had.
She bid me eat but I wasn't happy:
I had other things on my mind as I sat there, a foreboding of future misfortune.

> 1 Why does the narrative devote so much attention to these preparations?
>
> 2 What do you make of Odysseus' unfaithfulness to Penelope? Is he justified
>   because he is essentially forced to? What are his own feelings about the
>   situation?

10.375–417

Once Circe noticed that I was sitting there without   10.375
touching a thing and that I was deeply upset,
she came near and spoke in vigorous language:
"Why on earth are you sitting here like some mute, Odysseus,
sulking? You haven't touched any food or drink!
Are you suspicious, perhaps, of some new trick? There's no need   10.380
to fear: I've already sworn the mighty oath of the gods for you."
        I spoke in reply to her words:
"How could any fair-minded man, Circe,
bring himself to take any food or drink
before rescuing his men and seeing them before his eyes?   10.385
If you are going to order me around and make me eat and drink,
then free them, Circe: let me see my trusty men."
        At these words Circe went from the room,
wand in hand, and opened the pigsty doors.
What she drove out resembled full-grown hogs.   10.390
As they stood before her she approached them
one by one and spread a different, second potion over their bodies.
The bristles that had grown on their arms from that
baneful potion that she had given them earlier now fell!
They became men again, younger than before   10.395
and far more handsome and larger in appearance.
They recognized me and each of them embraced me.
A sweet longing for wailing overcame us all and the palace
resounded with a terrible din. Even the goddess herself was moved.
Resplendent among goddesses, she stood near me and said: 10.400
"Clever Odysseus, son of Laertes and offspring of Zeus,
go now to your swift ship on the seashore.
First draw it up onto the dry land
and put all your gear and goods in the caves.

Then come back and bring your trusty men with you."

     My stout heart was persuaded by what she said
and I set out for our swift ship on the beach.

The *Odyssey* and later literature: Plutarch's *Gryllus*

In this witty dialogue by the second-century AD philosopher Plutarch, one of Odysseus' men (Gryllus or 'Grunter' in Greek) here launches into his argument that it is preferable to remain a pig, since humans are such irrational creatures.

GRYLLUS   Stop, Odysseus! Not a word more! You see, we don't any of us think much of you either, for evidently it was a farce, that talk of your cleverness and your fame as one whose intelligence far surpassed the rest – a man who boggles at the simple matter of changing from worse to better because he hasn't considered the matter. For just as children dread the doctor's doses and run from lessons, the very things that, by changing them from invalids and fools, will make them healthier and wiser, just so you have shied away from the change from one shape to another. At this very moment you are not only living in fear and trembling as a companion of Circe, frightened that she may, before you know it, turn you into a pig or a wolf, but you are also trying to persuade us, who live in an abundance of good things, to abandon them, and with them the lady who provides them, and sail away with you, when we have again become men, the most unfortunate of all creatures!

ODYSSEUS   To me, Gryllus, you seem to have lost not only your shape, but your intelligence also under the influence of that drug. You have become infected with strange and completely perverted notions. Or was it rather an inclination to swinishness that conjured you into this shape?

GRYLLUS   Neither of these, king of the Cephallenians. But if it is your pleasure to discuss the matter instead of hurling abuse, I shall quickly make you see that we are right to prefer our present life in place of the former one, now that we have tried both.

Plutarch, *Beasts are Rational* or *Gryllus* 986c–e (tr. Cherniss and Helmbold 1957)

Myths of transformation are widespread in antiquity (compare the vast compendium in Ovid's *Metamorphoses*); Apuleius' *Metamorphoses* (also known as 'The Golden Ass', second century AD) features an extended narrative from the viewpoint of a human turned donkey, replete with Odyssean echoes. The motif of transformation inspires exploration of the definition of humanity.

Books 9–12: Much-travelled Odyssey **99**

I then found my trusty men at the ship,
wailing pitiably and shedding warm tears.
Whenever heifers have been fed and return   10.410
to the mess and sludge of the pen, all the farm calves surround them
and dance with glee: the pens can't
contain them: they run in a throng around their mothers,
mooing. *That's* how my men were when they saw me
through their tears. In their minds it seemed   10.415
as if they had reached their fatherland and the very city
of rugged Ithaca, where they were born and bred.

> • How does this homely simile affect our perception of the relationship
>   between Odysseus and his men? (Note too how Odysseus is a *mother* cow:
>   see note on **19.106–22**.) And why do the men associate Odysseus so closely
>   with their fatherland?

10.418–574   They wept as they addressed me in vigorous language:
"Now that you are back, Odysseus, beloved of Zeus, we're as happy
as we would be if we were in our fatherland Ithaca.   10.420
Come now, tell us how we lost the others."
        I replied to their question with gentle words:
"First let's draw up our ship onto the dry land,
and put all our gear and goods in these caves.
Then I want each one of you to hasten to follow me: 10.425
you're going to see your companions in Circe's palace
alive: eating and drinking! They've got plenty of food and drink there."
        They responded with quick obedience to what I had ordered them to do.
Eurylochus alone tried to keep the men back;
he addressed them in vigorous language and said: 10.430
"Wretched creatures! Where exactly are we going? How could you actually
                                                desire this disaster?
Fine! Go to Circe's palace! She will turn each and every one
of you into a pig or a wolf or a lion,
just so she can force us to guard her grand palace.
She'll do just what the Cyclops did to us when our friends   10.435
entered his cave and this foolhardy Odysseus started that conversation with him!
They perished as the result of the **recklessness** of this man!"

---

recklessness note how Eurylochus very sharply imputes recklessness to Odysseus, a
criticism that Odysseus has levelled against his men earlier in the poem (see note on
1.34 for discussion of this word). It is worth noting how Homer singles out Eurylochus
for characterization among Odysseus' otherwise frequently nameless men; Antinous and
Eurymachus are similarly distinguished among the suitors.

Once he'd had his say I deliberated whether
I should mightily draw my long-edged sword from my belt
and cut his head clean off his body and throw it to the ground,   10.440
even though he was a kinsman close to me by marriage, but my men
held me back, one after the other, and persuaded me:
"Let's allow him, beloved of Zeus, if you like,
to stay here by the ship and guard it.
Just take us to the mystic palace of Circe."   10.445
      With these words they began to make their way from our ship by the sea,
and even Eurylochus followed along, not staying back
by our hollow ship – I had terrified him with my threatening rebuke.
In the meantime Circe had kindly bathed the others
back in her palace and spread olive oil over their bodies;   10.450
she had clothed them in tunics and woollen robes.
We found them all in the palace, enjoying a feast.
When the men looked in one another's eyes and recognized each other,
they wept and the house echoed with the sound of their tears.
Circe then, resplendent among goddesses, drew close and addressed us: 10.455
"Clever Odysseus, son of Laertes and offspring of Zeus,
don't stir up these warm tears any more. I know for myself
both what you all have suffered on the teeming sea
and what your enemies have done to wipe you out on dry land.
Come now, drink my wine and eat my food: 10.460
refresh your minds and spirits!
You will be just as you were when you first left your fatherland
of rugged Ithaca. But if you constantly think of your difficult wanderings
you will become worn out and listless, nor will you ever
enjoy the pleasures of what I can offer you since you've been through such
                                 hardship."   10.465
      Our stout hearts were satisfied with what she had said.
We stayed fixed in her palace for an entire
year, feasting on plentiful meat and sweet drink.
At the end of a year, when the seasons had returned
and the months had rolled on and the long days come to fulfilment,   10.470
it was then that my trusty men summoned me and said:

"You surprise us, Odysseus! It's now time to **recall your fatherland** –
if in fact you are fated to be saved and to return
to your fatherland and well-founded house."
My stout heart was persuaded by what they had said.   10.475
We then sat there feasting on vast quantities of meat and sweet drink
the whole day long, until sunset,
and when the sun did finally set and sank into the gloom
there they slept, in the dark chambers of Circe's palace.
I climbed into Circe's very beautiful bed   10.480
and took her knees in supplication. The goddess listened to me
and as I addressed her the words flew from my mouth:
"Please make good your promise, Circe: you told me
you would send me home. My heart is now eager,
and my men are too: when you're not there they wear   10.485
down my heart with their grief."
        Circe, resplendent among goddesses, was quick to reply:
"Clever Odysseus, son of Laertes and offspring of Zeus,
I won't ask you to stay here in my home unwillingly.

---

recall your fatherland   in a remarkable reversal Odysseus must now be reminded of his
nostos; we must remember and contrast the urgency he felt over the danger presented
by the Lotus-eaters at **9.91–105**. Note how Odysseus can simply skip over an entire
uneventful year without elaboration; he does exactly the same in Book 7 when he states
very simply that he was with Calypso for seven years. Virgil memorably alludes to the
situation with Circe in his *Aeneid* Book 4 (lines 259–82), when Jupiter sends Mercury on a
mission very much like that of Hermes in *Odyssey* 5:

> As soon as his winged feet touched the roof of a Carthaginian hut, he caught
> sight of Aeneas laying the foundations of the citadel and putting up buildings.
> His sword was studded with yellow stars of jasper, and glowing with Tyrian purple
> there hung from his shoulders a rich cloak given him by Dido into which she had
> woven a fine cross-thread of gold. Mercury wasted no time: 'So now you are
> laying foundations for the high towers of Carthage and building a splendid city
> to please your wife? Have you entirely forgotten your own kingdom and your
> own destiny? The ruler of the gods himself, by whose divine will the heavens and
> the earth revolve, sends me down from bright Olympus and bids me bring these
> commands to you through the swift winds. What do you have in mind? What do
> you hope to achieve by idling your time away in the land of Libya? If the glory of
> such a destiny does not fire your heart, spare a thought for Ascanius as he grows
> to manhood, for the hopes of this Iulus who is your heir. You owe him the land
> of Rome and the kingdom of Italy.' No sooner had these words passed the lips
> of the Cyllenian god than he disappeared from mortal view and faded far into
> the insubstantial air. But the sight of him left Aeneas dumb and senseless. His
> hair stood on end with horror and the voice stuck in his throat. He longed to be
> away and leave behind him this land he had found so sweet. The warning, the
> command from the gods, had struck him like a thunderbolt.
>
> (tr. D. West 1990)

But you must first complete another journey and make your way　10.490
into the house of **Hades** and dread Persephone
so that you can consult the spirit of **Tiresias** of Thebes,
the blind seer, whose mind remains strong and ready.
Though he is dead Persephone has granted perception
and understanding to him alone; other spirits flit about like shadows."　10.495
My heart broke at her words:
I sat on the bed and wept: I felt as though
I no longer wanted to live and see the light of day.
But when I'd had my fill of wallowing in tears
I then replied to her and said:　10.500
"Exactly who will be my leader for this journey, Circe?
No one has ever made it to the house of Hades in a black ship!"
She, resplendent among goddesses, was quick to reply:
　　　"Clever Odysseus, son of Laertes and offspring of Zeus,
you mustn't worry about needing a guide on board:　10.505
once you've raised the mast and spread out the white sails,
take your seat and the winds of Boreas will carry you.
But once you have made your way across the stream of Ocean,
there you will find the woody headland and groves of Persephone,
the tall poplars and willows, so quick to lose their fruit.　10.510
　　　Beach your ship there by the deeply stirring waters of the Ocean
and make your own way into **the dank house of Hades**.
There the Pyriphlegethon river and the Cocytus flow
into Lake Acheron – Cocytus is a branch of the Styx –
there is a rock there where the two rivers join and make a tumultuous sound.　10.515
Draw near this rock, my warrior, and do as I tell you:

Hades　the lord of the Underworld, just as his brothers Zeus and Poseidon are lords of the sky and sea respectively. He famously abducted Persephone, much to the displeasure of her mother Demeter.

Tiresias　he is said to have become blind as the result of seeing Athena naked or angering Hera; either goddess then gives him the gift of prophecy in compensation. He is also well known for his role in the legends of Oedipus and Pentheus. Here Tiresias plays a role that is very similar to that of Proteus in Book 4; Odysseus' despondent response here is very much like that of Menelaus at 4.538–41. At the same time, however, a visit to the Underworld is naturally a distinctive achievement, and Odysseus might just welcome the fact that this will place him in the same category of heroes such as Heracles and Theseus. Virgil similarly takes Aeneas to the Underworld in Book 6 of the *Aeneid*; for more on the afterlife of this great theme, much imitated in later literature, see the end of *Odyssey* 11 and Hall 2008, Chapter 15.

the dank house of Hades　note that Odysseus never actually *descends* into the Underworld: the dead live across the stream of Ocean (see note on **5.275**) and the spirits of the dead will come up from below to visit him; the process is very much like consulting an oracle: there is no need for a descent.

dig a pit as wide and as long as your arm
and pour into it a drink-offering made to all the dead.
First use a mixture of honey and milk, then sweet wine,
and thirdly water. On top of this sprinkle white barley.   10.520
Then make an appeal to the fleeting ghosts of the dead
and tell them that once you reach Ithaca you will sacrifice to them in
                                your palace
the best young cow you have and that you will fill a pyre with objects you
                                hold dear,
and that you will sacrifice a sheep, separately, for Tiresias alone,
completely black, the finest from your flocks.   10.525
Once you have completed your prayer to the glorious tribes of the dead
then sacrifice a male ram and a black ewe
and position them in the direction of the Underworld, then turn yourself
                                around
and make for the Ocean. There many spirits
of the departed will approach you.   10.530
Then stir up your men and order them
to skin and sacrifice the flocks there that you slaughtered
with your pitiless bronze sword and tell them to pray to the gods,
to mighty Hades and dread Persephone.
You will need to draw your sharp sword from your belt   10.535
and sit there: don't allow the faint ghosts of the dead
to **come near the blood** until you consult Tiresias.
The seer will then soon come to you, captain,
and tell you the path and the distance
of your journey home and how to make it over the teeming sea."   10.540
      As she spoke Golden-throned Dawn approached.
Circe clothed me in a tunic and robe;
the nymph herself put on her long silvery mantle,
so finely woven and graceful, then put a beautiful golden belt
round her waist, and a head-dress on her head.   10.545
      I went round the palace stirring up the men
and addressed each one separately with gentle words:
"Let's wake up from sweet sleep
and make our move: Lady Circe has shown me the way."
Their stout hearts were persuaded by what I said.   10.550
      And yet as we left there was still more suffering for my men:

---

come near the blood   Circe's instructions are evocative of a variety of universally practised
food rituals concerning the dead even today, from the Hindu practice of Tarpan to the
Día de los Muertos in Latin America. Here the dead are thought of as living an enervated
existence, and they seem to need these offerings to bring them to their senses.

there was a certain Elpenor, quite young; not the ablest
hand in war nor the sharpest as far as wits go.
He was drunk and in his quest for fresh air lay down
on the roof of Circe's mystic palace, apart from the others.   10.555
When he heard the loud noise of the men stirring to go
he woke up suddenly **and forgot**
to go back down by the long staircase:
instead he fell down straight off the roof and broke
his neck – and his spirit departed for Hades.   10.560
I then addressed my men just before departing:
"I suppose you think, friends, that you are going to our homes
and beloved fatherland. Circe, however, has indicated a different path to me:
we must go to the house of Hades and dread Persephone
to consult the spirit of Tiresias of Thebes."   10.565
    Their hearts broke on hearing this.
They sat weeping right there and began to pull out their hair –
but the weeping was of no effect.
When we finally reached the beach and our swift
ship – all in despair and shedding warm tears –   10.570
then Circe came to the black ship:
she brought a black ewe and tied it up to the ship –
completely unbeknownst to me. Who can spot the motion
of the gods if they wish to remain unobserved?'

Book 11

In Book 11 Odysseus follows Circe's instructions to the letter and performs a
nekuia, the magical rite of summoning the ghosts of the dead. Elpenor is the
first to appear; he explains what happened and requests a burial. Tiresias then
tells Odysseus that Poseidon is angry with him for blinding Polyphemus and that
he must go home via the island of Thrinacia, where he must not touch the Sun
God's cows. The prophet also tells Odysseus of the suitors and assures him that
he will kill them; he then informs him that once he's killed them he must travel
again until he finds a race of people that do not know of ships and seafaring at all;
he then finally tells the hero that he will die peaceably in old age. Odysseus then
speaks with his dead mother Anticlea and learns more of the situation in Ithaca;
a lengthy catalogue of famous women now follows. As Odysseus concludes the

---

and forgot   a vivid and somewhat comic epilogue to all the solemnity surrounding a trip
to the Underworld. It is remarkable that Odysseus doesn't realize that he is missing a man;
he learns of this story directly from Elpenor's ghost in the next book. Elpenor's death also
seems to come as a kind of compensation for his leader's escape from the Underworld:
we might compare the roles of Enkidu in the *Epic of Gilgamesh* and Palinurus in the
Aeneid.

catalogue, he interrupts the narrative of his adventures and asks the Phaeacians: perhaps we should all go to bed now? Alcinous, however, is keen for more; intriguingly he says, 'you do not seem at all / a fraudulent or deceptive man, the kind of man / the black earth spawns everywhere in such numbers, / one who makes up lies about things that no one else could even see for themselves' (lines 363–6), and he compares Odysseus to a poet (369). He then asks his guest to tell of any Greek heroes he saw. As Odysseus resumes his narrative, he tells of his encounter with the ghost of Agamemnon, who explains how he died at the hands of Aegisthus; he curses Clytemnestra and warns Odysseus not to trust women. Achilles next appears and famously declares that he would prefer to be alive, even as a lowly slave, than to be 'king over all the dead' (lines 489–91). Ajax the son of Telamon now appears, whom Odysseus had defeated in a contest for the arms of Achilles and who had subsequently committed suicide in his shame at the defeat; Ajax movingly refuses to speak to Odysseus. A series of mythical characters now appears, including Tantalus, Sisyphus and Heracles. Odysseus longs to see more heroes (e.g. Theseus) but begins to fear danger as the spirits congregate; he rejoins his men and they set sail once again.

Book 12

12.1–141

'After our ship left the current of Ocean's
river and reached the swell of the broad sea
and then the island of Aeaea, where Early-born Dawn
dwells and dances to the rising of Helios,
there we beached our ship on the sand   12.5
and disembarked onto the seashore.
And there we fell asleep and awaited noble Dawn.
        When Early-born Rosy-fingered Dawn appeared
I then sent my men over to Circe's palace
to fetch the corpse of dead Elpenor.   12.10
We quickly cut down some trees for logs and through our tears
we prepared to bury him where the beach jutted out the furthest.
Once his corpse and weaponry had burnt
we heaped up the burial mound, put a stone pillar on it,
then fixed a broad-bladed oar on the very top.   12.15

---

fixed a broad-bladed oar   this is precisely how the ghost of Elpenor requested his burial when Odysseus met him in the Underworld in Book 11. The fact that such an unheroic figure can expect such a heroic burial may remind us of Telemachus' concern for a proper burial for his own truly heroic father (e.g. **1.239, 291**). The entire Elpenor episode is deftly woven to connect Books 10 and 12, which straddle the journey to the Underworld in Book 11. Circe also plays an important mythical role in Odysseus' journey to the Underworld, functioning both as gatekeeper and then as aide (compare the role of the Sibyl in Virgil's *Aeneid*).

The *Odyssey* and later literature: Dante's *Inferno*

> *Drawing its pinnacle this way and that,*
> *as though this truly were a tongue that spoke,*
> *it flung out utterance, declaring: 'Once*
> *I'd set my course from Circe (she had kept*
> *me near Gaeta for a year or more,*
> *before Aeneas, passing, named it that)*
> *no tenderness for son, no duty owed*
> *to ageing fatherhood, no love that should*
> *have brought my wife Penelope delight,*
> *could overcome in me my long desire,*
> *burning to understand how this world works,*
> *and know of human vices, worth and valour.*
> *Out, then, across the open depths, I put to sea,*
> *a single prow, and with me all my friends –*
> *the little crew that had not yet abandoned me.*
> *I saw both shorelines (one ran on to Spain,*
> *the other to Morocco), Sardinia*
> *and all those islands that our ocean bathes.*
> *I and my company were old and slow.*
> *And yet, arriving at that narrow sound*
> *where Hercules had once set up his mark –*
> *to warn that men should never pass beyond –*
> *I left Seville behind me on the right.*
> *To port already I had left Ceuta.*
> *"Brothers", I said, "a hundred thousand*
> *perils you have passed and reached the Occident.*
> *For us, so little time remains to keep*
> *the vigil of our living sense. Do not*
> *deny your will to win experience,*
> *behind the sun, of worlds where no man dwells.*
> *Hold clear in thought your seed and origin.*
> *You were not made to live as mindless brutes,*
> *but go in search of virtue and true knowledge."'*

Dante, *Inferno* Canto 26.88–120 (tr. Kirkpatrick 2006)

With these famous lines the ghost of Odysseus consults Dante and his guide in the Underworld, Virgil. Dante did not know Homer directly but the *Inferno* owes its inspiration to *Odyssey* Book 11, via Virgil especially. Dante's presentation of a restless and what some scholars call a 'centrifugal' (home-averse) Odysseus here was hugely influential, and arguably, as many have felt, not true to Homer's Odysseus – see especially Stanford 1968 and Boitani 1994 for good accounts of how the conception of Odysseus in western literature changed through time.

As we were busying ourselves with these things, Circe, of course,
was made aware of our arrival and she quickly
came to look after us. Her attendants followed and brought
food, plenty of meat and gleaming red wine.
Resplendent among goddesses she stood in our midst and said: 12.20
"You hardy creatures! You have gone down to the house of Hades while
                                                                                                          still alive!
You then have *two* deaths when others have only one!
But come now, spend the day eating my food and drinking
my wine right here: you will sail
when Dawn appears, and **I will show you your path** and tell   12.25
you all the details of what to expect so that you won't come to grief
and further suffering through any costly bad planning."
    Our stout hearts were satisfied with what Circe had said.
We then sat there feasting on vast quantities of meat and sweet drink
the whole day long, until sunset,   12.30

*The Sirens are variously depicted in antiquity, frequently as Harpies, with wings, though they
have no wings in Homer. What details of (or variations from) the narrative can you trace in this
1891 painting by J. W. Waterhouse?*

I will show you your path   Circe here seems to provide Odysseus with precisely the
same information about the way home that she said (**10.538–40**) Tiresias would give
him. For some this is an inconsistency that came about as the result of the conflation of
two separate traditions – as is frequent in the dynamics of oral poetry – one in which a
prophet is consulted in the Underworld, the other involving a Sibyl-type figure guarding
access and serving as guide to the Underworld. Yet it must be noted that apparently
only Tiresias knows about the suitors, and this (**11.115–17**) constitutes Odysseus' first
experience of learning about the situation back in Ithaca. Virgil reflects these two
figures in the *Aeneid*, including the Cumaean Sibyl, who accompanies Aeneas into the
Underworld, and Aeneas' father Anchises, who functions as the dead prophet-figure
who has important information for the hero. (Another female–male pair similarly assists
Menelaus in Book 4: Eidothea and The Old Man of the Sea.)

and when the sun finally did set and sink into the gloom
my men slept next to the ship's stern-cables
while Circe took me by the hand and sat me down,
away from my men. She lay beside me and took me through the details
of the journey.
I narrated everything that had taken place in due order to her,   12.35
then Lady Circe addressed me with these words:
        "While all of these tasks have now been completed, Odysseus,
                                                    you must listen
to what I am going to tell you now – and the gods themselves will fix them
                                                    in your mind.

You will first reach the Sirens: they enchant
everyone that approaches them.   12.40
If someone is ignorant enough to come close and listen to the voice
of these Sirens, he won't have his wife and little ones beside him,
rejoicing at his homecoming –
no: the Sirens will be sitting there in their island meadow,
charming this victim with their clear-voiced song, while the beach around
                                                    them swells   12.45
with men rotting on their bones as their skin shrinks tight.
Drive past these creatures, and soften some honey-sweet wax in your hands
and rub it into your men's ears so that none of them
can hear. But as for you, if you want to hear them,
tell your men to stand you straight up on the mast-box of your swift ship   12.50
and to tie up your hands and feet, tying the rope-ends there as well,
so that you can enjoy the sound of the Sirens.
And if you beg or even order your men to free you,
they must then tie you down with even more rope.
But once you and your men have made it past them,   12.55
now there's no longer any need for me to tell you exactly
which path to take – this will be up to you, and what

You will first reach the Sirens   Circe truly knows her Odysseus and devises here a cunning method to accommodate his curiosity (compare his insistence on going into Polyphemus' cave in Book 9). For the Sirens see below, lines 153 ff. Their song is so entrancing that it makes men incapable of any action at all. Their representation in ancient art varies, but they are most often portrayed as birds with women's faces. Homer's Sirens aren't actually given a great deal of detailed description. In some versions of the myth, they commit suicide if their intended victim manages to resist them. Nowadays the word Siren has come to represent the *femme fatale*, a dangerously alluring woman. It is typical (and telling of Greek society) that male heroes like Heracles, Theseus and Odysseus confront and overcome mythical monsters and dangerous women (or sometimes, as with Scylla below, a combination of the two!) on their heroic journey.

you want most. Let me explain the two options.
On the one side there will be overhanging crags, where
the great swell and surge of Dark-eyed **Amphitrite** roars.
The blessed gods in fact call these **the Wandering Rocks**,
and birds cannot pass through them, not even the tremulous
doves that take ambrosia to Father Zeus –
the smooth rock always snatches at least one of them away –
though Zeus always adds another to make their number complete.
No ship that has reached these crags has ever yet escaped:
the sea-surge and the fierce fiery storms
sweep away the shattered planks of ships and the bodies of men alike.
That famous seagoing ship the *Argo*, known to all men,
is the only one to have made it through, on its way from Aeëtes.
It too would have wrecked against the great crags
but **Hera** saw it through on account of her love for Jason.
There are also two other crags: one of them reaches up to wide heaven
at its sharp peak, and a dark cloud surrounds
it constantly, never going away. Sunlight never
touches its peak, neither in summer nor in autumn.
Mortal man could never climb or surmount it,
not even if he had twenty hands and twenty feet.
The rock is so smooth that it looks polished.
In the middle of this crag sits a shadowy cave
that faces the west in the direction of the Underworld, exactly where you
will be directing your hollow ship, noble Odysseus.
Even a powerful archer could not hit the cave
if he were to take aim from onboard.
This is where Scylla lives, shrieking terribly.
Her voice is in fact only as loud as the cry of a new-born
puppy, yet she herself is an evil monstrosity. No one would
take pleasure in seeing this beast, not even if a god were to come upon her.
Her feet, all twelve of them, hang like tentacles,

12.60

12.65

12.70

12.75

12.80

12.85

Amphitrite   Queen of the Sea and wife of Poseidon.

the Wandering Rocks   traditionally associated with the straits of the Bosphorus; Jason's famous ship the *Argo* must pass through them in his quest for the golden fleece (see **10.136**) in the land of King Aeëtes.

Hera   she supported Jason just as Athena now supports Odysseus. This passage is commonly taken as an allusion to a pre-Homeric epic about Jason and the Argonauts, now lost to us. It is a complimentary allusion but in keeping with the competitive nature of Greek poetry (see p. 10); Homer will outdo that poem by inventing even more – and more exotic – challenges for his hero.

and she has six very long necks, each with a 12.90
gruesome head containing three rows of teeth
set thick and close, full of the blackness of death.
Half of her body sits sunk in the hollows of the cave
but she holds her heads out of the dread pit
so that she can search around the crag and fish 12.95
for dolphins and dogfish or some other even bigger
prey: roaring Amphitrite furnishes countless such creatures there.
No sailor has ever claimed to have passed
by her unharmed: she uses her heads to snatch men
from their dark-prowed ships and take them away. 12.100
You will find the second crag close by but lying lower,
Odysseus; you could hit this one with an arrow.
There's a large wild fig-tree on it, with leaves in full bloom,
and under it famous Charybdis swallows the dark water.
Three times a day this monster gushes it forth and three times a day 12.105
she swallows it back down. I pray that you're not there when she swallows
                it down.

Not even Earth-shaker could rescue you from such evil!
Approach Scylla's crag and drive the ship

An intriguing fragment of a wine-mixing bowl depicting Scylla (fourth century BC); unfortunately we cannot determine the context.

quickly past her: **it's far better**
to lose six shipmates than all of them at once."   12.110
        I spoke in reply to her words:
"But come now, goddess, tell me truthfully:
can I escape this deadly Charybdis
and at the same time fight off that Scylla when she moves to hurt my men?"
        Circe, resplendent among goddesses, was quick to reply: 12.115
"You stubborn creature! Struggle and warfare are truly
what you love! Can you not give way even to the immortal gods?
You need to understand that Scylla is not mortal but an immortal abomination:
terrifying, baleful, savage and invincible.
You can't fight her: your only defence is flight.   12.120
If you were to waste any time at her crag gearing up for a fight,
I'm afraid that she'll hit you again with
those six heads and take six more men.
Just drive by her as quickly as you can, and call upon the goddess Force,
the mother of this Scylla, who brought into this world such a misfortune
                                        for mortals.   12.125
She will stop her from attacking you a second time.
        You will then reach the island of **Thrinacia**, where the many
cows and fat flocks of Helios graze.
There are seven herds of cows and seven good flocks of sheep,
and fifty creatures to each group. They do not give birth   12.130
and they do not die; goddesses are their shepherds,

---

it's far better   rather than face the Wandering Rocks, Odysseus must choose to sail by one of two crags, each inhabited by a monster (nowadays we still talk about being 'caught between Scylla and Charybdis' in describing a choice between two bad alternatives). Naturally, Scylla and Charybdis must owe their origin to folktale, in particular seamen's stories (sailors today still tell of giant squids and other monsters of the sea!), but there is much inventiveness here. It is tempting in fact to see the two not simply as a sea-monster and a whirlpool respectively but also as misogynistic representations of Circe and Calypso (see more generally Cohen 1995): Odysseus reconfigures his frustrating experiences with these goddesses as they now become monsters, derailing his *nostos*. 'Scylla' derives from the word 'puppy' and 'Charybdis' seems to mean 'the swallower'. In one myth Circe herself changed the nymph Scylla into this monster out of jealousy for the love of the sea-god Glaucus. Tradition located Scylla and Charybdis in the straits of Messina, between Italy and Sicily. Note the references to archery here and below – see on **1.259**.

Thrinacia   traditionally identified as Sicily (the name interpreted as meaning 'three-cornered' and as referring to Sicily's triangular shape). Here Circe repeats verbatim what Tiresias had told Odysseus in the last book: the warnings about the Sun God's cows are now explicit (see also on line 300).

the Fair-haired nymphs **Phaethousa** and **Lampetia**,
whom resplendent **Neaera** gave in childbirth to **Helios Hyperion**.
After their lady mother bore them and bred them
she settled them to live far away on the island of Thrinacia   12.135
so that they could take care of their father's flocks and curly-horned oxen.
Now, if you leave these creatures untouched and concentrate on your journey
                                                         home,
you will still reach Ithaca, I assure you, though at the price of great suffering.
But if you come to harm them then I can foresee doom and destruction
for your men and your ship. Even if you do manage to escape on your own, 12.140
your journey home will be slow and miserable, and you will lose all your men."

---

1   These are Circe's last words to Odysseus. How might you compare her to
    Calypso (see **5.1–277**)? What significant common features do they share in
    the description of their persons, genealogies, activities, surroundings and
    interactions with Odysseus? How do their characterizations differ?

2   How would you characterize Circe's and Calypso's feelings for Odysseus?

12.142–65   After she spoke Golden-throned Dawn came,
and Circe, resplendent among goddesses, retreated back into the island.
       Meanwhile I made my way to the ship and urged my men
to loosen the stern-cables and embark.   12.145
They quickly got on board and sat at the oar-locks.
Sitting all in order they began to strike the white-flecked sea with their oars,
and Fair-haired Circe, dread goddess who can speak with humans,
kindly sent a following wind behind our dark-prowed
ship to fill our sails – a perfect companion.   12.150
We took our positions, each of us working over our
assigned gear. The wind and our pilot steered the ship.
It was with a heavy heart that I then turned to my men:
"It is not right, friends, that only one or two of us know
the predictions that Circe revealed to me, resplendent among goddesses. 12.155
I want to tell you so that whether we die or escape
death and doom we will do so in full possession of the facts.

Phaethousa   the name means 'radiant'; Lampetia means 'shiny', and Neaera 'newly risen'.
The word Helios means 'sun' in Greek; his son was Phaethon, whose disastrous request
to drive his father's chariot across the sky led to his death. The name Hyperion is used
of both Helios' father and Helios himself (as at **1.8**). It means 'the one going above': like
Atlas (**1.52**), he was one of the Titans.

Circe first ordered us to avoid the sound
of the divinely voiced Sirens and their flowery meadow.
She said that only I could hear their voice, and that you must   12.160
tie me up with unbreakable knots so that I can remain securely in place
                    right here,
straight up on the mast-box, and you must tie the rope-ends here as well.
And if I beg or even order you to free me,
you must then tie me down with even more rope."
With these words I revealed the details of our journey to my men.   12.165

> •   Why might Odysseus share such information with his men in this particular
>   case? What other important information does he omit, and why might he
>   do so?

12.166–91   Our good ship was quick to reach
the island of the Sirens: a favourable wind had been driving us,
but then it immediately stopped and the sea became calm,
with a stillness in the air; some god had lulled the waves to sleep.
My men rose to lower the ship's sails   12.170
and store them in the hull of the ship; they then sat down
to the rowing and churned up the waters with their smoothly polished oars.
Meanwhile I used my sharp bronze sword to cut off little chunks of wax
from a large wax-wheel and squeezed it in my stout hands.
Immediately the wax grew warm, under the commanding strength   12.175
of the sun and the blazing beams of Lord Helios, son of Hyperion.
One after the other I rubbed the wax into all my men's ears;
they then set me straight up on the mast-box
and tied me up, hand and foot, and tied up the rope-ends there as well.
Then they took their positions and began to strike the white-flecked sea
                  with their oars.   12.180
When we were within shouting distance of the island,
moving fast, the Sirens noticed how close our swift
ship had come and they began to sing their clear-toned song:

---

the Sirens   the Greek indicates that there are only two of them; they are like Homer's
own Muse – they know everything (compare the prologue) – and yet they attempt to
enchant Odysseus by singing of the Trojan War, his proudest moment (compare Odysseus'
interactions with Demodocus in Book 8). It is thought that the Sirens may have featured
in the pre-Homeric *Argonautica* and that Jason's companion Orpheus defeated them
in song (see **12.69**); if so, we find Homer again competing with that poem by inventing
this memorable picture of long-suffering Odysseus, wriggling on the mast and longing
to hear more about himself. (It is thought that wax would normally be kept on board a
ship for emergency caulking.) The flattering words in line 184 are a direct quotation of
Iliad 9.673, where an important discussion between Agamemnon and Odysseus is taking
place; it is tempting to see in the Siren's proferred song the *Iliad* itself.

"Come here, famous Odysseus, great glory of the Achaeans,
and draw up your ship so that you can hear our voices.   12.185
No one has ever reached our island
without listening to the sound of our honey-mouthed tones.
Whenever someone visits us they enjoy it and return home much more
                                                         knowledgeable:
we know all the toil and suffering that the gods brought on
Argive and Trojan alike on the plains of Ilium,   12.190
and we know everything that happens over all the rich earth."

1	How might the Sirens be compared to Circe and Calypso, or Scylla and Charybdis?
2	What is at the root of the temptation that the Sirens are presenting to Odysseus? Why is this so irresistible to him?
3	On what other occasions has Odysseus decided to risk rather than avoid a dangerous situation?
4	Why do you think so many of the dangers that Odysseus faces are represented as female?
5	Can you comment on the role of *music* or *poetry* in the epic?
6	What of the role of *knowledge* in the *Odyssey*?

12.192–231   This was the beautiful utterance of the Sirens, and I deeply
wanted to hear more, so I ordered my men to free me,
shooting fierce glances with my eyes. They simply pressed on with the rowing,
and Perimedes and Eurylochus were quick to stand up   12.195
and tie me up tighter with more ropes.
Once we had sailed past them we could then
no longer hear the Sirens singing their song;
my trusty men immediately took out the wax
that I had rubbed into their ears and untied me from the ropes.   12.200
          We left that island behind but I soon then saw
smoke and a great sea-swell, and I heard a terrific crash.
The oars flew from my men's terrified hands
and clattered all along the current. They abandoned
their thin-bladed oars and the ship was held there, motionless.   12.205
I then made my way through the craft and stirred up my men;
standing close to each one I spoke to them with words of comfort:
"We have, my friends, further trials to experience.
But this fresh misfortune is no greater than when the Cyclops
so violently herded us up in his hollow cave.   12.210
Even under those circumstances it was my courage and my intelligent scheming
that saved us – here too I am persuaded that we will one day come to savour in
                                         our minds whatever takes place.
But come now: you must all do exactly what I tell you to do.

Sit at the oar-locks and strike the deep surf
with your blades: Zeus may very well grant   12.215
us escape and deliverance from the destruction we face here.
Now this is what I need you to do, steersman, and don't forget
it – you're the one in charge of steering:
keep the ship away from the smoke
and surge and make for this crag here: don't inadvertently let the   12.220
ship head over there and put us all at great risk."
      At this the men quickly obeyed my orders.
I had not yet raised the topic of Scylla, that inescapable evil:
I feared that the men would become terrified and stop
rowing, that they would huddle themselves deep in the hull.   12.225
I pushed out of my mind the grievous injunction
of Circe: she had told me not to gear up in armour at all.
I went down for my good weaponry and brought up
two long spears and mounted the platform at the ship's
prow. It had occurred to me that Scylla would first appear   12.230
from the rock there, at the prow, in her determination to make my men suffer.

> 1   Is it true that his men owe their escape from the Cyclops to Odysseus' quick
>   wit (lines 211–12)?
>
> 2   What do you make of Odysseus' treatment of and attitude towards his men
>   in this book? Is his disobedience to Circe here rash or heroic – or both?

12.232–59   And yet I found that I could not see anything, and my eyes
grew weary from looking everywhere for her on that misty crag.
With groans we began to sail up that narrow strait.
On the one side lay Scylla, and on the other famous Charybdis,   12.235
who was horribly sucking down the briny water of the sea.
Whenever she would vomit it back up she would stir it all up
like a seething cauldron over a roaring fire, and sea-spray would
rush upwards to the tops of both the crags.
But then, when she would swallow back down the briny water of the sea,   12.240
you could see her vigorously stirring away within, while the rocks
around roared deafeningly, and you could see the earth
below, dark in the sand. Green fear seized my men.
We were fixated on Charybdis, and feared dying there,
but it was just then that Scylla pitilessly grabbed **six** of my men   12.245
from our hollow ship, six of my best fighters.
I looked back into our swift ship for my men
and just then saw the hands and feet of those
who were being carried up above over our heads. In grief they

---

six   note that Polyphemus also killed six of Odysseus' men.

shouted out my name, but it was to be the last time.
They gasped for breath as they were taken up to the crag:
it was just as when a **fisherman**, sat atop a rock
with his fishing pole, baits his hook
and casts it into the sea; once he's caught one
he tosses the wriggling creature over to one side.   12.255
As they screamed she devoured them there at the mouth of her cave;
they stretched out their hands to me as she killed them so violently.
Out of all that these eyes have seen, and out of all the suffering
I've endured in my efforts to cross the sea, *that* was the most pitiful.

---

1   Does Odysseus' simile comparing his men to fish make their death seem
    more pitiful or does it trivialize it?

2   What does Odysseus appear to forget? (See lines 124–6 above.)

3   Does the narrative here succeed in maintaining your interest even though
    you know what to expect? Can you think of any purpose served by the
    frequent overlaps and repetitions in Homeric narrative?

12.260–302   After we had escaped the crags and Scylla   12.260
and dread Charybdis we quickly reached the peerless island
of the Sun God Hyperion – and there were the fine, broad-fronted cows
and the many fat flocks that belonged to him.
Even in our black ship, while still out on the sea,
I could hear the lowing of the cattle and the bleating   12.265
of the sheep on their way back to their pens. I instantly recalled
what the blind seer, Tiresias of Thebes, had said,
and what Aeaean Circe had said when she put me under strict instructions
to avoid the island of Helios, who brings delight to man.
With a heavy heart I addressed my men: 12.270
"You have suffered much, friends, but you must listen to what I have to
                                                                     say now:

I will tell you the prophecy of Tiresias
and Aeaean Circe, who put me under strict instructions
to avoid the island of Helios, who brings delight to men.
She said that a most fearsome evil awaits us here –   12.275
let's drive our black ship on, past this island."
          My men's hearts broke on hearing these words.
Eurylochus' reply sent a shudder down my spine:

---

fisherman   the fisherman simile is particularly vivid and grisly; it coheres with the image
at lines 439–40, also drawn from daily life (compare **9.384–8** and **10.410–17**). With the
subjectivity in lines 258–9 we remember that Odysseus is of course still narrating to his
audience in Phaeacia.

"You are a stubborn creature, Odysseus: you've an excess of might and
inexhaustible

physical strength. And now you're made entirely of iron   12.280
if you won't allow your men, sated with exhaustion
and lack of sleep, to disembark: here's a sea-girt
island where we could assemble a good meal –
but here you are telling us to drive off from the island through the mists
of the sea and wander off through the swiftly approaching night.   12.285
And it's at night-time that the difficult winds spring up and wipe out
ships. How could anyone escape immediate death
if a windstorm suddenly rises?
It could be Notus or blustering Zephyr – these winds
especially can shatter ships without the involvement of any particular
divinity.   12.290

Let's give in now to black night,
wait by our swift ship, and prepare a meal.
We will rise at dawn and push off onto the wide sea."
        The men approved what Eurylochus had said,
and at that moment I realized that some god was putting misfortune in
our path.   12.295

I replied to him in vigorous language:
"You and the rest here are forcing my hand, Eurylochus: I am but one man.
Come now, all of you must swear a mighty oath for me:
if we come upon a herd of cattle or a large flock
of sheep here, no one is permitted to succumb to wanton **recklessness**   12.300
and kill any such creature. Be content with
eating the food that immortal Circe has given us."

> • Do you think that Odysseus, as a leader, is being sufficiently clear with his
> men here and elsewhere in this book? What does he really think of them?

12.303–453   They were quick to obey my orders and swear that they wouldn't.
Once they had finished swearing the oath
we moored our good ship in a curved harbour,   12.305
near fresh water, and my men disembarked
from the ship and carefully prepared a meal.
Once they had sated their appetite for food and drink,
they recalled in tears their friends,

---

recklessness *atasthalia*, the word used at **1.34**; naturally, the Sun God's cows form a clear
parallel with Odysseus' livestock back in Ithaca, currently being devoured by the suitors.
Sacred animals were not unknown in ancient Greece (e.g. sacred snakes were kept on
the Acropolis in Athens); the episode resonates with the themes of taboo and 'forbidden
fruit'; for folkloric connections see Page 1973, chapter 4 and Segal 1994, chapter 10.

the ones whom Scylla had taken from the hollow ship and devoured.　12.310
Sweet sleep then fell upon them as they wept.
But when the third part of the night arrived and the stars ascended into the sky,
Cloud-gatherer Zeus stirred up a furious wind
in a deafening storm, covering land and sea alike
with clouds. Night sprang from the sky.　12.315
　　　　When Early-born Rosy-fingered Dawn appeared
we drew the ship into a hollow cave and beached it onshore –
it was a place where nymphs would gather to dance.
I called for an assembly and spoke amidst the men:
"Because we have food and drink in our swift ship,　12.320
my friends, let's keep our hands off the cattle and avoid any suffering here.
These cows and fat flocks belong to the dread god
Helios, who sees all and hears all."
　　　　Their stout hearts were satisfied with what I said,
but for a month Notus blew without ceasing and there was no　12.325
other wind blowing except for Eurus and Notus.
As long as the men had food and red wine on hand
they kept their hands off the cows because they wanted to survive.
But once the ship's supplies gave out
they were forced to begin roving over the island, hunting　12.330
for fish and birds, whatever they could catch,
using hook and line: starvation was beginning to wear them down.
It was then that I made my way up further into the island so that I could pray
to the gods in the hope that one of them might show me how to get back home.
As I made my way through the island and got some distance from my men,　12.335
I found a place where there was shelter from the wind; I washed my hands there
and prayed to all the gods who hold Olympus.
They then poured sweet sleep over my eyes;
meanwhile Eurylochus presented his baleful plan to the men:
"**Though you have suffered much**, my friends, listen to what I have to say.　12.340
All forms of death are hateful to wretched mortals
but to die and meet one's doom by starvation is the most miserable.
Come now, let's herd the best of these cattle that belong to Helios
and sacrifice them to the immortals who hold wide heaven.
And if we do reach our homeland of Ithaca　12.345
then we will immediately build a sumptuous temple
to Helios Hyperion and put many fine offerings in it.
But if he somehow becomes angry over his high-horned cows
and wants to destroy our ship and the other gods support him,

---

Though you have suffered much　the whole of line 340 is a direct quotation of Odysseus'
words at 271; note that Odysseus similarly falls asleep at **10.31**; he will reveal to his
audience how he came to know all of this at lines 389–90.

I would choose a quick death by drowning in the sea   12.350
over a slow death by starvation on a deserted island."
The men approved what Eurylochus had said,
then immediately herded up the best of the cattle that belonged to Helios –
the curved-horned, beautiful, broad-fronted beasts
were pasturing near our dark-prowed ship.   12.355
They surrounded them and plucked fresh leaves
from a tall oak tree because they had no white barley
in the well-benched ship; they then began their prayers to the gods.
Once they had finished praying and slaughtering and skinning the cows
they cut off the thighs and covered them with fat,   12.360
folding them up with a double fold and laying the raw flesh on top.
They had no wine to pour over the **blazing sacrifices**
so they made a libation using water and roasted the entrails completely.
After they had burnt the thighs and tasted the innards
they cut up the flesh and pierced the meat onto spits.   12.365
It was then that sweet sleep dissolved from my eyes
and I made for our swift ship on the seashore.
As I approached the curved craft

Sixteenth-century painter Pellegrino Tibaldi vividly catches the moment of suspense and horror,
even in the cow's eyes, as Eurylochus and the men prepare their feast.

blazing sacrifices   such sacrificial scenes are common in epic (e.g. *Iliad* 1.447–74): the
gods receive certain cuts (i.e. the entrails) while the rest goes to the humans; thus
sacrifices provided worshippers with meat on festivals and other important occasions.
Here Odysseus' men seem to be appeasing the gods in the hopes of forestalling their
anger at them for killing the sacred cattle.

then the sweet scent of the smoking fat came over me.
I cried out in pain and shouted loudly to the immortal gods: 12.370
"Father Zeus and you other blessed gods who live for ever,
you have used cruel sleep to lull me off to my destruction
while my men stayed here and devised this monstrosity!"
Long-robed Lampetia then went swiftly as messenger
to Helios Hyperion to say that we had killed his cows. 12.375
In deep anger he immediately addressed the immortals:
"Father Zeus and you other blessed gods who live for ever,
take vengeance on Odysseus' men!
They have insolently killed my cows! On my journeys into the starry
sky and on my descent back from heaven to earth as well, 12.380
it was the sight of these beasts that delighted me.
Now, if they do not pay a fair and just price for killing my animals
I will descend to the house of Hades and give my light only to the dead!"
        Cloud-gatherer Zeus then said in reply:
"Keep shining, Helios, among immortals 12.385
and mortals on the life-giving earth.
I will quickly strike their swift ship with my bright thunderbolt
and smash it into bits over the wine-dark sea."
(**I heard all this** from Fair-haired Calypso,
who had heard it from Messenger Hermes.) 12.390
When I returned to our ship by the seashore
my men were arguing intensely with one another; we were incapable
of coming up with any kind of solution – the cows were already dead!
The gods then began to produce **some prodigies**:
the skins of the cows began to crawl, and the meat on the spits, whether
                                                                    cooked 12.395
or raw, was mooing with the sound of the cows.
For six more days thereafter my trusty men
kept rounding up the best of Helios' cows and feasting on them.
        But then when Zeus son of Cronus brought the seventh day to pass,
the raging storm-winds abated 12.400
and we immediately embarked and set sail on the wide sea
after raising the mast and hoisting up the white sails.
Once we'd left the island no other land

I heard all this   compare Homer's concern for preserving narrative plausibility at **10.210–60**; such comments remind us of the unique position of greater knowledge enjoyed by the poet (see note on divine inspiration and the invocation of the Muse in the opening line of the epic, **1.1**).

some prodigies   these bad omens are paralleled with similar ones experienced by the suitors in Book 20; the men's improvised sacrifices at 356–65 above seem similarly ominous.

could be seen, just sea and sky,
but then the son of Cronus created a dark cloud   12.405
over our hollow ship, and the sea darkened underneath it.
Our ship ran further for only a little while, for Zephyr soon
came with a shriek and a raging storm;
a gust of wind then smashed the forestays on the mast,
both of them. The mast then fell backwards and all the gear   12.410
poured into the hull. Back at the stern the mast
struck the steersman flat on the head and crushed in one
fell swoop all the bones in his skull. He fell like an acrobat
from the stern-platform as his brave spirit departed from his bones.
Zeus then thundered and, at the very same moment, struck the ship with
                          lightning;   12.415
with this blast the ship began to spin around completely
and became full of brimstone as the men fell overboard.
They floated around the black ship on the waves,
bobbing like seagulls – and the gods prohibited any return home for them.
    Meanwhile I was making my way through the ship to where   12.420
a wave had loosened the keel from the hull. The surge was making off with
                          the bare keel
and had smashed the ship's mast against it, though the
backstay, made of leather, remained attached to the mast.
With this piece I then bound the keel and mast together,
perched myself on top of the two and found myself being carried off by the
                          baneful winds.   12.425
Zephyr then stopped blowing with his raging storm
but Notus quickly came next, bringing heartache:
I was following the path back to that deadly Charybdis.
I floated all night long, and with the return of sunlight
I had reached Scylla's crag and dire Charybdis.   12.430
The monster began to swallow up the salty water of the sea
but I lifted myself upwards towards the tall wild fig-tree
and clung to it **like a bat**. And yet I could not

---

like a bat   a striking image drawn from real life; Odysseus simply means that he clung
to the fig-tree from morning (line 429) till evening. The image could not contrast with
his current situation more starkly. The picture of Odysseus patiently clinging to the fig-
tree perfectly realizes the endurance of 'long-suffering' Odysseus; it is remarkable that
the suitors' ghosts in the Underworld are compared to bats (24.6), as Odysseus is here;
these are the only two mentions of bats in all of Homer (compare the men as seagulls at
12.419). We should also compare the image of Odysseus clinging to the underside of the
ram as he escapes Polyphemus' cave at **9.435**. This image is followed by another (lines
439–41) that returns the narrative to the civilized world familiar to Odysseus as ruler and
law-giver on his own island.

find any firm footing or climb onto it
because the roots were too far away and the branches were too high: 12.435
they were vast and long, overshadowing Charybdis.
I refused to let go until that monster vomited back out
the mast and the keel. I waited in eager expectation and in time
they returned. When a man gets up to leave the assembly for his supper
after judging the many contentious cases that young men bring to court,   12.440
that was the time that the ship's timber appeared out of the mouth of Charybdis.
I let go of the tree with my hands and feet and fell down,
crashing down in between the two long pieces of wood.
I perched myself on top of them and began to row with my hands.
The Father of men and gods prevented Scylla from seeing   12.445
me, otherwise I would not have escaped flat-out annihilation.
    For nine days after this I floated along, and on the tenth night
the gods drove me towards the island of Ogygia, where Fair-haired
Calypso dwells, dread goddess who can speak with humans.
She loved me and took care of me. But why go on with this part of the
                                   story?   12.450

I related this narrative yesterday, here in your palace,
to yourself and to your good wife. And naturally I am loath
to repeat again what was told clearly enough then.'

1   With these words Odysseus has now explained to the Phaeacians how he
lost 12 ships and hundreds of men in the course of a couple of years; he
mentioned briefly in Book 7 that he had spent the following seven years
with Calypso on Ogygia. What do you make of Odysseus' great narrative?
How much of the narrative seems appropriate to his own situation in
Phaeacia? Is there any element of self-criticism discernible?

2   Think about Book 9's Polyphemus in particular: why does Homer have
Odysseus spend so much time on that single episode?

3   Which episodes highlight which qualities in Odysseus?

4   Does Odysseus always come across in a positive light? Since Odysseus is
actually speaking, how does Homer manage to suggest any subtleties in
characterizing him?

5   Think back over the various occasions at which the gods have been said to
be involved in the lives of mortals. Under what circumstances are the gods
suspected of involvement? To put it another way, what exactly *do* the gods
do over the course of the poem? Homeric epic is famously characterized as
exhibiting so-called 'double-motivation', i.e. certain things have both divine
and human origin. The effect can be fruitfully compared to the magical
realism that we associate today with the fiction of Kafka, Márquez and
Rushdie.

Part Four (Books 13–20): Homecoming

With Books 13–20 we find a dramatic shift in pace and tone: Odysseus finally achieves his *nostos* at the outset and very little action follows; the emphasis now is more on speech and characterization. Everything seems to be slowly leading up to the final showdown between Odysseus and the suitors, and the leisurely pace is Homer's way of building up suspense on a truly grand scale. The only vital action that takes place is the reunion of Odysseus and Telemachus in Book 16, and Odysseus' interview with Penelope in Book 19: does she recognize him or not? Otherwise Odysseus spends his time learning whom he can trust and whom not, all the while plotting how to destroy the suitors. Ultimately it is his wife who comes up with a critical part of the plan: the contest of the bow (Book 22). Some readers have faulted these books for their lack of action, but Odysseus' position is precarious: if he appears openly to all 108 of these mighty suitors he runs the risk of ambush (like his son), hence Athena's plan for a disguise – all in an echo of Odysseus' other great trick, the Trojan Horse.

Book 13

As Book 13 opens the Phaeacians are struck dumb with amazement at the close of Odysseus' story. King Alcinous urges all the Phaeacian chieftains to join him in giving Odysseus suitable gifts. On the next day they take this treasure down to the ship, then return to the palace for another meal, with another performance by Demodocus. As the sun sets, Odysseus asks to be allowed to leave and prays for his host's prosperity. The king and queen send Odysseus off with a crew of 52 men for this night-time journey; curiously enough the Phaeacians make Odysseus a bed aboard the ship; they push off and Odysseus sleeps a sleep that 'closely resembles death' (line 80). The ship is miraculously fast, faster than a falcon, 'the fastest of things that fly' (line 87). With the rise of the morning star the ship arrives at Ithaca and the Phaeacians deposit Odysseus, still asleep, onshore with all his treasure intact, next to an olive tree, symbol of Athena's protection. Poseidon notices that Odysseus has reached home safely, and Zeus grants his brother permission to turn the Phaeacian ship, now almost home again, into stone. Alcinous recognizes the shocking phenomenon as the fulfilment of an old prophecy. (Polyphemus has a similar moment of recollection at **9.506–21**.)

1   Why does Odysseus make a mysterious night-time journey? Do you find any symbolism here?

2   What else has happened when Odysseus falls asleep aboard a ship?

3   Why does Odysseus seem always to bring trouble to those he visits? (Compare **10.72–5.**)

The scene suddenly shifts back to Ithaca as Odysseus awakes; he does not recognize his fatherland, and Athena has poured a mist around him to keep others from recognizing him prematurely. Athena eventually appears to Odysseus in the guise of a handsome young shepherd boy and tells him that he is in Ithaca; Odysseus in turn responds guardedly, claiming that he is a fugitive from Crete who served in the Trojan War. Athena smiles and transforms herself into the mortal form of a woman, playfully chiding Odysseus for lying to her. She promises to look after him and his treasure, but he has hardships to face. Odysseus protests that she abandoned him after Troy until he reached Scheria, and insists that she's trying to deceive him now. Athena explains that she did not want to offend Poseidon. The two of them now work together to hide Odysseus' treasure safely in a nearby cave, then, sitting together against an olive tree, plot 'the destruction of the reckless suitors' (line 373). Athena tells Odysseus that he must make his way to the loyal swineherd Eumaeus' hut while she returns to Sparta to summon Telemachus. She then transforms Odysseus into an old beggar.

What aspects of Athena do you find in this painting of the goddess by Gustav Klimt (1898)? What, for instance, do you make of her eyes?

Book 14

As Book 14 opens, Odysseus finds Eumaeus in his hut out in the countryside of Ithaca. Farm dogs rush to attack Odysseus, but Eumaeus scares them off. The swineherd instantly attests to his loyalty towards his missing master and offers the 'old man' room and board. He spreads a thick goatskin from his own bed for Odysseus; Odysseus is pleased and prays for Zeus to grant Eumaeus all he wishes for. Eumaeus explains that he is only doing what is right since 'Zeus looks after strangers'; he adds that the gods have kept his former master Odysseus from returning home from Troy and that Odysseus had treated him kindly, giving him home, land and a wife. He curses Helen. Eumaeus then generously sacrifices and roasts two pigs – young ones, since it's the suitors who get the fattened swine – and urges Odysseus to eat. Over the meal he bitterly explains the situation with the suitors, highlighting the fact that the suitors don't even sacrifice to Zeus despite all the feasting, and adding more information for us as readers as he describes the vast extent of Odysseus' wealth: no twenty Ithacans put together have as much as Odysseus had. Odysseus eats his meal without a word, 'meditating misfortune for the suitors' (line 110), then asks Eumaeus to name his missing master: he might have some news of him. Eumaeus becomes suspicious here, and says that Odysseus might just be yet another lying vagrant offering false news to the vulnerable Penelope in return for some hospitality. But he talks himself out of this since he is convinced that Odysseus is dead anyway and therefore no one can in fact have any news of him. In deep reverence he eventually names his master, lamenting his loss.

The *Odyssey* and later literature: Joyce's *Ulysses*

In one of the innumerable allusions to the *Odyssey* in Joyce's *Ulysses* (see Zajovi 2004 for an overview), we find Bloom (Odysseus) and Stephen (Telemachus) in an analogous 'cabman's shelter' (Eumaeus' hut). The *Odyssey* was hugely popular in early twentieth-century modernist literature; here Joyce nicely captures the atmosphere of hospitality, chat, and tall tales.

Mr Bloom and Stephen entered the cabman's shelter, an unpretentious wooden structure, where, prior to then, he had rarely, if ever, been before; the former having previously whispered to the latter a few hints anent the keeper of it, said to be the once famous Skin-the-Goat, Fitzharris, the invincible, though he wouldn't vouch for the actual facts, which quite possibly there was not one vestige of truth in. A few moments later saw our two noctambules safely seated in a discreet corner, only to be greeted by stares from the decidedly miscellaneous collection of waifs and strays and other nondescript specimens of the genus homo, already there engaged in eating and drinking, diversified by conversation, for whom they seemingly formed an object of marked curiosity.

> *—Now touching a cup of coffee, Mr Bloom ventured to plausibly suggest to break the ice, it occurs to me you ought to sample something in the shape of solid food, say a roll of some description.*

James Joyce, *Ulysses* (pp. 715–16 Penguin edn.)

Odysseus immediately asserts to Eumaeus that his master is indeed returning and will be back within a year. To prove his trustworthiness he refuses to take any reward for this news until the hero has actually returned. Eumaeus dismisses the report and expresses concern for Telemachus; he knows the suitors are plotting to kill him. He then asks his visitor where he's from and how he reached Ithaca.

There follows the second of Odysseus' 'Cretan tales': this one a much longer and more elaborate variant on the one originally told to Athena in the previous book; in many places there are echoes of Odysseus' narrative in Books 9–12. He claims that while in Egypt he learned that Odysseus was coming back to Ithaca soon. Eumaeus finds the narrative moving but refuses to accept that Odysseus is still alive and, ironically, asserts that his guest is lying. Odysseus objects; Eumaeus remains sceptical and urges that they eat supper, all the while cursing the suitors and praying piously for Odysseus' return. There follows a detailed description of a heroic feast, resonant of such great scenes in the *Odyssey* and the *Iliad*, yet set in a humble swineherd's hut. With the onset of harsh weather, Odysseus tests the swineherd to see whether he will give him a cloak for the night. Now he launches into yet another yarn, about a night raid at Troy he was asked to join. The weather was similarly bad then, and Odysseus and Menelaus were co-captains with himself. He had foolishly left his cloak behind and complained of the cold to Odysseus, who then craftily arranged for him to have one. Eumaeus catches the hint and asserts that Telemachus will give the old beggar a cloak, but then ultimately finds a cloak for Odysseus, who falls asleep happy in the knowledge that he and his property are being so well looked after. Eumaeus goes out to sleep among the pigs.

> • Note the importance of using *speech* to get things done in the *Odyssey*. Can you recall other episodes that illustrate this theme? How do those episodes compare with this one?

Book 15

The scene now changes to Sparta, where we left Telemachus in Book 4. It is night-time, and the anxious Telemachus cannot sleep. Athena appears to him and urges him to get moving: Eurymachus, she asserts, is close to marrying his mother, and Penelope, like any woman, cannot be trusted and cannot wait any longer for marriage. She warns him of the suitors' ambush and tells him to find Eumaeus at once. At daybreak his departure is accompanied by a favourable omen: an eagle flies by, carrying a goose in its talons (and prefiguring Penelope's dream in Book 19). Helen interprets the omen as a symbol for Odysseus' triumph over the suitors. On the way home Telemachus stops at Pylos (compare Book 3), where a fugitive approaches him as a suppliant: it is a prophet named **Theoclymenus**, who has killed a fellow countryman (motive mysteriously unexplained) and is now seeking to avoid death at the hands of the man's kinsmen – a prefiguration of

---

The *Odyssey* and later literature: Shakespeare's *Troilus and Cressida*

Odysseus was renowned in antiquity for his cunning use of speech, beginning with the *Iliad*, where he suppresses mutiny in Book 2 by rousing animosity against Thersites, and in Book 9 is chosen to accompany the embassy to Achilles in order to persuade the great warrior to return to the fight. Shakespeare's Ulysses in *Troilus and Cressida* owes a great deal to this Odysseus; his famous speech on 'degree' (or rank) is worth quoting in part here; it is his analysis of why Troy hasn't been taken yet:

The speciality of rule hath been neglected,
And look how many Grecian tents do stand
Hollow upon this plain, so many hollow factions.
When that the general is not like the hive
To whom the foragers shall all repair,
What honey is expected? Degree being vizarded,
Th'unworthiest shows as fairly in the mask.
The heavens themselves, the planets and this centre
Observe degree, priority, and place,
Insisture, course, proportion, season, form,
Office, and custom in all line of order.
And therefore is the glorious planet Sol
In noble eminence enthroned and sphered
Amidst the other, whose med'cinable eye
Corrects the influence of evil planets
And posts like the commandment of a king
Sans check to good and bad; but when the planets
In evil mixture to disorder wander,
What plagues and what portents, what mutiny,
What raging of the sea, shaking of earth,
Commotion in the winds, frights, changes, horrors,
Divert and crack, rend and deracinate,
The unity and married calm of states
Quite from their fixture! O, when degree is shaked,
Which is the ladder of all high designs,
The enterprise is sick.
[…]

Theoclymenus   his name can be translated 'God-listener'; he plays an important part at the end of Book 20. He forms a neat foil to Odysseus' seer Tiresias (Books 10–11), and invites us to compare Telemachus and his father more closely.

> The general's disdained
> By him one step below, he by the next,
> That next by him beneath – so every step,
> Exampled by the first pace that is sick
> Of his superior, grows to an envious fever
> Of pale and bloodless emulation;
> And 'tis this fever that keeps Troy on foot,
> Not her own sinews. To end a tale of length,
> Troy in our weakness stands, not in her strength.
>
> Shakespeare, *Troilus and Cressida* 1.3.78–103 and 130–8

the close of the *Odyssey*. Telemachus generously welcomes the prophet on board his ship and they set sail.

The scene now switches back to Ithaca. Odysseus wants to test the loyalty of Eumaeus yet again. He seeks advice as to whether he should go and beg among the suitors and do some work for them. Eumaeus denounces the suitors and warns Odysseus not to go: he will find only trouble there and he should wait here for Telemachus to return: he will treat him kindly. Odysseus then asks about his own mother and father: are they alive or dead? Laertes is alive but in constant mourning, and Anticlea died of grief. Eumaeus reminisces over how Anticlea brought him up along with Ctimene, Odysseus' sister. Odysseus asks Eumaeus how he came to be part of the family, and Eumaeus is only too happy to tell. As if to mirror Odysseus' long-winded Cretan tale, the swineherd now narrates the story of how he was a king's son who was betrayed by his nurse into being kidnapped by pirates. The miniature epic resonates with many themes of the larger whole: deception, craft, sailing, narrative, palace culture. Eventually Laertes purchased Eumaeus as a slave. Odysseus is grateful for the story.

The scene now changes yet again to Telemachus and the narrative pace quickens: he has made it ashore on Ithaca safely. He sends his men ahead to the city and sets out for Eumaeus' hut. Theoclymenus asks: should I stay with you or go to Odysseus' palace? Telemachus knows better than to send him to the palace but actually contemplates sending him to the house of Eurymachus, who he admits to be the best of the suitors. But another divine portent appears: a falcon flies by on the (auspicious) right, carrying a pigeon. Theoclymenus interprets it as a favourable omen and tells Telemachus that his family will rule over Ithaca for ever; Telemachus then asks a close friend to look after Theoclymenus. The book closes as Telemachus finds the loyal Eumaeus asleep again among the pigs.

Book 16

Book 16 opens at daybreak: Odysseus notices that the dogs don't bark at Telemachus: they recognize their master. Eumaeus greets Telemachus warmly, 'as a father', and the latter asks for news of the palace. They share a meal with Odysseus, and Telemachus asks about this stranger. Eumaeus urges Telemachus to give the stranger hospitality; Telemachus replies that he will indeed look after him, but will not permit him to go to the palace for fear that the suitors will abuse him. Odysseus keeps his identity hidden from his son and declares that he is willing to fight the suitors. Telemachus explains his humiliating situation to

---

The *Odyssey* and later literature: Ralph Ellison's *Invisible Man*

The idea of being invisible has long appealed to philosophical explorations of right and wrong, and in the case of Ralph Ellison's *Invisible Man* (1952), racism. These are the opening words of the novel (see Hall 2008, pp. 53–7 for further connections):

I am an invisible man.

No, I am not a spook like those who haunted Edgar Allan Poe; nor am I one of your Hollywood-movie ectoplasms. I am a man of substance, of flesh and bone, fiber and liquids – and I might even be said to possess a mind. I am invisible, understand, simply because people refuse to see me. Like the bodiless heads you see sometimes in circus sideshows, it is as though I have been surrounded by mirrors of hard, distorting glass. When they approach me they see only my surroundings, themselves, or figments of their imagination – indeed, everything and anything except me.

Nor is my invisibility exactly a matter of a biochemical accident to my epidermis. That invisibility to which I refer occurs because of a peculiar disposition of the eyes of those with whom I come in contact. A matter of construction of their inner *eyes, those eyes with which they look through their physical eyes upon reality. I am not complaining, nor am I protesting either. It is sometimes advantageous to be unseen, although it is most often rather wearing on the nerves. Then too, you're constantly being bumped against by those of poor vision. Or again, you often doubt if you really exist. You wonder whether you aren't simply a phantom in other people's minds. Say, a figure in a nightmare which the sleeper tries with all his strength to destroy. It's when you feel like this that, out of resentment, you begin to bump people back. And, let me confess, you feel that way most of the time. You ache with the need to convince yourself that you do exist in the real world, that you're a part of all the sound and anguish, and you strike out with your fists, you curse and you swear to make them recognize you.*

Herodotus and Plato preserve the myth of the shepherd Gyges, who stumbles upon a magic ring granting invisibility which he then uses to become king. We might extend the notion of invisibility to Odysseus' status as a returning veteran of war; psychiatrist Jonathan Shay has argued persuasively (2002) that much of Odysseus' experience back in Ithaca resembles the plight of such veterans and that his behaviour shows traces of combat trauma.

this old beggar, then instructs Eumaeus to go and tell Penelope that he is safe. The swineherd departs and Athena now appears to Odysseus alone, in the guise of a woman, and tells him to reveal his identity to Telemachus; she then transforms and improves his appearance. Telemachus is astonished as Odysseus reveals himself and refuses to believe that he is not some god come to earth. Odysseus perseveres and the two share a happy, tearful reunion. Odysseus goes on to tell some of his story and the two plot the death of the suitors. Telemachus doubts they can take on the 108 suitors and all their attendants successfully, but Odysseus assures him that Athena and Zeus will help them, and he unfolds his plan: Telemachus is to return to the palace in the morning and put Odysseus' weapons in a storeroom, distracting the suitors with an excuse. Eumaeus will then bring Odysseus to the palace, disguised again as an old beggar. Telemachus must not flinch if the suitors abuse him, nor must he tell anyone that Odysseus has returned, not even his mother. Odysseus will gauge the loyalty of the slaves first hand.

Eumaeus now departs from the palace, having delivered his message to Penelope. The suitors are outraged at the news and recall their ambush, expressing fears that their fellow Ithacans will hear of their failed plan; they must therefore consider murdering Telemachus immediately and decide on a husband for Penelope – or abandon the palace altogether. Penelope learns of the debate through the faithful Medon and rebukes the suitors, Antinous in particular. Eurymachus replies that

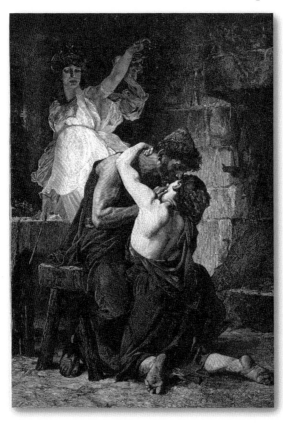

A touching nineteenth-century version of the reunion of Odysseus and Telemachus (presided over by Athena) by Henri Lucien Doucet.

no one will touch Telemachus – unless the gods will it. Just before Eumaeus returns to his hut, Athena transforms Odysseus once again into an old beggar, and the three share a meal and go to bed.

Book 17

In the morning Telemachus urges Eumaeus to take Odysseus into the town of Ithaca, where his prospects of begging will be better. Telemachus returns to the palace and is reunited with Euryclea and Penelope. He makes for the place of assembly and collects the prophet Theoclymenus, bringing him back to the palace. He offers him hospitality and then tells Penelope about his journey to visit Nestor and Menelaus, revealing what the latter told him about Odysseus: he is stuck on Ogygia with Calypso. Theoclymenus then interrupts to assert that Odysseus is actually on Ithaca right now: an omen has told him so. Penelope hopes that this is true; Telemachus does not say anything.

The suitors are now seen playing sports and feasting as Eumaeus and Odysseus make for the palace. On their way they meet the nasty goatherd Melanthius, henchman to the suitors, who curses them and tries to knock Odysseus down; the latter debates whether to kill him on the spot but resists the temptation. As they approach the palace, Odysseus hears the music of Phemius the poet; in a particularly pathetic scene, Odysseus' old and tick-ridden dog Argus ('Flash' or 'Swifty') lifts his head from a pile of manure and wags his tail in recognition of his old master, now home after 19 years. Eumaeus does not notice as Odysseus sheds a tear; the swineherd tells Odysseus of the former prowess and current neglect of Argus, and the dog passes away.

Eumaeus is now reunited with Telemachus and the latter instructs his father to start begging among the suitors. Athena mysteriously stands next to Odysseus and urges him to beg as well so that he can 'know which are just and which are unjust', despite the fact that, as Homer now tells us clearly, she is not going to 'defend any of them from misfortune'. As Odysseus collects food from the suitors they enquire after his identity and Melanthius tells them that Eumaeus has brought him. Antinous chastizes Eumaeus for bringing yet another beggar into their midst. Eumaeus begins to argue but Telemachus stops him and criticizes Antinous for his stinginess; the latter responds by picking up a footstool to throw at Odysseus as a 'gift' for the beggar. (The sarcasm is reminiscent of Polyphemus' 'gifts' at **9.370**.) Odysseus approaches Antinous and flatters him: he is the best of the suitors and should accordingly give generously; Odysseus then briefly retells his 'Cretan tale' of how he was once rich but lost all. Antinous is unmoved and refuses to give him anything; when Odysseus finds fault with him the suitor hurls the footstool at him. Once struck, Odysseus withdraws and protests that Antinous is unjust; the suitors actually agree and warn Antinous that the beggar could be some god, testing men.

Penelope, outside the main dining-hall, learns that the beggar has been struck and mutters a curse on Antinous. She then tells Eumaeus to send the beggar to her so that she can welcome him and see whether he knows anything of Odysseus 'because he seems like a much-wandered man'. Eumaeus praises the old beggar's storytelling skills and compares him to a poet; he says that he does indeed have news of Odysseus. Penelope excitedly demands to see the man and promises that she will give him clothes if what he says is true; Telemachus now sneezes, a favourable omen. Odysseus tells Eumaeus that he will see Penelope in private after sunset, in order to avoid bringing further attention to himself among the suitors; Penelope consents and Eumaeus heads back home.

Book 18

Another beggar, Irus, now enters the palace and tries to drive Odysseus away with threats. Odysseus asks him to leave him alone. Antinous overhears the beggars arguing and, finding it entertaining, eggs them on to fight and offers prizes to the winner. Odysseus asks for a fair fight and Telemachus guarantees it. As Odysseus prepares to fight, Athena makes him look larger and the suitors are astonished. Irus becomes frightened but Antinous orders him to fight. Odysseus ponders just how badly he should defeat the beggar, aware that he might arouse suspicion with too great a show of strength. He takes a blow but then knocks Irus down.

An early twentieth-century rendition of Odysseus' fight with Irus by Lovis Corinth vividly captures the chaos amid the suitors.

The suitors find it all very amusing and congratulate the victor, who warns them that Odysseus is 'very close' and that they will have a fight on their hands if they stay in the palace. Homer states that one of the suitors, Amphinomus, then grew sad and 'saw in his heart the misfortune to come, / but did not escape doom and destruction since Athena had bound him / to fall at the hands and lance of Telemachus' (lines 154–6).

Athena then inspires Penelope to enter the hall 'so that she might open / the hearts of the suitors and so that she might seem more valuable / in the eyes of her husband and son than previously' (lines 160–2). The goddess then causes Penelope to have a quick sleep and makes her more beautiful. On making her entrance, Penelope rouses the passion of the suitors. She chastizes Telemachus for letting the stranger fight with Irus. Eurymachus praises Penelope's beauty but she disagrees: she tells the company that all her beauty was lost on the day that Odysseus left for Troy, and she recalls in detail their moment of parting, even quoting Odysseus' order for her to remarry once Telemachus becomes an adult. As she criticizes the suitors for their behaviour, Odysseus is impressed and delighted with his wife's cunning. Antinous emphatically asserts that the suitors will not leave the palace until she chooses a husband; he tells his fellow suitors to bring in more gifts and they do so.

As the company now turns to dancing and music, Odysseus addresses the slave-girls, urging them to tend to Penelope, who has now returned to her rooms. The girls ridicule him, in particular one Melantho, sister of the goatherd Melanthius. Homer describes how Penelope had reared her as her own daughter but the girl was selfish and she was in fact sleeping with Eurymachus. Melantho lashes out at

A representation from the mid-fifth century BC of Penelope at the loom, with Telemachus. How would you describe their moods?

Odysseus, who then threatens to report her to Telemachus, who will 'cut her into pieces'. The girls retreat inside in terror.

Homer states that Athena then inspires the suitors to become even more reckless in order to wound Odysseus more deeply. Eurymachus taunts Odysseus as a lazy beggar and the latter replies that he is a hard worker, warning him yet again of Odysseus' return. In anger the suitor flings a footstool at Odysseus but misses; the suitors complain that all of this is unseemly. Telemachus boldly criticizes them, and they 'bite their lips / in surprise'. Amphinomus urges the company to leave the stranger alone and let Telemachus look after him; more drinking and libations follow, and the suitors eventually leave for their homes.

Book 19

19.1–46

But illustrious Odysseus remained in the palace,
plotting to murder the suitors with the aid of Athena.
He was quick to address Telemachus excitedly:
'We must put every last weapon in storage,
Telemachus, and when the suitors begin looking for them and asking
                        awkward questions   19.5
you will have to persuade and placate them like this:
"I have put them in storage owing to the smoke: they are not in the same state
                        as they were
when Odysseus left them as he set out for Troy:
all this smoke has scorched them and ruined them.
But the gods have also put an even more important reason in my mind: 19.10
if you men have accidentally had a bit too much to drink and start fighting,
you could harm one another and ruin the feasting
and the wooing – weapons have a way of attracting only more weapons to
                        themselves."'

        Satisfied with his father's instructions, Telemachus
next summoned the nurse Euryclea and spoke: 19.15
'Come now, good mother, please tell the slave-girls to stop whatever they're
                        doing and stay put
so that I can put my father's good armour
in storage: ever since his departure it's lain neglected throughout the house
and the smoke is tarnishing it. I was just a child when he left
but now I want to put it where it can't get scorched.'   19.20
His beloved nurse Euryclea then replied:
'How I wish you would spare a thought for the
upkeep of the house, my child, and look after everything we have here.
But come, tell me, who do you want to come along and carry the lamp for you?
You said the slave-girls should stay put but they could do it.'   19.25
Shrewd Telemachus said in reply:

Direct speech in Homer

Direct speech is an important component of the poetry of Homer, as Socrates notes in Plato's *Republic* (392d–393b). Often a speech will repeat what has already been described in the narrative. An interesting example of this is the description of Eurylochus' encounter with Circe in Book 10. First we are given a description of it in the narrative (though we must remember that this is itself a story within a story, since it is part of Odysseus' retelling of his exploits to his Phaeacian audience that extends through Books 9–12). Then Eurylochus recounts the same incident as he tells the story of his escape to Odysseus (**10.251–60**); his compressed version includes phrases identical to those used in the narrative. In the opening lines of Book 19 we have a variant, in which Odysseus gives Telemachus instructions which Telemachus then paraphrases as he in turn instructs Euryclea. This practice is unusual in modern literature and might seem to us repetitive, but in oral poetry these embedded speeches (which make up a large proportion of the overall narrative) can function as a poem's building blocks, as it were: an oral poet doesn't memorize a poem word for word, but has in mind the outline structure, and then builds up a poem out of these larger elements. Thus speeches, like ring composition, often provide an organizing principle for both the poet and his audience, as well as serving other important roles such as developing characterization.

'This guest here of ours will do it for me: I cannot tolerate someone who
would take
advantage of our generosity without doing any work for it, even if he has
come from far away.'
Euryclea was too surprised to say anything in reply.
She shut the doors of the good hall.   19.30
      Odysseus and his illustrious son then sprang up
and began to bring in the helmets, the bossed shields,
and the sharp spears. **Pallas Athena went before them,**
carrying a golden lamp and creating a beautiful light.
Telemachus was quick to say to Odysseus: 19.35
'What a miracle – I really can't believe what I'm seeing, father!
The walls of our hall, the good column-bases,
the fir beams, the columns themselves that stretch so high –

Pallas Athena went before them Athena's direct involvement in the action of the *Odyssey* is neatly encapsulated here: it is illuminating (providing light for Odysseus and Telemachus to see where to store the weapons), and will prove deadly. Athena's patronage of Odysseus in our epic is an extension of the favour she shows him in the *Iliad* (10.245 and 23.782–3; see Clay 1997 and Kearns 2004 for overviews).

everything seems to be glowing, as if there's a burning lamp on hand!
One of the gods who hold wide heaven must be inside.'   19.40
          Clever Odysseus then said in reply:
'Be quiet, my child, and don't let your curiosity get the better of you:
this is the way of the gods who hold Olympus.
You ought to go to bed. I'll stay here:
I want to get some information from the slave-girls and your mother –   19.45
and she, in all her sorrows, will have some questions for me, too.'

> 1 Does Athena's intervention enhance or detract from Odysseus' status as a
>   hero?
> 2 What character traits has Telemachus exhibited in the second half of the
>   poem? As they collaborate here, do you see any ways in which he is similar
>   to his father?

19.47–122   At these words Telemachus left the hall,
lit a torch, and made for the bed
that he always slept in when sweet sleep came over him.
There he lay and waited for bright Dawn.   19.50
Now illustrious Odysseus remained in the hall,
plotting to murder the suitors with the aid of Athena.
          Shrewd Penelope then came in from her bedchamber,
looking **like Artemis, or golden Aphrodite**.
They put a chair for her next to the fire, one adorned with ivory and
                                                          silver spirals,   19.55
and she sat down. The carpenter Icmalius had made it
long ago; there was a footstool attached to it
underneath, and a large fleece had been spread over it.
As shrewd Penelope took her place there
her white-armed slave-girls returned from the hall   19.60
carrying a great deal of food, tables,
and the cups from which the arrogant suitors had drunk.
They shook the hot coals out from the braziers and piled a great
deal of wood on top for heat and warmth.
Meanwhile Melantho rounded on Odysseus for a second time: 19.65
'Are you still knocking about, stranger, and making a nuisance
of yourself this evening? Getting an eyeful of the women, are you?
Get out of here, you wretch! You've had your share of the meal.
Begone or I'll pelt you with this coal as you find the door!'

like Artemis, or golden Aphrodite   a striking, sharply contrasting double simile: Artemis
is the patron goddess of, among other things (e.g. hunting and childbirth), virgins (see
also Nausicaa at **6.102, 152**), while Aphrodite is the goddess of sex and love. In what ways
might we consider Penelope to be like Artemis or Aphrodite?

Clever Odysseus looked at her with a scowl and said: 19.70
'Who do you think you are? Why are you so angry with me?
Is it because I haven't bathed in days, I'm shabbily dressed,
and I go around Ithaca begging? I do this out of necessity –
it's what wandering beggars do!
I used to have a normal house,   19.75
I used to be rich, and I used to give regularly to beggars,
such as I am now, no matter who they were or what they needed.
I had countless slaves and all the other things
that make for prosperity and what we call the good life.
But Zeus, son of Cronus, **wiped it all out** – I suppose it was his plan for me. 19.80
You too, my lady, should watch out: you could lose all
this beauty of yours that currently makes you everybody's favourite.
Your mistress Penelope might get angry with you and make life difficult for you,
or Odysseus could come back: there's still a place for hope.
But even if he is dead and isn't coming back,   19.85
Apollo has now shown his favour to the great
Telemachus and no slave-girl will get away
with anything on his watch: he's not a child any more.'
Shrewd Penelope heard what Odysseus was saying
and addressed Melantho sharply: 19.90
'You shameless, brazen-faced bitch! I know very well
the crimes you're committing and you'll pay for them with your life!
And you knew full well that I in my sorry state was intending
to question our guest about my husband right here
in the palace – you heard it from me directly!'   19.95
    With these words she then turned to her housekeeper Eurynome:
'Bring a chair over here, Eurynome, and spread a fleece over it:
let's give our guest a seat and a chance to talk and
hear from me as well. I want to put some questions to him.'
    Eurynome was quick to comply: she brought in   19.100
a well-polished chair and spread a fleece over it.
Much-suffering, illustrious Odysseus took a seat.
    Shrewd Penelope was the first to speak:
'Let me first ask you something, stranger.

---

wiped it all out we frequently find in Greek literature the sobering sentiment that human wealth and good fortune are fragile and quickly overturned. Such reversals become a mainstay of tragedy, but there are many examples also in the *Iliad* and the *Odyssey* (as when Nestor reminds Telemachus of the dire fate that Zeus plotted for many of the Greeks after they had sacked Troy, *Odyssey* 3.130–5).

Apollo the god of young boys and their coming of age, the archer god who often extracts violent revenge, the god of prophecy and new beginnings who is frequently invoked before momentous undertakings.

Who are you? What is your city? **Who are your parents?'** 19.105
     In reply clever Odysseus said:
'No one on the face of the earth can compete with you,
my lady: your fame reaches broad heaven itself.
It's like that of some **peerless king**, who piously
rules over a mighty and multitudinous country – 19.110
he maintains law and order, his fertile earth brings forth
wheat and barley, his trees are heavy with fruit,
his flocks multiply steadily, his sea teems with fish,
his people thrive under him, and all this is down to his good leadership.
For this reason, then, ask me about other things while I'm here with you, 19.115
don't ask me about my family or my fatherland:
I am a man of many sorrows and you'll only fill my heart
with more pain by making me remember. And it's not right
for someone to sit weeping and wailing in someone
else's house: constant mourning is always a very bad thing. 19.120
And I don't want any of the slave-girls, much less you, to get angry with me
and say that I'm afloat on a sea of tears because I'm drunk.'

---

1   The current chaos contrasts sharply with Odysseus' idyllic picture here. Is he criticizing Penelope, or just being wistful?

2   What sort of vision of the world underlies the simile of the king? What other echoes of this world-view can be detected in the *Odyssey*?

3   As you read the interview, think of the other interviews and displays of hospitality in the *Odyssey*: does this encounter conform to the usual pattern of *xeinia*?

Who are you?, Who are your parents? the practice of *xeinia* (guest-friendship) seems to have been primarily cultivated among aristocratic families as a way of building alliances. When Telemachus shows up at the palaces of Nestor and Menelaus, his lavish reception is in large part due to the friendship that has existed between their families down the generations, a relationship that is reinforced by the ceremonial exchanging of guest-gifts. However, both kings welcome in the young Telemachus and offer him food before they ask him his identity. Thus *xeinia* extends beyond the obligations incurred through reciprocal family ties into benevolence towards those who cannot reciprocate, such as beggars – as happens here when Penelope entertains an apparent nobody.

peerless king Odysseus' comparison of Penelope with a king is one of the remarkable gender-reversal similes in Homer. Another example is when Odysseus himself is strikingly compared to a crying woman on hearing Demodocus' singing (8.523–31); see H. Foley 2009 and Moulton 1975 for a good overview of Homeric similes in general. The simile foregrounds Penelope's status and importance in the palace; the fame, piety and leadership of this king, and the law and order in his country – surely an echo of how Ithaca used to be – make her a kind of Odysseus. Note how Odysseus initially evades Penelope's request to reveal his identity, just as he did on Scheria with Arete and Alcinous.

Shrewd Penelope then said in reply:
'When the Argives sailed for Ilium, stranger, and my husband
Odysseus with them, the immortals wiped out   19.125
what made me special: my figure and my good looks.
If he were to come back and tend to my life here,
whatever fame I enjoy now would be greater and all the better for it.
But as it is I am in deep pain because the gods have beset me with so
                                            much misfortune.

The men, you see, who control the islands   19.130
of Dulichium, Samé, and woody Zacynthus,
and those who live in sunny Ithaca as well,
are pursuing my unwilling hand in marriage and exhausting our resources
                                            here in the palace.
This is why I do not normally receive strangers or suppliants,
and I've given up on those **work-at-large** heralds.   19.135
I simply miss Odysseus so much that I'm dying inside.
Meanwhile the men here are pushing for marriage. But I am spinning out
                                            plans to trick them.
My first idea, that of the shroud, came from the gods themselves:
I was to install a vast loom for long, fine threads here in the palace
and begin weaving on it. I said to them: 19.140
"I know, lads, that you're pursuing me because my good Odysseus has died,
but stop pushing for this marriage until I finish
the shroud – I don't want to lose all this work in vain –
it's for Lord Laertes' burial, when fate overtakes
him and leads him to the misery of death.   19.145
I don't want a single Achaean woman here in Ithaca to get angry with me
because a man who has so much goes buried without a proper shroud."
        Their stout hearts were satisfied with what I said.
In the daytime then I used to weave at the massive loom
but at night I would bring in torches and unravel it.   19.150
This went on for three years, unnoticed, and the Achaeans believed me!
But in the fourth year, when the seasons came round,
the months passed, and many days were fulfilled,
the men then found out through the slave-girls, those
uncaring bitches; they caught me and rounded on me.   19.155
Then I had to finish it – I was forced to.
At present, then, I can't escape a marriage and I haven't yet

---

work-at-large   the adjective refers to the fact that heralds, like some skilled craftsmen
(including carpenters, doctors and poets), are employed in various places of work and are
essentially independent (though the suitors force the poets Phemius and Medon to work
for them: compare **22.344–60**).

found any way round it; my parents are pushing hard
for me to get married and my son is distressed because he can see that these

men are

eating us out of house and home, and he is now perfectly capable   19.160
of managing a house and assuming the role Zeus has in store for him.
But never mind: tell me where you and your family come from.
You can't have been born to an **old tree or a rock**!'
Clever Odysseus then said in reply:
'With all due respect, good **woman**, can you not stop asking me   19.165
about my family, **wife** of Odysseus, son of Laertes?
Never mind. I will tell you. But you will just be making my situation
more painful than it already is. This is only natural for someone
who's been away from his fatherland as long as I have,
wandering in suffering from city to city.   19.170
Anyway, I'll tell you what you're wanting to know.
There is a certain country called **Crete**: it's a sea-girt island, beautiful
and fertile, sitting in the middle of the wine-dark sea. Countless people
live there, inhabiting ninety cities,
and everyone speaks a different language. There are Achaeans,   19.175
great-hearted Eteocretans, Cydonians,
long-haired Dorians, and noble Pelasgians.
Among these cities you will find populous Cnossus, where **Minos**
was king, Zeus' companion every nine years.
He was my father's father, great-hearted Deucalion,   19.180
who raised King Idomeneus and me as brothers.
Idomeneus then, being older and the stronger, went with the sons

---

old tree or a rock   apparently a proverb referring to a myth of mankind's origins –
Penelope's point is simply that the old beggar must have human parents.

woman, wife   the same word in Greek (*gynē*, from which our 'gynaecology' is derived);
so ironically, whenever Odysseus addresses Penelope he could be taken to be calling her
'wife'; it is striking that Penelope is the only woman in the epic whom he addresses with
this word.

Crete   yet another lying 'Cretan tale' from Odysseus: first to Athena (Book 13), then
Eumaeus (Book 14), now Penelope; the tales vary in interesting ways but all have the
patina of reality (see Haft 1984 for intriguing possibilities as to why Odysseus chooses
Crete, crossroads of a rich and long-lasting trading empire; Odysseus' Cretan alias thus
provides him with an especially plausible explanation for his wanderings). The association
of Cretans with lying became proverbial in the ancient world (e.g. Paul's remark in the
New Testament, Titus 1:12), probably as a result of these stories told by Odysseus.

Minos   the legendary king of Crete who fed young Athenians to the monstrous Minotaur
in his labyrinth (and ended up as a judge in the Underworld); with the help of Ariadne's
thread the great hero Theseus killed this beast. There was a tradition that Minos consulted
with Zeus once every nine years in a cave on Mount Ida, birthplace of Zeus.

Penelope and weaving

Penelope explains her great trick of weaving and unweaving Laertes' shroud, for which she is justifiably famous. Indeed, many scholars trace her name back to *pēnē*, the Greek word for weft (also known as woof): the yarn that is attached to the shuttle and drawn through the warp in the process of weaving. In this clever ruse she shows herself her husband's equal, possessed of just as much *metis* as he (see note on **9.384** and also Book 18). However, Penelope's action is also dangerous and has put her and Telemachus in a precarious and urgent situation with the suitors, who have complained bitterly of this trick in Book 2. The slave-girls' disloyalty will explain just how careful and distrustful Penelope feels she must be. The process of weaving, traditional women's work, is a good figure for poetic composition (see also note on **5.61**); Penelope's *unravelling* suits the narrative complexity of the *Odyssey* in particular – both in terms of narrative *flashbacks* and in terms of *misleading* narrative – and it underscores Penelope's importance to Homer: it is no great leap of faith to take her as a figure for the author (see Clayton 2004, chapter 4). In a neat symbol, Penelope's weaving of her father-in-law's shroud (the cloth used to wrap a corpse in burial) replaces the wedding trousseau that a bride-to-be would assemble in anticipation of her marriage.

of Atreus to Ilium in his curved ships. As for me,
I am his well-known younger brother named **Aethon**.

> • What do you make of Odysseus' tone here? Does he seem at ease, in control of the situation? Or is he nervous?

19.185–212

And that's where I saw Odysseus and gave him guest-gifts: 19.185
a forceful wind had driven him past Malea
and brought him to Crete on his way to Troy.
He put in at Amnisus, where there is a cave of Elethyia –
it's a difficult and dangerous harbour and he barely survived the storm.
Once he reached Cnossus he immediately asked for Idomeneus,   19.190
claiming that he was his special friend and guest,
but by that time it had been ten or eleven days since
Idomeneus had left for Ilium in his curved ships.
I then brought him to my palace and hosted him well;
I had plenty on hand and showered hospitality on him.   19.195
For his men as well, the ones who were accompanying him,
I raised a collection from my countrymen and gave them barley, gleaming wine,
and cows for sacrificing, so that they would be content.

Aethon   could mean 'shining', 'blazing' or perhaps 'dark-complexioned'; it is a common epithet for metallic objects in Homer.

Does Penelope recognize her husband?

There are many ways in which we can interpret the words and actions of Penelope in the rest of this book. Scholars are divided on whether or not Penelope recognizes Odysseus at this point. The conventional view is that she does not: Athena ensures that Penelope is unable to recognize Odysseus (see **19.476–9**) until the killing of the suitors has been accomplished, and it is only after Athena reverses Odysseus' disguise as a beggar (see **23.156–63**) that Penelope is able to recognize her husband. Yet the suggestion that she recognizes him and conceals this from him is attractive, and gives much more weight to her character, meaning to her choices (see note on line 581), and sophistication to the epic (see Ahl and Roisman 1996, Clayton 2004, and Heitman 2005 for good discussions and further bibliography). Other major interpretations of Penelope's behaviour suggest that the poem is simply inconsistent here as the result of being the product of an oral tradition, that Penelope only recognizes Odysseus subconsciously, or that she doesn't recognize him until Book 23; even for a major commentator the situation 'has never been successfully explained' (Russo 1992, p. 7). We should remember, however, that Helen recognizes Telemachus immediately on seeing him when he visits her in Book 4 (whereas Menelaus does not), Circe correctly identifies Odysseus in Book 10, Athena immediately sees through Odysseus' lies in Book 13, and that even Argus the dog recognizes his master in Book 17. Even Eumaeus seems suspicious. Is it credible that so shrewd a woman does not recognize her husband, despite his disguise?

A number of factors could help explain why Penelope might not disclose her recognition. She cannot expose Odysseus rashly for fear of the suitors. She also has reasons of her own for caution: if this is Odysseus, why doesn't he trust her enough to tell her himself? What will he make of her behaviour towards the suitors? And where exactly has he been all this time? He has, after all, slept with two other women; Penelope knows about Calypso. Note the testing to which she subjects him in the lines that follow – this is normally Odysseus' role. If she does recognize her husband, then, how might we explain these tears? Perhaps she is just as much in control of her emotions as he is.

Those illustrious Achaeans stayed with me for twelve days:
the mighty wind Boreas was hemming them in; you couldn't even   19.200
stand up straight – some god had stirred it up.
But on the thirteenth day the wind settled and they pushed off.'
With these words Odysseus had told **many lies** – but they were believable.

many lies   line 203 is remarkably close to Hesiod's *Theogony* line 27, where the Muses say, 'we know how to tell many lies – but they are like the truth' (more literal than 'were believable', as above, though the Greek words are the same). The line in Hesiod has been interpreted by some as an early definition of literary fiction. We don't know for sure whether Hesiod or Homer came first, but it is interesting to consider what the possible implications of such an allusion (in either direction) might be.

Meanwhile Penelope wept as she listened, melting into tears.
Up on the mountain-tops, Eurus and Zephyr will blow   19.205
and melt the snow up there,
and when it melts, it makes the rivers flow full.
That's exactly how Penelope's beautiful cheeks melted with tears
as she wept for the **man** that was sitting right next to her. Odysseus
pitied his crying wife, but only on the inside: 19.210
his eyes stood stiff as horn or iron
on his face as he craftily concealed his own tears.

> •   Why is Odysseus lying? What do you think of the use of deception by
>   Odysseus, Telemachus, Penelope and others in the poem?

19.213–360   Once she had had her fill of tearful weeping,
Penelope spoke again in reply to his story:
'Very well then, stranger, I'm minded to test you   19.215
and find out whether you really did host my husband
and his godlike men over there in your palace, as you claim.
Tell me what clothes he was wearing
and describe him and the men who were following him.'
Clever Odysseus then said in reply: 19.220
'So much time has passed, my good lady, that it's difficult
to say: by now it's been twenty years
since he went off and left my fatherland.
But I can tell you what comes to my mind's eye:
your noble Odysseus had a colourful woollen **cloak**,   19.225
double-ply. Now on it there was a **buckle** made of gold,
with two fasteners, and on the surface of this there was an ornament featuring
a dog pinning down a fawn with his two front legs,
choking it as it struggled for breath. Everyone admired how
the golden dog was throttling the golden fawn in its grip,   19.230
and how the fawn was eagerly scrambling to escape with its last breath of life.

---

man   the Greek can be translated as 'husband' (see on the word 'woman' in line 165) and
is the first word of the poem.

cloak, buckle   Odysseus chooses items which *he knows* that Penelope will recognize as gifts
from herself: has the delicate dance of reunion and reconciliation begun, with the couple
developing a coded language of their own? (Note too that the buckle can be taken as a
symbol for marriage, with a dominant male and subdued female – typical of ancient Greek
concepts of marriage.) The ironies of the exchanges here and following are delightfully
rich (all the richer if we accept the possibility that Penelope recognizes Odysseus). Note
that the pieces here are both 'finely made', resonating with the theme of craft and skill in
the epic. Recognition via concrete objects or 'tokens' such as hair or footprints (compare
also the scar-scene below and Penelope's words at **23.109**) begins here in epic, then gains
prominence in Attic tragedy and New Comedy, and it forms a central idea in Aristotle's
famous analysis of tragedy in his *Poetics* (1452a).

As for the tunic on him, I noticed it was very fine and sheer,
like the skin of an onion when it dries.
It was soft, and glistening like sunshine.
The women-folk thought highly of that piece. 19.235
Now I need to tell you something and you must not forget it:
I don't know whether Odysseus ever wore these things when he was here
at home,
or whether one of his men gave them to him when he boarded his swift ship
for Troy,
or perhaps some host gave them to him – Odysseus had
so many friends, and few of the Achaeans were like him. 19.240
I even gave him a bronze sword and a colourful
double-ply tunic, of good quality, edged with a fringe.
I gave him a respectful send-off in that well-benched ship of his.
He also had a herald in his company, a man just a little older
than himself. I can describe him for you as well: 19.245
he was hunch-backed, had dark skin and curly hair –
Eurybates was his name. Odysseus valued him most
of all his men because the man was quite clever.'
At these words the desire for yet more weeping overwhelmed Penelope:
she had recognized these tokens that Odysseus had described so clearly for
her. 19.250

Once she had had her fill of tearful weeping,
Penelope spoke in reply:
'Up to this point, stranger, you were just a figure for pity, but now, as far
as I'm concerned, you will be shown love and respect while here in my palace.
It was *I* who gave Odysseus the clothes you've described: 19.255
I folded them up and brought them out from our bedchamber, and *I* put that
shining buckle on that cloak –
I wanted him to stand out. But he is not mine to welcome back
home from his journey to his fatherland:
Odysseus was doomed when he left on his hollow
ship to see a city that can only be called by its real name: **Troyble**.' 19.260
Clever Odysseus then said in reply:
'With all due respect, good woman, don't ruin your beautiful skin, wife
of Odysseus, son of Laertes, and don't break your
heart with this crying over your husband. And yet I won't hold it against you:
when a woman loses her wedded husband, the man she's made love to, 19.265
the man she's had children with – she weeps – even if she's not got
an Odysseus in her life – and he, they say, was like the gods!

Troyble   Penelope's hatred for Troy is so strong that she cannot bear to name it properly;
Fagles 1996 translates '*Destroy*'; see note on **1.62** for such puns.

Now stop this weeping and listen very carefully to what I have to say.
I will speak truthfully to you and I won't hold back:
I have heard about Odysseus' homecoming.   19.270
He's close, in the fertile land of the Thesprotians, very much
alive and heaping up a great deal of good treasure
as he visits these people. But he lost his trusty
men and his hollow ship out on the wine-dark sea
as he was making his way from the island of Thrinacia – Zeus and the Sun
                                                            God   19.275
were angry with him because his men killed the Sun God's cows.
Each one of them lost their lives on the wild sea.
As for him, he rode his ship's keel till the waves spat him up on dry land
in the country of the Phaeacians, a people very close to the gods.
They treated him like a god   19.280
and gave him many gifts and wanted to send him back
home unharmed – Odysseus would have in fact been here
long ago, but it seemed more profitable to him
to visit more countries and acquire more **treasure**.
Odysseus knows more about acquisition than any   19.285
other man; no other mortal can compete with him in this!
Now I have all this from Phedon, king of the Thesprotians.
He poured a libation right there in front of me in his house and swore directly
that a ship and sailors were ready for the job
of sending Odysseus back to his fatherland.   19.290
But he sent me on beforehand because a Thesprotian ship
happened to be making for the rich wheatfields of Dulichium.
He even showed me all the goods that Odysseus has assembled –
there's so many of them there in Phedon's palace
that they could keep a family going for ten generations!   19.295
But he said that Odysseus had gone to **Dodona** so that he could
hear the plan of Zeus from the tall oak tree
concerning his return to his fatherland:
he has been away so long and needs to know whether to come back openly
                                                        or in secret.
He is, therefore, safe, and he will return   19.300
very soon: he will not be absent from his family and fatherland
much longer. I swear these things to you on oath!

---

treasure on its importance to a Homeric hero, see note on **10.42**. Acquiring (and retaining) property will be of special interest to Odysseus now: he can see with his own eyes just how much the suitors are draining his resources.

Dodona Zeus' oracle at Dodona (in north-west Greece) and Apollo's oracle at Delphi were the most famous oracles in antiquity; at Dodona the priests observed the rustling of oak-leaves to obtain information about the will of the gods (see Eidinow 2007).

May Zeus be my witness, highest and best of the gods,
and may the hearth of peerless Odysseus that I have now reached also be

                                                     my witness:

all these things are falling into place just as I have described them.   19.305
Odysseus will be here within this very **feast day**,
just as the moon begins its cycle afresh.'
Shrewd Penelope then said in reply:
'I pray that what you have said will come to pass:
for these words you will find friendship and generosity   19.310
here, enough so that someone who met you would think you a lucky man.
But it seems to my mind that *this* is how it's going to be:
those in charge here aren't like Odysseus was –
if indeed he ever existed – when it comes to treating
strangers appropriately. Odysseus won't, in fact, come home,   19.315
and you won't get any kind of send-off.
But come, girls, wash our guest's hands and feet and make him a bed
with a mattress, some cloaks and some good linens,
so that he can sleep warmly.
In the morning give him a bath and spread oil over his body –   19.320
I hope he won't mind sitting next to Telemachus for a meal
here in the hall. And if any of those obnoxious suitors gives him
any grief there will be trouble: no matter how angry
they get at him it won't make any difference.
How else, indeed, will you know, stranger, whether I am in fact   19.325
any more clever or thoughtful than any other woman?
Certainly not by taking a meal all dirty and shabbily dressed
in my hall! **Human beings don't live for ever**:
when someone is cruel and treats others harshly,
everyone prays that he will suffer while   19.330
he's alive, and when he's dead everyone mocks him.
But when someone is good and treats others in the right way,
strangers spread his good reputation,
and word gets round that he is just and good.'

---

feast day   a rare word of uncertain meaning; it could mean day, month or year, yet in this context it seems best to take it as indicating 'within the next 24 hours' because of Penelope's decisive actions that follow (lines 572–81). In the next book (lines 156 and 278) it is revealed that the next day is in fact a festival day, sacred to Apollo (god of archery, appropriately enough).

Human beings don't live for ever   most Greeks don't seem to have sought comfort in the hope of an afterlife (about which their ideas were rather vague) nor in the idea of wrongdoing being punished in the hereafter. In these lines we see another way in which a person could achieve immortality of a sort, by securing a good and lasting reputation (*kleos*).

Clever Odysseus then said in reply: 19.335
'With all due respect, good woman, I cannot stand cloaks
and good linens, wife of Odysseus, son of Laertes,
not since I left the snow-clad mountains
of Crete in my long-oared ship.
Let me sleep my sleepless nights as I have in the past: 19.340
many's the night I have spent in shabby linens
waiting for bright, Well-throned Dawn.
And I don't like foot-baths and I won't
let any of your slave-girls working
here in the palace touch me –   19.345
unless, perhaps, there's an old, kind lady about,
one who's been through as much as I have.
I wouldn't mind if *she* touches my feet.'
Shrewd Penelope then said in return:
'Out of all the foreign guests I've entertained here, my stranger, 19.350
I've never had one as clever as you:
everything you say is carefully thought out.
I do have an old woman here, a very thoughtful woman:
she took my poor Odysseus in her arms when his mother
gave birth and reared him from a baby;   19.355
though she's lost her former strength she can wash your feet.
Come now, get up, shrewd Euryclea,
here's someone to wash who's as old as your master Odysseus, and
these feet and hands resemble his too, come to think of it.
Misfortune makes people grow old quickly.'   19.360

> 1   Why does Odysseus request that an old woman bathe him? Note what
>   Melantho says to him at lines 65–9.
>
> 2   What about Penelope's final words here: do they seem to imply that she is
>   still oblivious about Odysseus' identity or do they suggest that she already
>   knows?
>
> 3   Who is testing whom at this point?

19.361–443   At these words the old woman put her hands to her face,
burst into tears, and lamented:
'I am all but useless to you now, **Odysseus, my child**! Despite your

---

Odysseus, my child   Euryclea's apostrophe (i.e. direct address to someone absent) to
her putatively missing master is one of the most ironic moments in the epic. Some see
a comic flavour suffusing this book (the ancient critic Longinus famously called the
Odyssey 'a kind of comedy of manners' (*On Sublimity* 9.15)), a stark contrast with the
grim slaughter of the suitors that is to come. For others the irony further heightens the
pathos of Euryclea's grief.

piety, Zeus has singled you out for his wrath.
Never yet has any mortal burnt as many fat thighs 19.365
or choice hecatombs to Zeus Thunderer
as you have in your prayers for
a safe old age and for a son to be proud of.
But as it is, Zeus has wiped out the day of your homecoming – and for you
alone!

Perhaps the womenfolk in the good house 19.370
of some distant host mocked Odysseus,
stranger, as all these bitches mock you,
and perhaps you refuse to let them wash you so that you can
avoid their insults and obscenities. But shrewd Penelope,
daughter of Icarius, has asked me to do this and I am willing. 19.375
I will wash your feet for your sake and
for Penelope's – my heart is deeply
troubled here. But come now, listen to what I have to say:
many's the needy guest we have hosted here
but I think no one has ever resembled Odysseus so closely 19.380
as you do in the way you look, the way you talk – and these feet!'
Clever Odysseus then said in reply:
'Everyone who has seen the two of us
says the same, old lady: we look very much alike,
exactly as you've observed just now.' 19.385
    At these words the old woman took a shining bowl
for washing his feet, poured cold water

On the reverse side of the cup shown on p. 134, Euryclea washes the feet of Odysseus. Curiously she is named 'Antiphata' on the cup, and Eumaeus (also named) looks on from the right.

in, then drew off some warm water and added it in. Odysseus
was sitting at the hearth but **quickly turned** to face the dark:
it had suddenly occurred to him that if the old lady took him in hand   19.390
she might notice his scar and expose all he was trying to do.
Euryclea came close to her master and began to wash. She recognized
the scar at once. A boar had gouged Odysseus with its white tusk
one day when the hero was making for Parnassus to visit Autolycus and his
                                                                            sons.

This was his mother's good father, and he had no rival   19.395
when it came to trickery and manipulating oaths. The god Hermes had
                                                            given Autolycus
these skills because he had pleased him with the burnt thighs
of his lambs and young goats. The god watched over him kindly.
Now this Autolycus had come to the fertile country of Ithaca
one day and found the new-born son of Anticlea, his daughter.   19.400
At the end of a meal Euryclea placed the baby
Odysseus on his lap and said:
'Think of a name to give your grandson,
Autolycus – you have prayed constantly for this day.'
        The new grandfather then said in reply: 19.405
'Be sure to use the name that I give him, son-in-law and daughter of mine.
Now, I have come here, *odious* to
man and woman alike across this fertile land,
and for this reason let his name be *Odysseus*. Meanwhile,

---

quickly turned   if the final outcome is never in doubt, suspense is created through other
means: Odysseus thinks he is on the verge of being discovered, then manoeuvres his way
to safety – only to then make a very simple mistake. The plot in these closing books is full
of intrigue, close calls and other forms of delay that draw us in. The famous digression
that follows, coming precisely at such a climactic moment, marks a high point in Homeric
poetry.

odious   for the pun on Odysseus' name see **1.62**; it is as though anger, and in particular
the wrath of Poseidon – i.e. the famous story of Odysseus' adventures on his *nostos* – is
what defines and makes Odysseus. And for us as Homer's audience *this* is his *kleos*, and
not necessarily his accomplishments in Troy. Just as Autolycus angers others by taking
advantage of them, so Odysseus angers Polyphemus (Book 9) and the families of the
suitors (Book 24). Autolycus, whose name means something like 'the wolf himself', stole
a cap (decorated with white boar's tusks: see line 465) that Odysseus wore on a night
raid in *Iliad* 10 (line 267), and he was known to be good at stealing cattle: an intriguing
echo of Helios' cattle in Book 10. In some traditions Autolycus was the son of Hermes,
giving Odysseus a divine lineage and direct connection to the patron god of trickery
(see Stanford 1968 and Hall 2008, chapter 11 for more on how later authors developed
Odysseus' reputation for craftiness).

when he **grows up** and comes to his maternal family 19.410
in **Parnassus**, where I have all my acquisitions,
I will give him some of these and send him off happy.'
Now this is why Odysseus had gone to him: he wanted his grandfather to
                                     give him
these fine gifts. Autolycus and his sons greeted him
warmly, with embraces and kind words. 19.415
His mother's mother Amphithea held him in her arms
and kissed his head and his handsome eyes.
Autolycus then ordered his good sons
to prepare the meal, and they obeyed his instructions
by bringing in a five-year-old bull straight away. 19.420
They busied themselves with skinning it, then butchering the whole thing,
then carefully cutting up the meat and piercing it on spits.
They expertly roasted it and distributed the portions.
They spent the whole day feasting, until
the sun set, and no one went hungry for his fair share. 19.425
When the sun sank and descended into the gloom,
the entire party went to bed and partook of the gift of sleep.
       When Early-born Rosy-fingered Dawn appeared
they made for the hunt: all the sons of Autolycus
and their dogs. Noble Odysseus joined 19.430
them. They made it to steep Mount Parnassus, all decked out
with trees, and quickly found themselves in the breezy foothills.
As the sun rose from the gentle, deep currents of Ocean
and fell fresh on the fields,
the hunting party entered a glen. The dogs ran 19.435
ahead, sniffing for tracks, while the men
followed behind, with noble Odysseus in their
company, sticking close to the dogs and wielding a long hunting-spear.
A huge boar lay there in a dense lair.
Neither the force of the wet winds could penetrate that lair, 19.440
nor the blasts of the sun's rays,
nor could any rain get in: it was too thickly
set with its vast heap of leaves.

---

grows up   physical challenges involving hunting or survival in the wild are often elements of coming-of-age rituals for young men in cultures around the world: we can compare Telemachus' trip to Nestor and Menelaus as a similar ritual passage into adulthood.

Parnassus   a mountain sacred to Apollo and one of the traditional homes of the Muses.

1   It is noteworthy that the same words are used when Odysseus makes a makeshift hut for himself on landing in Scheria at the beginning of Book 6. What might we gain by comparing Odysseus to this boar?

2   What might we make of the theme of hunting and 'sniffing for tracks' (line 436), introduced so subtly here? To what larger themes in the poem can this be connected?

19.444–75

The noise of the men and the dogs running reached the creature's ears
as they closed in on him: he emerged opposite the hunters from the thicket, 19.445
bristles standing on end and fire shooting from his eyes,
and then stood right close to them. Odysseus was the first
to rush at him, long spear held high in his stout hand,
aiming for a stab, but the beast was too quick and gouged him
just above the knee: he had darted towards him at an angle and tore off   19.450
a good piece of flesh with his tusk, though he did not reach the bone.
But Odysseus had struck him **over the right shoulder**,
and the point of the bright lance went all the way through.
The beast fell to the earth squealing as his life flitted away.
The sons of Autolycus then busied themselves over the creature   19.455
and carefully bound the wound of noble,
divine Odysseus. They uttered an incantation to stop the dark
blood from flowing, and soon they were back at their father's palace.
Autolycus and his sons nursed Odysseus
back to good health and gave him splendid gifts;   19.460
they sent him back to his fatherland Ithaca speedily
and in good spirits. His own father and lady mother were
delighted to welcome Odysseus back home and asked him all about
how he got his scar. He narrated to them in detail
how the boar had gouged him with his white tusk while on the hunting   19.465
expedition at Mount Parnassus with the sons of Autolycus.
And *this* was the scar that the old woman now touched;
she recognized it by touch alone. She dropped his foot,
and his lower leg then fell in the bronze bowl, which then clattered
and tipped over; the water shot out across the floor.   19.470
Joy and pain simultaneously overwhelmed the old lady: her eyes
filled with tears: her voice froze in her throat.
Taking Odysseus by the chin she said:
'It's you, my child! *You are Odysseus!* I couldn't
recognize my master until I had a chance to get my hands on him!'   19.475

---

over the right shoulder   the *Iliad* is full of detailed and vivid descriptions of the ways in which combatants are killed on the battlefield; the duel here between Odysseus and the boar is reminiscent of these (note too the similarly Iliadic death of the stag at **10.163**).

1 Why does Homer go into so much detail about this hunting expedition? And why right now?

2 How do Homeric digressions compare to modern narrative techniques (e.g. flashbacks in films)?

3 Taking someone by the chin is a gesture of supplication (see note on **6.141–4**): why does Euryclea do this?

4 What is gained by having a series of recognition scenes? Is the way in which individuals (Eumaeus, Telemachus, Euryclea) recognize Odysseus personalized?

19.476–553

She shot a glance at Penelope:
she wanted to tell her that her husband was in the room.
Though she sat opposite them, Penelope could not see or notice what
was happening
because Athena had diverted her attention. Meanwhile Odysseus
reached and **grabbed Euryclea** by the throat with his right hand   19.480
and pulled her close with his left, saying:
'Why, good mother, do you want to destroy me? It was you who nursed me –
on this very breast! After all my suffering I have now
returned to my fatherland after nineteen years.
But now that some god has illuminated your mind and you understand
what is happening,   19.485
keep quiet: no one else in the palace can know.
I'm going to tell you something – and I will certainly hold to it:
if the gods use me to defeat these good suitors
I won't spare you, even though you were my nurse, when
I come to kill the slave-girls here in my palace!'   19.490
In turn shrewd Euryclea then addressed him:
'What a thing to say, my child!
You know how strong and firm I am: I won't give in!
I will be like a sturdy rock, or iron.
But I want to tell you something, and don't you forget it: 19.495
if the gods do use you to defeat these good suitors,
I can tell you which of the women-folk here
in the palace have dishonoured you and which are innocent.'
            Clever Odysseus said in reply:
'Why would you tell me, good mother? There's no need: 19.500
I can see them for myself and I know what's what.
Just keep what I've said to yourself and entrust everything to the gods.'
            At these words the old woman went back through the hall
to fetch more bathing-water since all of the first lot had been spilt.
After she had bathed him and spread rich oil over him,   19.505
Odysseus then drew his chair closer to the fire

---

grabbed Euryclea   compare Odysseus' similarly rough treatment of an ally at **4.284–9**. Is his behaviour justifiable?

in order to get warmer, and kept his scar covered in his rags.
Shrewd Penelope now began their conversation:
  'I would still like to ask you a little more, stranger.
Soon it will be time for pleasant rest,   19.510
and sleep comes sweetly to everyone, even the troubled.
As for me, the gods have given me immeasurable suffering.
I while away my days in lamentation, weeping
as I attend to my tasks here in the house, and those of the slave-girls.
But when night comes and sleep overtakes everyone else,   19.515
I lie in my bed as painful anxieties swarm
over my beating heart and drive me to more tears.
This is what happened to **the daughter of Pandareus**, the nightingale of
                                                             the greenwood,
when she sings so beautifully at the beginning of spring
and flits among the thick foliage of the trees   19.520
as she pours out her many-toned music, varying the tune so frequently.
She's lamenting for her beloved son Itylus, child of King Zethus,
whom one day she killed unwittingly with a bronze sword.
And this is how my heart is torn in two different directions:
am I to stay here, living with my son and carefully guarding all we have,   19.525
our property, our slave-girls, and our high-roofed palace,
showing due respect to my husband's bed and to my reputation?
Or am I to attach myself to whichever Achaean manages to woo me best
here in this palace by bringing me more marriage-gifts than I can count?
When my son was young and still a senseless child,   19.530
he wouldn't allow me to leave Odysseus' palace and marry,
but now that he's grown up and reached the prime of youth
he begs me to leave and go home:
he's fretting over our property, which the Achaeans are now consuming.
  But come now: please listen to a **dream** of mine and interpret it
                                                             for me.   19.535

---

the daughter of Pandareus   this is Aedon ('nightingale' in Greek – literally 'singing
one'); in a case of mistaken identity – surely an appropriate theme for this context – she
accidentally killed her son and was then transformed into a nightingale. She had meant to
kill her sister Niobe's son out of jealousy for her fertility. Note again the bird and singing
imagery; these are common enough terms for describing Greek female lamentation yet
are so apposite for our poem in particular (Nagy (1996) sees the bird and her song as a
symbol for Homeric poetry). Compare also Calypso's use of mythological examples at
5.118–28.

dream   Penelope's dream is extraordinary, not least because it offers an interpretation
of itself *within itself*; for an overview of the problems and the scholarship see Rozokoki
2001; the theme of interpretation and its difficulties relates to the broader theme of
intelligence in the epic – and our own task as readers (note too the omens in Book 15).

In my dream I have twenty geese at home; they come in from their pond
and start eating their grain; I look on and am delighted to see them.
But then a huge curved-beak eagle comes from Mount Neritus,
breaks all their poor necks and kills them. They then lie dead
en masse throughout the house while the eagle flies off into the bright sky.   19.540
In my dream I then begin to weep and wail
and the fair-haired women of Achaea gather round me;
I'm miserable because the eagle has killed my geese!
But the eagle then comes back, comes to rest on one of the rafters,
and speaks words of warning to me with a human voice: 19.545
"Be brave, daughter of far-famed Icarius!
This is no dream, it is reality and it will come to pass.
These geese are your suitors, and I, though once an
eagle, am now your husband. I have come back
and I will unleash destruction on all the suitors – and it won't be pretty."   19.550
     When the eagle said this I woke up suddenly from honeyed sleep.
I looked anxiously for my geese and found them in the palace,
munching grain at their trough, precisely where they were before.'

> 1   What are we to make of Penelope's feelings for her geese?
>
> 2   Why does Penelope tell this intimate dream to Odysseus?

19.554–604   Clever Odysseus then said in reply:
'There's no other way you can take this dream,   19.555
my lady! Odysseus himself explained
to you how it will happen: disaster is on hand for each
one of the suitors, and not a single one will escape the fate of death.'
     Shrewd Penelope then said in reply:
'Dreams are tricky, stranger, and hard   19.560
to interpret: not everything comes true for everyone.
There are **two pairs of gates**, you see, for fleeting dreams:
one pair is made of horn, the other of ivory.
Some dreams come through the gates of sawn **ivory**,
and these are the ones that **deceive**, bringing only empty words in tow.   19.565
But dreams that come out through the polished **horns**,
these are the ones that **come true**, as anyone can see.
But I think that my terrible dream did not come to me

---

two pairs of gates this is the earliest appearance of this legend and it is probably
Homer's invention (see Haller 2009); Virgil draws directly on this passage in *Aeneid* 6 by
having Aeneas emerge (mysteriously enough) from the Underworld through the gates
of ivory. In the Greek 'ivory' is punningly similar to the word for 'deceive', and 'horns' is
similar to the words for 'come true'.

through these gates of horn: my boy and I would have welcomed it if so.
I want to tell you one more thing, and don't forget it: 19.570
the morning that comes to take me away from the house
of Odysseus will be accursed. I will therefore set up a contest,
one with the axes that he used to stand up all in a row
here in his palace; they were **like keel-props**, all twelve of them.
He would stand off at a distance and shoot an arrow right through them.   19.575
This is the contest that I will now set up for my suitors,
and whoever can manage to string the bow with his hands
and shoot an arrow through all twelve of the axes,
he's the one I will marry. I'll then leave this palace behind,
where I was first a bride. It's a good house, full of what you need to get by. 19.580
I think that even **in my dreams** I will remember it.'
Clever Odysseus then said in reply:
'Don't postpone this contest,
revered wife of Odysseus, son of Laertes!
Clever Odysseus will come here before   19.585
any of these suitors can take that well-polished bow,
string it, and shoot through the iron!'
        Shrewd Penelope then said in reply:
'No sleep would come to take me, stranger, if you were willing
to sit by me here in the palace and entertain me.   19.590
But people need sleep at some point
or other: the immortals have given to each man
his own time and place on life-giving earth.

---

like keel-props the axes are arranged in a row; apparently the heads are stuck in the earth and resemble props that would hold up a boat in dry dock; at the end of the handle is perhaps some kind of a hole through which an arrow can pass. Note that Odysseus would regularly practise this feat: Penelope is confident that Odysseus can do it; note too the hero's enthusiasm in the lines that follow. See Fernández-Galiano 1992, 131–47 and Page 1973, appendix for a detailed study, the latter complete with parallels of similar tests of strength from myth and folktale across the world.

in my dreams in a further, dazzling play of language (compare note on **9.384**), the contest of the bow can be connected with the dreams that pass through the gates of horn, since Homeric bows are always made of horn: Penelope could thus be encouraging Odysseus here to make her dream *come true* by means of the horn in the bow. According to this reading, she has decided to force the issue of her marriage by setting the contest for the bow knowing that Odysseus has arrived and will win the contest. We may compare the way Odysseus chooses tokens of identity (above in lines 220–47) which he knows full well Penelope will recognize. An alternative explanation is that Homer has conflated portions of a tale involving an *ignorant* Penelope with portions of a tale involving a *fully informed*, conspiring Penelope (see box on p. 143).

As for me, I'm going upstairs
to lie down on the **bed** that has become a bed of sorrows for me,   19.595
constantly tear-stained since the time Odysseus
left to see a city that can only be called by its real name: Troyble.
That's where I'll sleep: you can lie down here in the house –
spread some bedding down on the floor or get the girls to put some down
                                                                                for you.'

With these words Penelope went up to her bright upper rooms,   19.600
but she was not alone: her slave-girls followed her.
She made it up to her rooms with the women
and then wept for her husband Odysseus until
Bright-eyed Athena poured sweet sleep over her eyes.

> 1   What do you make of Penelope's tone here? How would you characterize
>   the emotional range of this encounter?
>
> 2   What other tests has Odysseus prevailed in over the course of the poem so
>   far?
>
> 3   Can you comment on the role of 'testing' in the epic in general? What is it
>   that some characters are looking for from or in other characters?

Book 20

In Book 20 Odysseus now goes to the forecourt to sleep but he lies awake, plotting
the destruction of the suitors. As the slave-girls flit by cheerfully to sleep with their
lovers he contemplates killing them on the spot but soliloquizes: he's seen worse,
particularly in Polyphemus' cave. Homer vividly compares the hero's heart to
a female dog, her pups' safety threatened, then to a meat pudding, boiling over
a fire. Athena then appears to Odysseus in the guise of a woman and tells him
to calm down. Odysseus replies that he's afraid of taking on all the suitors by
himself, and then asks her what will happen afterwards if he is successful. Athena
reassures him and tells him to get some sleep.

The scene changes to Penelope's bedroom: the good wife of Odysseus is also now
awake and she prays to Artemis for death – she wants to meet her husband in the
Underworld and not become the wife of 'a lesser husband'. She states that she's
just had a dream that a man resembling Odysseus was lying by her side. It is now
morning and Odysseus can hear Penelope; in a significant line he feels that she
has already recognized him (94). He prays to Zeus for an omen; the god sends
a thunderbolt. A poor, exhausted slave-woman also hears the omen and prays
aloud that this will be the last day that the suitors occupy the hall. Odysseus hears
the prayer and is delighted.

---

bed   mention of the bed prefigures the great scene of reunion in **23.171–343**.

Telemachus asks Euryclea after his guest's well-being, in fear that Penelope has been careless. The faithful slave-woman reassures him that his mother looked after him. Telemachus departs for an assembly in the city while Euryclea orders the slave-girls to get to work: today is a special festival day. Eumaeus turns up with pigs for the suitors and converses with Odysseus but they are interrupted by Melanthius, here with goats for the suitors, who rebukes Odysseus for his continued presence in the palace. Odysseus does not reply. We now meet the cowherd Philoetius, who asks Eumaeus about the stranger, noting that he looks like a king who has fallen on hard times. Philoetius greets the beggar warmly and declares his love for his supposedly dead master Odysseus, faulting the greedy and violent suitors. Odysseus responds equally warmly and asserts that the hero will return soon.

The suitors are now seen plotting the death of Telemachus but a portent appears: an eagle clutching a pigeon. Amphinomus declares it unpropitious: they will not manage to kill Odysseus' son. They then enter the palace and the feasting begins; Telemachus boldly asserts that he will protect the stranger and that the suitors had better leave him alone; they again are amazed at his self-confidence. Even Antinous consents to respect Telemachus' wishes. Athena is then said again to inspire the suitors' recklessness in order to wound Odysseus even further. One Ctesippus insultingly hurls an ox-hoof at Odysseus, which misses its mark; Telemachus chides Ctesippus and asserts that he is grown up now and will not tolerate such violence any longer. One of the suitors speaks up in defence of Telemachus, surprisingly, but urges the young man to agree to letting his mother marry: Odysseus is never coming back. Telemachus replies that he wants her to remarry but hopes that things will not turn out this way; in a haunting passage Athena causes the suitors to laugh wildly, 'with jaws not their own', and their food becomes bloody. The prophet Theoclymenus takes all this to be very bad indeed and claims to see the 'walls spattered with blood' and ghosts in the courtyard. The suitors laugh only harder at this and Theoclymenus departs, making for the house of a close friend of Telemachus. The suitors mock Telemachus for his choice in guests: an old beggar and a crazy prophet. Son and father exchange glances and the book closes with Penelope just outside the door, hearing every word. Homer tells us that this will be the last meal of the suitors.

Part Five (Books 21–24): *Nemesis*

With Books 21–24 we have finally reached the great climax of the epic: the stringing of the bow (21), the slaughter of the suitors (22), the reunion of Odysseus and Penelope (23), and the resolution of the situation in Ithaca (24). Of central concern here is Odysseus' *nemesis*: 'retribution' or 'righteous anger aroused by injustice'. Odysseus' mass-killing seems harsh, but it is arguably necessary within the world of the epic; likewise Zeus and Athena's intervention in Book 24 is effective, but it may leave us unsatisfied. Book 23 has been chosen as a focus for this part of the epic because of the unforgettable and complex cross-questioning between Odysseus and Penelope.

Book 21

At the opening of Book 21 Athena inspires Penelope to start the contest of the bow. In a poignant scene, Penelope collects the bow in tears (there is a brief digression here relating how Odysseus got the bow as a guest-gift). She announces the terms of the contest to the suitors and Eumaeus and Telemachus set up the axes. Telemachus himself then tries to string the bow; on his fourth attempt he is about to succeed but Odysseus prohibits him with a quick glance. The suitors then attempt to string the bow, all in vain; the chief suitors, Antinous and Eurymachus, hold off for the moment. Odysseus then leaves the hall in the company of Eumaeus and Philoetius and reveals himself and his intentions to them. They return to find Eurymachus taking the bow; he fails to string it; Antinous urges him not to worry and recommends postponing further attempts until tomorrow, after due sacrifices to Apollo the Archer. Odysseus now requests an attempt; the suitors mock and warn him not to try. In a sharp and witty exchange, Penelope now intervenes and assures the suitors that if this strong, old beggar manages to string the bow then she won't marry him but give him some fine gifts and send him off on his way.

Telemachus now gets involved and in (contrived?) anger sends his mother to her rooms, asserting his authority: he will decide who can try the bow. Penelope makes off and Eumaeus then brings the bow to Odysseus amid the shouting and scorn of the suitors. Telemachus' angry insistence that Eumaeus take the bow to the old beggar distracts the suitors, and the weapon finally reaches Odysseus' hands. Eumaeus tells Euryclea to keep the slave-girls out of the way and to guard the door of the hall as Philoetius locks down the courtyard. In a famous and important simile Odysseus now strings the bow 'just as a musically accomplished lyre-player / can easily loop a string over a new peg / and attach the finely braided

The *Odyssey* in later literature: Plato's *Ion*

This colourful specimen of Socratic debate is from Plato's *Ion*, a dialogue about poetry (fourth century BC).

SOCRATES   Hold on Ion; tell me this. Don't keep any secrets from me. When you recite epic poetry well and you have the most stunning effect on your spectators, either when you sing of Odysseus – how he leapt into the doorway, his identity now obvious to the suitors, and he poured out arrows at his feet – or when you sing of Achilles charging at Hector, or when you sing a pitiful episode about Andromache or Hecuba or Priam, are you at that time in your right mind, or do you get beside yourself? And doesn't your soul, in its enthusiasm, believe that it is present at the actions you describe, whether they're in Ithaca or in Troy or wherever the epic actually takes place?

ION   What a vivid example you've given me, Socrates! I won't keep secrets from you. Listen, when I tell a sad story, my eyes are full of tears; and when I tell a story that's frightening or awful, my hair stands on end with fear and my heart jumps.

SOCRATES   Well, Ion, should we say this man is in his right mind at times like these: when he's at festivals or celebrations, all dressed up in fancy […] finery – or when he's standing among millions of friendly people and he's frightened, though no one is undressing him or doing him any harm? Is he in his right mind then?

ION   Lord no, Socrates. Not at all, to tell the truth.

Plato, *Ion* 535b–535d (tr. Paul Woodruff in Cooper 1997)

As Socrates manages to cast doubt on the sanity of poetic 'inspiration', we get a tantalizing glimpse here into the otherwise little-known world of the rhapsode: probably 'song stitcher' in Greek. It is unclear how to connect these performers with the original conditions of the composition of Homeric poetry (some even called themselves *Homeridae* or 'sons of Homer'), but in the historical period they were celebrated for their recitation of Homer and they competed publicly for prizes. The *Ion* forms part of Plato's famous attack on Homer: he comes to eject the Poet from his ideal state in the *Republic* (Books 2, 3 and 10). It should come as no surprise that Socrates lists this moment in the *Odyssey* first out of all the dramatic moments in Homeric poetry.

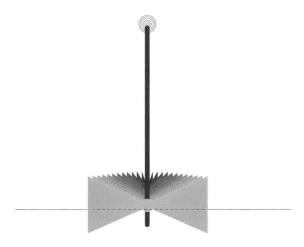

A reconstruction of the arrangement of the axes for the contest, based on Page 1973, p. 112.

sheep's gut to both ends of the lyre' (lines 406–8). Odysseus then twangs the bowstring and 'a beautiful sound sprang up, like the voice of a swallow' (411). As the suitors cower in terror, Zeus sends a favourable omen of thunder. Odysseus selects an arrow, takes aim and lets fly: the arrow makes it clean through the axe-handles. At the very close of the book, Odysseus announces grimly that 'it's time for a meal' and 'some entertainment'; Telemachus dons his armour and takes his place at his father's side.

Book 22

22.1–43
Clever Odysseus then stripped off his rags
and leapt onto the massive **threshold**, bow and quiver
full of **arrows** in his hands. He emptied the swift missiles
out on the floor at his feet and addressed the suitors:
'This decisive contest of ours is now over!   22.5
I will now take aim at **another target**, one that no one has hit yet –

---

threshold   a strategic position that enables Odysseus to entrap the suitors in the main hall but a symbolic one as well, since he is now making his transformation from beggar to hero. For the architecture of Homeric palaces see Bennet 1997, Osborne 2004 and Cline 2010.

arrows   Odysseus' bow is massive and it seems that he kneels or sits here and during the contest of the bow in the preceding book; hence the arrows are 'at his feet' (see note on **1.259**).

another target   compare the grim humour at the close of Book 21 and at **9.368–70**.

I might just hit it if Apollo will give me this glory!'
With these words he directed a bitter arrow at Antinous,
who was on the verge of lifting a fine, gold,
double-handled cup; he was lifting it to his lips   22.10
for a sip. Death was the furthest thing
from his mind. Who would have thought that one single man, among so
                                                                    many men
at that feast, even if he was quite powerful,
would bring him evil death and black destruction?
Odysseus took aim and the arrow struck Antinous in the throat;   22.15
the tip went straight through his soft neck.
The man flipped over backwards as the cup fell from his hands
with the blow, and a thick stream of blood and gore
flew from his nose. He kicked his table with his feet
and pushed it away, spilling his food on the ground.   22.20
His bread and meat grew red with blood. Now the suitors burst
into an uproar throughout the room when they saw the fallen man;
panic-stricken they leapt up from their chairs
and glanced frantically at the well-built walls of the hall:
but there was no shield or stout lance there for them to take.   22.25
They lashed out at Odysseus with these angry words:
'Shooting at men is ill-advised, stranger! No more contests
for you! Your fate is sealed.
You've just killed the finest
young man in Ithaca, and vultures will prey upon your flesh for this!'   22.30
To a man the suitors were at a loss: naturally they thought that this beggar
had not willingly killed Antinous. But the fools had no conception
of how tightly the noose of death now stood around their necks.
        Clever Odysseus scowled at them and said:
'You thought that I would never return from Troy,   22.35
you bastards! You've been pillaging my house,
raping my slave-girls,
and wooing my wife on the sly while I was still alive!
Have you no fear of the gods who hold wide heaven,
or of what angry men are capable of when they seek revenge?   22.40
The noose of death now stands around all your necks!'
Sickening fear overcame the suitors at these words;
each of them looked frantically about for a way to escape sheer destruction.

22.44–339   Book 22 contains the complete narrative of the slaying of the suitors from start to finish. This is Odysseus' *aristeia*, or moment of glory on the battlefield, such as is given to important heroes in the *Iliad*. (Beyond the numerous graphic killing-scenes like this one there are many verbal echoes of the *Iliad*, such as the flesh-eating vultures at line 30 above (compare *Iliad* 4.237), and the 'noose of death' or 'moment of death' at line 33 (compare *Iliad* 7.402).) Odysseus' first victim is Antinous. In disbelief the suitors round on Odysseus without yet fully realizing who he is; the next-ranking suitor, Eurymachus, tries to come to (not ungenerous) terms with Odysseus but the hero refuses; Eurymachus summons the suitors to declare war and is immediately shot down. Telemachus brings down the next suitor, then makes for the armour he had been instructed to store away; Odysseus keeps the suitors at bay with his archery. The disloyal Melanthius then manages to fetch armour for the suitors; Odysseus tells Eumaeus and Philoetius to seize him; they do so and hoist him up high on one of the columns in the hall. Now both sides, fully armoured, face one another: it's four versus more than one hundred suitors! Athena now appears in the guise of Mentor, and Odysseus, suspecting it is the goddess, urges him to join battle; she chides Odysseus for requiring any help: 'she wanted to test the strength and might of Odysseus / and his glorious son a bit more'. The suitors threaten this 'Mentor' with death; Athena turns into a swallow and disappears. In a book positively bristling with echoes of the grisly fight-scenes from the *Iliad*, the suitors rally, then Odysseus and his men rally. Athena sends the suitors' javelins awry as Odysseus' reach his targets. One Leodes, priest to the suitors, begs forgiveness from Odysseus but is mercilessly killed. The poet Phemius now needs to think of a plan quickly.

22.340–60   Phemius placed his hollow lyre on the ground,   22.340
between the mixing-bowl and the chair with the silver studs,
then lurched for Odysseus and took him by the knees.
He begged him feverishly:
'I beseech you, Odysseus! Show some decency and have mercy on me!
You will come to regret it if you kill a poet   22.345
who performs for both god and man!
I have no teacher: it is the gods who implant all the different
poems in my mind and it would only be fitting for me to sing to you
as to a god. Don't then think of cutting my throat.
Telemachus, your beloved son, could in fact tell you   22.350
that I came to your house to perform at meals
for the suitors completely against my will:
they were too numerous and too powerful by far for me to resist.'
Mighty Telemachus heard Phemius talking close by and he was quick to address
Odysseus; he spoke with an air of divinity about him: 22.355
'Stop: don't stab this perfectly innocent man with your sword.

We should spare Medon the herald as well: he always
looked after me here in our palace when I was young –
unless Philoetius or the swineherd has killed him,
or he encountered you on your rampage through the hall.'

22.360

1   How do Phemius' words add to the role of the poet as portrayed in Homer?
    (Compare the prologue in Book 1, Phemius in Book 1 and Demodocus in
    Book 8.)
2   How might this portrayal relate to Homer and his contemporary audience?
3   At what point do the suitors recognize Odysseus?

22.361–501 (end)

Thus the loyal herald Medon is also spared, on Telemachus' word. The suitors
are now all dead and Odysseus summons Euryclea, who rejoices to find her
master 'all spattered with blood and gore like a lion / when it has come from
feeding on a cow in the fields' (lines 402–3). Odysseus urges piety and now
wants to know which of the slave-girls have been loyal and which not; 12 have
not. Odysseus now grimly orders the disloyal girls to come and assist him and
his men in cleaning up the hall and dispensing with the corpses; Telemachus
is to stab them to death afterwards. Once the hall is clean, Telemachus
intriguingly does not follow these instructions to the letter; he does not want
to 'take their lives with a clean / death', and in a particularly chilling scene he
hangs them all at once like trapped birds. Odysseus fumigates the hall with
brimstone and is reunited with the loyal slave-women – Penelope has been
asleep in her room all this time: 'one of the gods has put her in a deep sleep'.

*In this fourth-century BC frieze from a hero-shrine in Lycia we find Odysseus clothed as he faces
the suitors, whereas in Homer he is naked, typical of a hero, even when fighting.*

Book 23

23.1–68 The old woman now triumphantly made her way to the upper rooms
to tell her mistress that her beloved husband was in the palace.
Euryclea's legs bustled as she scrambled up the stairs.
She stood **at the head** of the bed and said:
'Wake up, dear child Penelope! You need to see   23.5
with these eyes of yours what you've been hoping for all this time!
He's back: *Odysseus has come home!* Though he took enough time to get here
he's killed the proud suitors who have caused all this trouble in his
home, devouring his property and mistreating his son!'
Shrewd Penelope then replied: 23.10
'The gods have made you insane, dear mother. They can
turn even the cleverest of people into fools –
though they can also put a fool on the path of wisdom –
but it's *they* who have harmed you. You used to be sound of mind!
Why on earth are you mocking the depth of my pain   23.15
with such pointless words? And now you've woken me up from the pleasures
of a sleep that came over me like a wave and held me tight.
I've not slept like this since Odysseus
went to see a city that can only be called by its real name: Troyble.
Come on then, get yourself back downstairs and go back to the hall.   23.20
If any of my other women, you know,
had come and woken me and said these things
I would have sent them back to the hall
packing and crying. You're lucky you're so old.'
    Nurse Euryclea then replied: 23.25
'I promise I'm not mocking you, dear child! It's true:
he's back: Odysseus has come home – it's just as I say!
He was the stranger that suffered such disgrace here in the palace.
Telemachus has known for a while that he was here
but he wisely concealed his father's intentions   23.30
so that Odysseus could pay back those overbearing suitors for their insolence.'
    At these words Penelope leapt with joy from her bed
and flung her arms around the old woman. With tears in her eyes
she addressed her excitedly:
'Come now, dear mother, and tell me truly   23.35
whether the man has in fact come home, as you claim, and tell me
exactly how he attacked those shameless suitors
all on his own: there were far too many of them in that hall!'

---

at the head Euryclea literally stands 'above Penelope's head', the typical position for a
visitor in a dream (e.g. **6.21**).

Nurse Euryclea then replied:

'I didn't see it for myself: I could only hear the groans   23.40
of the dying. We were all sat in a corner of the well-made
rooms, stunned while the well-fitted doors kept us in,
until your son Telemachus called for me
from the hall – his father had sent him to call for me.
I then found Odysseus standing among the dead   23.45
bodies: they lay on top of one another all around him,
clutching the hard earth with their hands. You would have been delighted
                                                      with the scene!

He was all spattered with blood and gore like a lion!
And now they are all lying in a heap at the gates
of the courtyard while he's now fumigating the good house with brimstone – 23.50
he lit up a huge fire to do it. And he sent me here to call for you.
Follow me! You and Odysseus can now start making your way down the path
of happiness – you both have suffered so much!
Now finally the hope you have nourished for so long has come to pass:
the man is here, alive, and waiting at the hearth! He found you   23.55
and his own child here in his palace! The suitors may have treated him
badly indeed, but he made them pay for it – right here at home.'

Violence in the ancient world

Ancient ethics were somewhat different from ours. While we might at least
try to turn the other cheek if we are wronged, the dominant ethical code
in the ancient world was to 'help your friends and harm your enemies'.
Especially in the early period, before the widespread development of law-
courts and law-codes, it was family members who carried out vendetta justice
(see line 57). So, for example, the punishment meted out on Melanthius
(his extremities – nose, ears, genitals, hands and feet are cut off, 22.474–7)
is typical of revenge killings: the idea being that this mutilation would
prevent the dead man's spirit from carrying out revenge. Homer presents the
punishments vividly and matter-of-factly, without any attempt to gloss over
them. Some commentators think that the severity of the punishment that
Odysseus executes on the suitors and their accomplices has been carefully
prepared for over several books by the degree of abuse that he is subjected
to by them, deliberately exacerbated by Athena (Books 18 and 20); that they
treated a beggar so badly is particularly shocking, since beggars are under the
special protection of Zeus. So both the violence that Odysseus exacts and the
enjoyment of it by Euryclea here would possibly have seemed less troubling
to an ancient audience than to us, though both Penelope and Odysseus urge
Euryclea not to flaunt her joy openly (see note on line 59), and the problem
of revenge forms the theme of Greece's only surviving trilogy, Aeschylus'
magnificent *Oresteia* (see **1.30**).

Shrewd Penelope then replied:
'Don't flaunt your **excitement**, dear mother.
You know how welcome Odysseus would be to everyone here   23.60
in the palace, especially to me and the son we both brought into this world.
But the story you're telling here simply isn't true:
it's one of the gods who has killed the good suitors,
out of anger at their insolence and the bad things they did.
They didn't care for a single human being on earth,   23.65
whether he was important or not! It didn't matter who it was who came here.
And it's for this reason – their **recklessness** – that they've met with misfortune.
But as for
Odysseus, he got lost on his way home, far from Achaea, and died on the way.'

---

1   How would you characterize Penelope's emotions here? Is she relieved, frightened, or both?

2   How would you judge the tone of this exchange? How does it compare with the longer exchange between Penelope and Odysseus that is to follow?

3   Does it surprise you that Penelope doesn't believe Euryclea's news?

4   If Penelope recognized her husband all along (see box on p. 143), then why does she continue to put off acknowledging his identity now that the suitors have been killed?

5   Do you feel that the slaughter of the suitors is morally justified?

6   Attributing *atasthalia* to someone, even oneself, is a moral judgement, one that depends on a notion of personal responsibility. Can you think of ways of describing the *Odyssey* as a poem about personal responsibility? How might the gods factor in?

23.69–122   Nurse Euryclea then replied:
'What a thing to say, my child!   23.70
You've denied that your husband will ever come home – but he's
sitting here at the hearth, inside! Will you ever believe?
Come on, let me tell you about another obvious piece of evidence I have:
the scar, the one that boar made with his white tusk one day long ago.
I noticed it when I was giving him his bath! I wanted to tell   23.75
you but then he grabbed me by the mouth and refused
to let me speak – it was very clever of him.

---

excitement   Odysseus similarly bids Euryclea not to celebrate aloud the death of the suitors at 22.411–12.

recklessness   the key term *atasthalia* (compare **1.34**). For some commentators, Euryclea's attitude is symptomatic of a 'new' morality exhibited in the *Odyssey* as contrasted with the *Iliad*: in the latter we (and the gods) are concerned with individual *honour* (Greek *timē*) whereas in the former we (and the gods) are concerned with *justice* (*dikē*, or *themis*), even if it necessitates extreme violence: yet it would seem that Homer subverts this point of view to some degree – see Finley 1979, chapter 5, Gould 1992 and Adkins 1997.

Follow me! I will bet my very life on this,
and if I let you down, then kill me in the cruellest way you can think of.'
    Shrewd Penelope then replied: 23.80
'Clever though you are, dear mother, it would be
difficult even for you to derail the gods' intentions.
Come on then, let's make for my son: I want to see
the dead suitors and the man who killed them.'
    With these words Penelope descended the staircase. She was
genuinely **torn**   23.85
in two directions: was she to sit aloof and put further questions to her husband,
or stand close, kiss his head, and take his hands in hers?
She crossed the stone threshold and entered the hall,
taking her seat along the wall, opposite Odysseus.
The fire blazed. He then took his seat next to the huge   23.90
column, glancing at the floor, waiting to see whether his strong
partner would have anything to say to him: he knew she had seen him now.
She sat for a long time without making a sound, her mind beset with shock.
At one moment she would glance at him in the face
but at the next she would not acknowledge him, sitting there in his
disgusting rags.   23.95

Telemachus spoke up and attacked her:
'What kind of mother are you, you cruel-hearted thing?
Why on earth are you sitting apart from my father, off on your own? You
won't even
sit next to him and ask him a single thing!
No other woman would steel her heart and be so standoffish   23.100
to her own husband, especially one who's spent nineteen hard
years toiling to get back to her and his fatherland!
Your heart has always been harder than stone!'
    Shrewd Penelope then said in reply:
'No, my child, it's just that I'm stunned: 23.105
I can't even say a word or formulate a question –
I can barely sit here looking at him. But if Odysseus really

---

torn in two directions Homer uses exactly the same language of deliberation that he uses of Odysseus (e.g. **9.300–5**), and indeed of so many heroes in the *Iliad*: shrewd Penelope is about to use her wits. Why does Penelope hesitate? Why does she come to test her husband like this? She supplies an answer in lines 215–17 but her true motivation may be more complex (see note on **19.203**). The couple sit together in the hall as they did the night before (**19.506** ff.), but the circumstances could not be more different: the warm fire of that earlier scene is now a fire fumigating the room of the stench of slaughter. For the marital tension in this scene it is helpful to recall the interactions between Menelaus and Helen in Book 4. Even strangers get a bath in keeping with *xeinia*; Odysseus is simply left here in his disgusting rags (95).

> **The *Odyssey* in later literature: Derek Walcott's *Odyssey***
>
> Derek Walcott here envisages quite a different conversation between
> Penelope and Odysseus in his 1993 stage version of the *Odyssey* (II.vi), but
> he arguably captures some of the moral and emotional ambiguities latent in
> Homer perfectly.
>
> PENELOPE You had to wade this deep in blood?
>
> ODYSSEUS   To reach your shore.
>
> PENELOPE This cunning beggar is the smartest of suitors.
>
> ODYSSEUS To claim his house.
>
> PENELOPE   What house? You mean this abattoir?
>
> ODYSSEUS To kill your swine, Circe.
>
> PENELOPE   And make their mistress yours?
>
> ODYSSEUS WHAT DID YOU WANT ME TO DO? IT'S YOU I KILLED
>   FOR!
>
> PENELOPE IT'S FOR THIS I KEPT MY THIGHS CROSSED FOR
>   TWENTY YEARS?
>
> ODYSSEUS Call out to Antinous! See if he answers.
>
> PENELOPE He has gone to his own dark bed.
>
> ODYSSEUS   Alone at least.
>
> Margaret Atwood's *The Penelopiad* (2005) similarly envisions a haunting
> retelling of the story, told at points from the perspective of the maids killed at
> the end of Book 22.

has come home and sits before me now, then the two of us
will acknowledge one another – it's better this way. We've got some special
                                            means of recognition,
you see, hidden ones that nobody else but us will know.'   23.110
Long-suffering, resplendent Odysseus smiled at these words,
and he was quick to address Telemachus in vigorous language:
'Enough: let your mother test me, Telemachus, right here
in the palace. She will be quick to acknowledge me and it's better this way.
She won't do it at the moment and she'll just keep on humiliating me   23.115
because I look a state and I've got these rags on.

---

means of recognition   see the note on **19.225–6**. The Greek word here is *sēma*, literally
'sign', from which we get 'semantics' and 'semiotics', etc. We find a great many such 'signs'
in the *Odyssey*, ranging from linguistic puns (**19.407**) and divine omens (Telemachus'
sneeze at the end of Book 17) to physical symbols of complex relationships (Odysseus'
bow is a guest-gift) – they seem designed to suggest the importance of *interpretation* in
the epic.

But the best thing to do is just let us talk.
If someone had just come in and killed only one of these men –
one that had no family to avenge him later on –
well, he'd be quick to take his leave, even abandon his fatherland, and avoid
the kinsmen. 23.120
As it is, we've killed Ithaca's finest lads, men who protected
this city. I want you to go and start thinking about what we will need to
do about this.'

> 1 Odysseus has indeed hit upon a major problem. What do you think are
> Penelope's thoughts on this?
>
> 2 What do you think of Penelope's state of mind in general, now that her
> long-lost husband is back, and how has Homer managed to convey this?

23.123–8 Shrewd Telemachus then replied in turn:
'That would be something that only you can deal with, father! They say that
your wits are second to none and that no mortal 23.125
on earth could vie with you in this.
But I'm willing to do whatever you say and I can promise
that I won't let you down as far as is humanly possible.'

> • What do you make of Telemachus' characterization in this exchange? Is it
> consistent with his portrayal elsewhere in the epic, and if so, how?

23.129–230 Clever Odysseus then said to him in reply:
'Fine: let me tell you what seems best to me. 23.130
First have a bath and then dress yourselves
and tell the palace slave-girls to find some clothes to wear.
Meanwhile tell the divine poet to take his clear-toned lyre
and lead you in a lively dance:
if someone were to come up the road or if the neighbours were to hear, 23.135
I want them to think that a wedding is taking place.
I don't want word of how we killed the suitors
to get out until we've got out of the palace and been to
the orchards on the estate. Once there we'll be able
to see how Zeus wants to resolve this situation.' 23.140

I want them to think   Odysseus' clever plan of mass deception is both ominous and
ironic. The (forced?) rejoicing when so much slaughter has just taken place may strike us
as out of keeping with Odysseus and Penelope's injunctions to the household for piety
and humility (end of Book 22 and line 59 above); the suggestion that a wedding is taking
place may damage Penelope's reputation (see lines 149–51) but it is actually quite fitting
for the reunion and reconciliation of the hero and his wife that is currently under way.

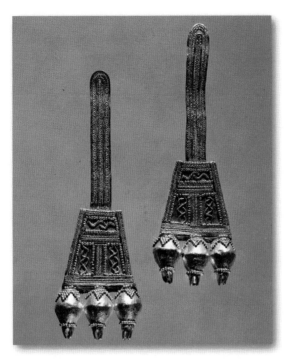

These eighth-century BC earring pendants illustrate Homer's point about craftsmanship (line 161) amply.

Telemachus and the others listened carefully to his words and were quick
to comply.

They first had a bath and then dressed themselves;
the slave-girls also prepared themselves. Then the divine poet took up
his hollow lyre and stirred up their desire
for sweet song and good dancing.   23.145
The huge palace resounded with the sound of the feet
of the men and beautiful women as they danced.
If anyone standing outside the palace had heard they would have said:
'Ah! Someone's getting married to the much sought-after Queen!
Cruel-hearted creature: her attempts to defend the home of her wedded   23.150
husband didn't last. She didn't wait for him to return.'
That's the kind of thing people were saying, and they had no idea what
had actually transpired.
        Meanwhile the house steward Eurynome bathed great-hearted
Odysseus and spread oil over his body,
then clothed him in a tunic and a fine mantle.   23.155
Then Athena streamed down beauty from his head,
making him larger and stronger in appearance, and making his curly
hair cascade down his head; it resembled a hyacinth.

---

making him larger in a further echo of a wedding theme, these exact lines (i.e. lines
157–62) appear at **6.230–5**, when Odysseus appears to Nausicaa, a potential bride (see
question 2 on p. 60 for the metapoetic resonances here).

Just as when a skilled craftsman gilds silver
with gold – someone whom Hephaestus and Pallas Athena have instructed   23.160
in every kind of craftsmanship, someone who can make delightful works of art –
that's exactly how Athena showered Odysseus with beauty on head and
                                                   shoulders.

He left the bath looking like one of the immortal gods.
He returned to sit back down on the chair he had left,
sitting opposite his wife, and he addressed her: 23.165
'You surprise me, Penelope: the gods who hold Olympus have made you
the hardest-hearted woman of all women by far.
No other woman would steel her heart and be so standoffish
to her husband, especially one who's spent nineteen hard
years toiling to get back to her and his fatherland!   23.170
But come now, good mother Euryclea, and spread me a bed
I can sleep on. This woman has a heart of iron.'
      Shrewd Penelope then replied:
'You surprise me, Odysseus: I'm not being offish! I'm not taking this lightly
but at the same time I'm not about to fall at your feet: **I know what kind**
                                        of man you were   23.175
when you left Ithaca on that long-oared ship.
Come on, Euryclea, fetch the man that stout bedstead
out from my well-made bedroom, the bedstead he himself made.
Put the thing out here for him and then spread some bedding over it:
some fleece, some thick spreads, and some bright linens.'   23.180
Penelope had said this to test her husband. Odysseus then
grew angry with his clever wife and said:
'That was a painful thing to say, woman!
Who's moved my **bed** from where it was?! That would be a difficult job indeed,

---

I know what kind of man you were   a puzzling, elusive statement: what does Penelope
mean? Commentators themselves disagree widely; if, however, Penelope sees it fit to
'test her husband' (line 181) she may simply be alluding to Odysseus' craftiness, or in
the worst case, his untrustworthiness. By putting Penelope in this role Homer seems to
be encouraging us to compare her to Athena, who similarly tests (and tricks) Odysseus
(e.g. 22.237–8).

bed   the bed is naturally a metonym (i.e. one word standing in for another, related
word) for their relationship and suggesting that it has been damaged is an extraordinary
show of bravura and craftiness on Penelope's part; she *knows* that even a hint of infidelity
will enrage her husband with jealousy. (We may compare the 'means of recognition' (line
109) that appear at **19.220–48**.) In one tradition (probably post-Homeric but we cannot
know) Penelope slept with *all of her suitors* and gave birth to the god Pan (meaning 'all'
in Greek)! Odysseus' extensive reaction is highly emotional (notice the repetition of 'I')
and Penelope gets just the reaction she wants: he still cares about their relationship. On
the olive tree see 5.477 and 13.122 (also note **5.236**, **9.319** and **9.378**).

even for someone who knows what he's doing, unless Zeus himself 23.185
were to help him and move it at the touch of his hand.
But no living mortal, not even a strapping youth,
could move that bed – the secret lies in
how it was made, and *I'm* the only one who made it.
There once was a small, long-leafed olive tree growing on the premises here, 23.190
blooming and fully grown. It was as thick as a column.
I made it the centre of the bedchamber and built around it, finishing it off
with tight-fitting stones and a solid roof overhead.
I put a pair of doors at the entrance, closely fitted.
I then sheared off the boughs and leaves from the tree 23.195
and then reduced the trunk by cutting from the roots up and planing what
                                was left with a knife;
I used a carpenter's line and it was expert work.
I turned it into a bedpost and drilled holes all through it,
and starting from this I fashioned the bed and then finished the job
by decorating it with gold and silver and ivory. 23.200
I then fitted it with strap-work of bright purple.
That's the secret of how it was made, woman, but how am I to know
whether it still remains in place or whether
some other man has cut away the base of the tree from underneath and
                                moved the bed elsewhere?'
        Penelope's knees gave way, her heart gave way **at these words**: 23.205
she acknowledged the secret that Odysseus had so amply described to her.
With tears in her eyes she then rushed straight for him and threw
her hands around his neck, kissed his head, and said:
'Don't be angry with me over this, Odysseus: you're the one
who's so **intelligent** here! It's **the gods** – it's *they* who have been making
                                  us suffer: 23.210
they have been jealous at the prospect of us spending our youth
and old age in happiness and faithfulness to one another.

---

at these words it is worth noting that Odysseus (once again) achieves his goal at this crucial juncture through the power of words – the craftsmanship of his detailed description (*ekphrasis*) matches his handiwork as woodworker.

intelligent Penelope seems to be flattering Odysseus, perhaps even indulging him in his belief that he could deceive her (especially at lines 215–17) – we must remember that her epithet 'shrewd' means literally '*more* clever'. However, Penelope's tone is difficult to judge and commentators vary quite widely on several points – at the least this could be taken as resulting from the emotional complexity of the scene and the richness of Penelope's characterization.

the gods in a startling echo we may compare her feelings towards the gods with Calypso's words at **5.118–29** and Odysseus' at **12.371–3**.

Let's not get into a fight just because
I didn't show you any affection when I first saw you.
It's been my constant, deepest worry, you see, that   23.215
some smooth-talker would come and trick
me: there are lots of bad people with bad intentions out there.
Not even **Helen** of Argos, with that divine lineage of hers,
would have ended up in a stranger's bed
had she known that the mighty sons of Achaea   23.220
would come to bring her back to her fatherland.
It was a god, I tell you, that drove her to commit such a shameless act,
and it was this god who put that blind and baneful mischief in her
heart that introduced such suffering into our lives.
As it is, you've now so amply recognized the secrets   23.225
of our bed, a bed that no other mortal has seen
but you and I and that one slave-girl
Actoris, the one that my father gave me when I was coming to live with you;
she used to watch over the doors of our snug bedroom –
oh, you've won me over – though I know I've been hard on you.'   23.230

- Why does Penelope compare herself to Helen? What is the point of the
  comparison?

23.231–78 At these words an intense desire to weep overwhelmed Odysseus:
he cried as he took his woman into his arms, his clever woman.
It was **just as when** shipwrecked, swimming men finally spot sweet land:
Poseidon has blasted their well-made ship
on the sea, ravaging it with wind and mighty waves.   23.235
Only a few of them have swum to dry land in safety from the white-flecked
sea, and the brine has thickened in clumps on their skin;
they have escaped disaster and rejoice to find their feet on the earth.

Helen in the famous legend of the judgement of Paris, Aphrodite promised Helen to
Paris as a reward for choosing her as the most beautiful of goddesses, thus starting the
Trojan War; on mischief (line 223) or 'destructive infatuation' (*atē*) see **4.261**. Helen and
Penelope are actually first cousins through their fathers, Icarius and Tyndareus.

Actoris truly a puzzle: at the least a small, verisimilar detail, at the worst a possible dig
at some past impropriety of Odysseus' – we often hear of masters taking advantage of
slaves in antiquity (see note on **1.428**). Whatever the explanation, Penelope is clearly in
an excited state of mind.

just as when the simile is truly striking and it suggests that *Odysseus* has been in a
precarious position: he may have won the contest of the bow but will Penelope take him
back? Line 230 makes it clear that she has. Note the impressive twist on the typical sunrise
formula in the lines that follow.

That's what Odysseus was like as Penelope looked at him with relief,
and she refused to take her white arms off his neck.   23.240
Rosy-fingered Dawn would have risen on the two of them, sat there weeping,
but Bright-eyed Athena had other plans.
She held the long night fast in the West and pulled Golden-throned
Dawn back to the edge of Ocean; she wouldn't even let her begin to yoke
her swift-footed horses that bring sunshine to men,   23.245
Lampus and Phaethon, the colts that drive Dawn's chariot.
          In time clever Odysseus then addressed his wife:
'We have not yet reached the end of all our trials,
Penelope: immeasurably hard work remains:
it's dangerous and difficult but I've got to finish it off.   23.250
On the day I went down to the house of Hades
the spirit of Tiresias prophesied to me;
I went to him to ask how I could get my men and myself home safely.
But come on, let's go to bed and enjoy the pleasures
of sweet sleep while we can.'   23.255
          Shrewd Penelope then said in reply:
'The bed is yours for the taking whenever
you like: clearly it's the gods who have brought you back
to your well-built home and your fatherland.
But since you've got this on your mind and a god has moved you to speak
                                                             of it,   23.260
come on, tell me about **this next trial**: I'll know about it later on anyway,
                                              I should think,
and in the meantime there's no harm in hearing about it now.'
Clever Odysseus then addressed her in reply:
'You surprise me, Penelope: why are you so keen to get me talking
again? Fine: I'll tell you and I won't keep back a thing.   23.265
But you won't be happy with this, and I'm not
either. Tiresias told me that I had to take a good
oar in hand and go to countless cities
until I reached some people who have never seen the sea,
people who do not take salt with their food.   23.270
These people will know nothing of our crimson-prowed ships
nor our good oars that make our ships fly.
I won't conceal the clear token he spoke of:
he said that when I meet a fellow traveller

---

this next trial   note Penelope's insistence on hearing more about this – it could hardly
come as welcome news to her.

who says that I'm carrying a **winnowing-fan** on my good shoulders,   23.275
that's when I have to plant the oar in the earth
and make a splendid sacrifice to Lord Poseidon:
a ram, a bull and a lusty male boar.

> • Do you think that Odysseus is annoyed in lines 264–5 – and if so, why?

23.279–343   Then he said I must come back and sacrifice whole hecatombs
to the immortal gods who hold wide heaven,   23.280
to each of them, one after the other. He said that a gentle death
awaits me, one from the sea, and one that will take me
when I'm exhausted from living to a ripe old age. He said that those around me
will be happy, and that all these things will come to pass.'
Shrewd Penelope then said in reply: 23.285
'If the gods are actually going to make the final years of your life so good
then there's reason to hope you can escape further misfortune at their hands.'
They carried on like this for some time
while Eurynome and Euryclea prepared their bed
with soft linens by torchlight.   23.290
They were quick to make the bed snug and tight with spreads;
Euryclea then went back to bed
while the house-steward Eurynome, torch in hand,
urged the couple to go to bed.
She brought them to their bedchamber then made her way back. They
were happy   23.295
to repeat their old **rituals of bedtime**.
Meanwhile Telemachus, Philoetius and Eumaeus
brought the dancing to an end and told the slave-girls to stop,
then they finally put themselves to bed in the shadows of the palace.
Odysseus and Penelope made sweet love to one another,   23.300
then turned to the delights of talk: they each told their own story:
the magnificent woman told of all she endured in the palace
while she sat watching the destructive suitors

---

winnowing-fan Tiresias' prophecy featured in Book 11 (see note on **10.492**); a winnowing-fan is used to thresh wheat and resembles an oar; a complete landlubber would naturally not know what an oar is. The prophecy is echoed in folklore from a wide variety of times and places: see Segal 1994, chapter 9. Later traditions made Odysseus travel through Greece and even Italy, fathering a number of children (see note on **10.347**) – according to some traditions he becomes grandfather to Homer himself!

rituals of bedtime there is a good discussion in Heubeck 1992 of the now discredited view that an 'original' version of the *Odyssey* actually ended here. Can you think of how such a view could have arisen?

slaughtering their oxen and good flocks
and drinking cup after cup of wine – all because of her.   23.305
Then Odysseus, offspring of Zeus, told of all the pain he had inflicted
on others and how much suffering he had gone through himself,
down to the last detail. She was captivated with his story and wouldn't
let sleep touch her eyes until he had told her everything.
He began with his victory over the Cicones, then his   23.310
visit to the fertile land of the Lotus-eaters.
He told her about the atrocities of Polyphemus, and how he avenged
the stalwart men that the monster had so cruelly devoured.
He told of how he made it to Aeolus, who had welcomed him kindly
and sent him off for home, but it was not yet fated for him to reach   23.315
his fatherland: a storm blasted him
and brought him back, wretch that he was, to the teeming sea.
He explained how he arrived in the Laestrygonian city of Telepylus,
and how the natives there wiped out his ships and every one of his
well-armoured men: he and his black ship were the only things to escape.   23.320
He told her the story of Circe's deceptive tricks,
and how he went in his many-benched ship
to the dank house of Hades to consult
the spirit of Tiresias of Thebes. It was there that he saw all his companions
and the mother who had given him birth and brought him up when he
                                                          was small.   23.325
He told her that he heard the loud voice of the Sirens,
and that he reached the Wandering Rocks and dread Scylla
and Charybdis; no one had ever escaped Scylla unharmed.
He told her how his men had killed the cattle of the Sun God,
and how High-thundering Zeus had struck his swift ship   23.330
with a smoking thunderbolt; all his good men died
together, but he had escaped their evil fate.
He explained how he then reached the island of Ogygia and the nymph Calypso,
who detained him there in her desire to have him for a husband.
She had looked after him there among the hollow caves and promised that 23.335
she would make him immortal and ageless for the rest of his days,
but she could not reach him: she never managed to persuade him.
He told of how he then came to the Phaeacians, after a huge struggle on the sea:
they honoured him deeply, like a god,
gave him bronze, gold and plenty of good garments,   23.340
then sent him off via ship to Ithaca.
This was the last story he could tell her before sweet sleep
overwhelmed every inch of his body and made him forget all his cares.

1   In which book is each of the episodes described by Odysseus recounted?

2   Where does the 'flashback' achieved through Odysseus' story-within-a-story told to the Phaeacians begin?

3   How many books are devoted to the wanderings of Odysseus, and how many to events on Ithaca?

4   What do you make of Odysseus' summary of the *Odyssey*? Homer says 'down to the last detail' (line 308), yet Odysseus seems to omit the problems he encountered with the Cicones (see **9.47** ff.), and we are intriguingly left to guess whether Odysseus told Penelope that he was with Circe for one year and Calypso for seven.

23.344–72 (end)   But Bright-eyed Athena once again had other plans.

The moment she expected that Odysseus had satisfied himself   23.345
with the pleasures of being with his wife and finally enjoying some sleep,
she immediately stirred up Golden-throned, Early-born Dawn
from Ocean so that she could bring the light of day to the world. Odysseus
                                                                then rose
from the soft bed and instructed his wife:
'The two of us, Penelope, have had our glut   23.350
of trials: you've been here weeping over
my homecoming while I've been trying to make it back,
despite the best efforts of Zeus and the other gods to derail me and make
                                                                me suffer.
Now that we've finally enjoyed the pleasures of this bed together once again
I need you to look after everything I've got here in the palace   23.355
while I look to the flocks that the overbearing suitors have wiped out.
I'll conduct some raids to get the majority back and the Achaeans will give me
the rest: they'll have to fill each and every pen and stall we have.
Listen: I need to go to the orchards on the estate
to see my good father who has suffered so much endless grief.   23.360
I know you're sharp, Penelope, but listen carefully to me:
when the sun rises there's going to be some talk in town
about the suitors I've killed here in the palace.
When it comes I want you to retreat upstairs and find a place to sit
among all your slave-girls: don't let anyone see you, and don't ask any
                                                                questions.'   23.365
        With these words he suited up in his fine armour,
got Telemachus and the farmhands moving,
then told them to arm up and prepare for a battle.
They were quick to comply and geared up in bronze,
opened the doors, and made their way outside. Odysseus led the way.   23.370
Sunshine fell on the earth as Athena
kept them concealed in darkness and swiftly led them away from Ithaca town.

The *Odyssey* in later literature: Nikos Kazantzakis' *Odyssey*

Nikos Kazantzakis' continuation of the *Odyssey* (1938) is a modernist
extravaganza that sees Odysseus leave Ithaca, elope with Helen, overthrow
Crete, and enjoy a veritable host of surreal and existentialist adventures
(some include the Buddha), culminating with our hero's death in Antarctica!
This is how it begins:

Unmoved, Odysseus mounted to his lofty bed
and for the last time lay beside his luckless wife.
A sweet and satisfying sleep relaxed his brain,
but just before cock crow his crimson rooster leapt
and shrilled in the large courtyard by the well's dark rim.
The archer heard in sleep his glad three-crested cock,
dashed to his feet and buckled on his iron sword,
then hung his twisted hornbow down his sunburnt back
and drew the door bolt softly, not to wake his wife.
But she had lain all night unsleeping, with closed eyes,
her mute, incurably pale lips drawn tight with pain,
and when the bronze bolt creaked, she slightly raised her lids
and saw in dawn's dim light her husband stealing off.

Kazantzakis, The Odyssey 2.1445–7 (tr. K. Friar)

Odysseus is more or less a continuation of the restless and 'centripetal'
Odysseus discussed on p. 107. This Odysseus is also given voice in the famous
lines that open and close Tennyson's *Ulysses* (1842) (1–7 and 65–70):

It little profits that an idle king,
By this still hearth, among these barren crags,
Match'd with an aged wife, I mete and dole
Unequal laws unto a savage race,
That hoard, and sleep, and feed, and know not me.
I cannot rest from travel: I will drink
Life to the lees.

Tho' much is taken, much abides; and tho'
We are not now that strength which in old days
Moved earth and heaven; that which we are, we are;
One equal temper of heroic hearts,
Made weak by time and fate, but strong in will
To strive, to seek, to find, and not to yield.

Book 24

Book 24 begins colourfully with the descent of the unburied suitors' souls into the Underworld; they are compared to bats shrieking and flitting in a cave as Hermes leads them down. In a moving scene we find Achilles in discussion with Agamemnon – the two had been so hostile to one another in the *Iliad* – but in keeping with the theme of (sometimes uneasy?) reconciliation that dominates Book 23, the pair seem to be getting along. The topic of their conversation, suitably, is burial. Achilles expresses pity for the way Agamemnon died, and the latter describes the magnificent burial of Achilles to the hero himself. Agamemnon then notices the suitors and asks one of them what could possibly explain the sudden appearance of such vast numbers; ironically the suitor had hosted Agamemnon in Ithaca (in an instance of *xeinia* again) when the latter had come to persuade Odysseus to join him in the campaign against Troy 20 years ago. On hearing this, Agamemnon praises Penelope in words so fitting for such a self-reflective poem: 'Perfect Penelope, daughter of Icarius! / What a mind! You never forgot your wedded husband / Odysseus. And now people won't forget her and what she's done – / ever! The gods will give mortals / a poem, one that will elevate and delight sharp Penelope!' (lines 194–8).

The scene rapidly changes back to Ithaca, where Odysseus goes to find his father Laertes. In a disquieting exchange, Odysseus initially tries to test his father by concealing his identity with yet another false tale of origins. (Perhaps Odysseus is still smarting from the way Penelope responded to his own self-disclosure?) But on seeing his father's desperation, Odysseus suddenly abandons the attempt and is tearfully reunited with Laertes. Odysseus and his loyal team then assemble at Laertes' farm and prepare for the final showdown with the suitors' families, who have now caught wind of what happened, and are coming to collect the dead – and to seek vengeance on Odysseus. Some Ithacans urge restraint: the suitors brought this on themselves; but the majority want blood, Antinous' father in particular. In a moving speech he points out that Odysseus is responsible for the death of many Ithacans: not only the hundreds he lost on his way back from Troy (compare the prologue), but also now all the suitors! In an echo of the divine councils of Books 1 and 5, Athena then appeals to Zeus: what should be done? The king of gods and men has the solution: let Odysseus be king of Ithaca again and 'we'll make the Achaeans forget about how their sons / and brothers were killed. Let both parties agree to regard one another kindly, / just as before, and let there be plenty of peace and wealth on hand' (lines 404–6). Just before this happens, however, Athena encourages Laertes, overjoyed to be fighting alongside his son and grandson, to hurl a javelin at Antinous' father; it strikes the man dead immediately. Odysseus and his team make to attack but Athena herself intervenes directly with a divine apparition and urges everyone to stop fighting; Zeus confirms with an omen. The Ithacans retreat and Odysseus is happy to stop; in the last three lines of the epic, Athena transforms herself once again into the guise of Mentor and 'compelled both sides to swear lasting oaths'.

The *Odyssey* in later literature: Derek Walcott's *Omeros*

In the following lines from his 1990 *Omeros* (chapter LVI, part iii), Derek Walcott has perfectly captured the self-referentiality of the *Odyssey*: the 'dog-eared manuscript' is of course the *Odyssey* (see chapter XXXVIII, part i, where the *Odyssey* has been turned down by publishers!). Even 'Mr Joyce' makes an appearance in the poem (chapter XXXIX, part iii): something about the *Odyssey* inspires allusion, interpretation and emulation.

> 'I saw you in London,' I said, 'sunning on the steps
> of St Martin-in-the-Fields, your dog-eared manuscript
> clutched to your heaving chest. The queues at the bus-stops
>
> smiled at your seaman's shuffle, and a curate kicked
> you until you waddled down to the summery Thames.'
> 'That's because I'm a heathen. They don't know my age.
>
> Even the nightingales have forgotten their names.
> The goat declines, head down, with these rocks for a stage
> bare of tragedy. The Aegean's chimera
>
> is a camera, you get my drift, a drifter
> is the hero of my book.'
>   'I never read it,'
> I said. 'Not all the way through.'
>   The lift of the
>
> arching eyebrows paralyzed me like Medusa's
> shield, and I turned cold the moment I had said it.
> 'Those gods with hyphens, like Hollywood producers,'
>
> I heard my mouth babbling as ice glazed over my chest.
> 'The gods and the demi-gods aren't much use to us.'
> 'Forget the gods,' Omeros growled, 'and read the rest.'

The book remains one of the most problematic of the *Odyssey* for many reasons; we may compare the complex reconciliation effected here with that of Odysseus and Penelope (Fajardo-Acosta 1990 has argued for a tragic interpretation of the conclusion); in metapoetic terms we could reflect on the problem of 'ending' for Homer: just as Odysseus must continue journeying, any ending to the *Odyssey* will feel arbitrary; Homer seems to be drawing attention to the very nature of plot and closure itself, getting his audience to see its function as one defining element of a text, but perhaps not the only or most important one. What do we as readers want in a poem anyway? The *plot* of the *Odyssey* is obviously necessary

– and compellingly so – for the poem – but what matters most is how it's handled and presented (see note on **5.41**), and what other effects can be achieved in the meantime.

> 1 Can you make a case for and against the total destruction of the 108 suitors (plus attendants)?
>
> 2 Think back over events since Odysseus' return to Ithaca in Book 13: what are the key events that mark his homecoming, and at what point can he be said to have fully achieved it?
>
> 3 How satisfactory do you find this conclusion to the poem? Civilization and justice have been restored, but at what cost?
>
> 4 Much of the *Odyssey* is realistic, earthy and gritty, yet much is not. Can you comment on realism versus fantasy in the poem?

Further reading

Some suggestions

It is difficult, but perhaps not impossible, to come to terms with the *Odyssey* without knowing the *Iliad*. One of the best things a reader new to the *Odyssey* can do is to read that epic; as with the *Odyssey* I recommend **Lattimore's** translations (1961 and 1967) above all. I can also strongly recommend having a good guide to Greek myth handy; though I have tried to explain many of the mythological references in the notes, a text such as **Grimal** 1986 will prove useful.

I recommend consulting another translation as well as that of Lattimore: **Fagles** 1996, **Fitzgerald** 1962, **Cook** 1993 and **Lombardo** 2000 are all outstanding, and there are even audio recordings available of Fagles. As for secondary literature, **Griffin's** short introductions are commendable (1980a and 2004), as well as **Jones's** commentary on the entire *Odyssey* (1988) and that of **Morrison** (2003); **Ahl and Roisman** 1996 is an unconventional commentary but highly readable and stimulating. The scholarly standard Oxford commentary (here cited as **S. West** 1988, **Hainsworth** 1988, **Heubeck** 1989 and 1992, **Russo** 1992 and **Fernández-Galiano** 1992) may occasionally baffle the reader without Greek, but there is a wealth of learning and good sense here; so with the briefer and older **Stanford** (1959). The two recent 'Companion' volumes to Homer, **Morris and Powell** 1997 and **Fowler** 2004, are invaluable as first points of departure into the vast world of Homeric scholarship and provide answers to many questions that cannot be dealt with here. As for contextualizing more fully Homer and the *Odyssey* within the society that engendered them, I recommend **Finley** 1979, **Latacz** 1996 and **Powell** 2007.

Monographs on the *Odyssey* abound; among the most accessible are **Dimock** 1989, **Segal** 1994, **Clay** 1997 and **Louden** 1999. There are good collections of essays in **Emlyn-Jones et al.** 1992, **Schein** 1996, **McAuslan and Walcott** 1998 and **Doherty** 2009. I have made some reference in the notes to the extensive and lively reception of Homer and the *Odyssey*, particularly in Western literature (and in the visual arts); **Stanford** 1968, **Boitani** 1994 and **Hall** 2008 provide good overviews on this subject. I should stress, however, that it is important to view the *Odyssey* with fresh eyes, and not to allow later versions of Odysseus and his story to dim our perception of those features that stand in the original.

Works cited

Adkins, A. 1997. 'Homeric Ethics', in **Morris** and **Powell**. 1997.

Ahl, F. and **H. M. Roisman**, 1996. *The* Odyssey *Re-formed*. Ithaca, NY.

Antonaccio, C. M. 2007. 'Colonization: Greece on the Move, 900–480', in **Shapiro** 2007.

Arnold, M. 1861 *On Translating Homer*. London.

Bennet, J. 1997. 'Homer and the Bronze Age', in **Morris** and **Powell** 1997.

Bernadete, S. 1997. *The Bow and the Lyre: A Platonic Reading of the* Odyssey. London.

Boitani, P. 1994. *The Shadow of Ulysses: Figures of a Myth*. Oxford and New York.

Booth, W. C. 1983. *The Rhetoric of Fiction*. Chicago, IL.

Chadwick, J. 1990. 'The Descent of the Greek Epic', *Journal of Hellenic Studies* 110: 174–7.

Cherniss, H. and **W. C. Helmbold** (trs.) 1957. *Plutarch's* Moralia. Vol. 12. Cambridge, MA.

Clay, J. S. 1997. *The Wrath of Athena: Gods and Men in the* Odyssey. London and Lanham, MD.

Clayton, B. 2004. *A Penelopean Poetics: Reweaving the Feminine in Homer's* Odyssey. Lanham, MD.

Cline, E. (ed.) 2010. *The Oxford Handbook of the Bronze Age Aegean*. New York.

Cohen, B. (ed.) 1995. *The Distaff Side: Representing the Female in Homer's* Odyssey. New York.

Cook, A. S. (tr.) 1993. *Homer: The* Odyssey. New York and London.

Cooper, J. M. (ed.) 1997. *Plato: Complete Works*. Indianapolis and Cambridge.

Dalley, S. 1989. *Myths from Mesopotamia: Creation, the Flood, Gilgamesh and Others*. Oxford.

De Jong, I. J. F. 2001. *A Narratological Commentary on the* Odyssey. Cambridge.

Deneen, P. J. 2000. *The Odyssey of Political Theory: The Politics of Departure and Return*. Lanham, MD.

Dimock, G. E. 1989. *The Unity of the* Odyssey. Amherst, MA.

Dodds, E. R. 1951. *The Greeks and the Irrational*. Berkeley, CA.

Doherty, L. (ed.) 2009. *Oxford Readings in Homer's* Odyssey. Oxford.

Edmunds, L. and **R. W. Wallace** (eds.) 1997. *Poet, Public and Performance in Ancient Greece*. Baltimore, MD.

Edwards, M. W. 1997. *Homer: Poet of the* Iliad. Baltimore, MD.

—— 2002. *Sound, Sense and Rhythm: Listening to Greek and Latin Poetry*. Princeton, NJ.

Eidinow, E. 2007. *Oracles, Curses and Risk among the Ancient Greeks.* Oxford.

Emlyn-Jones, C., L. Hardwick and **J. Purkis** (eds.) 1992. *Homer: Readings and Images.* London.

Fagles, R. (tr.) 1996. *Homer: The* Odyssey. New York and London.

Fajardo-Acosta, F. 1990. *The Hero's Failure in the Tragedy of Odysseus: A Revisionist Analysis.* Lewiston, NY.

Fernández-Galiano, M. 1992. *A Commentary on Homer's* Odyssey. Vol. 3. Oxford.

Finley, M. I. 1979. *The World of Odysseus.* Second edition of original 1956 edition. Harmondsworth.

Fitzgerald, R. 1962. *Homer: The* Odyssey. London.

Foley, H. 2009. '"Reverse Similes" and Sex Roles in the *Odyssey*', in **Doherty** 2009. Reprint of original 1978 article.

Foley, J. M. 1999. *Homer's Traditional Art.* University Park, PA.

Fowler, R. (ed.) 2004. *The Cambridge Companion to Homer.* Cambridge.

Gentili, B. 1988. *Poetry and its Public in Ancient Greece: From Homer to the Fifth Century.* Baltimore, MD and London.

Goldhill, S. 1991. *The Poet's Voice: Essays on Poetics and Greek Literature.* Cambridge.

Gould, T. 1992. '"Modern" Patterns of Dramatic Violence in the *Odyssey*', in **Buitron et al.** 1992. *The* Odyssey *and Ancient Art: An Epic in Word and Image.* Annandale-on-Hudson, NY.

Graziosi, B. 2002. *Inventing Homer: The Early Reception of Epic.* Cambridge.

—— 2008. *Journal of Hellenic Studies* 128: 178–80.

Griffin, J. 1980a. *Homer.* Oxford.

—— 1980b. *Homer on Life and Death.* Oxford.

—— 2004. *Homer: The* Odyssey. Cambridge.

Grimal, P. 1986. *The Dictionary of Classical Mythology.* Oxford.

Haft, A. J. 1984. 'Odysseus, Idomeneus and Meriones: The Cretan Lies of *Odyssey* 13–19', *Classical Journal* 79: 289–306.

Hainsworth, J. B. 1988. *A Commentary on Homer's* Odyssey. Vol. 1. Oxford.

Hall, E. 2008. *The Return of Ulysses: A Cultural History of Homer's* Odyssey. London.

Haller, B. 2009. 'The Gates of Horn and Ivory in *Odyssey* 19: Penelope's Call for Deeds, Not Words', *Classical Philology* 104: 397–417.

Hansen, W. 1997. 'Homer and the Folktale' in **Morris** and **Powell** 1997.

Heitman, R. 2005. *Taking Her Seriously: Penelope and the Plot of Homer's* Odyssey. Ann Arbor, MI.

Heubeck, A. 1989. *A Commentary on Homer's* Odyssey. Vol. 2. Oxford.

—— 1992. *A Commentary on Homer's* Odyssey. Vol. 3. Oxford.

Horrocks, G. 1997. 'Homer's Dialect' in **Morris** and **Powell** 1997.

Janko, R. 1998. Review of **Morris** and **Powell** 1997, *Bryn Mawr Classical Review* 98.5.20 (online).

Jones, P. 1988. *Homer's* Odyssey: *A Companion to the English Translation of Richard Lattimore.* Bristol.

Kearns, E. 2004. 'The Gods in the Homeric Epics', in **Fowler** 2004.

Kirkpatrick, R. (tr.) 2006. *Dante Alighieri: The* Divine Comedy 1: Inferno. London.

Latacz, J. 1996. *Homer: His Art and His World.* Ann Arbor, MI.

Lattimore, R. (tr.) 1961. *The* Iliad *of Homer.* Chicago, IL.

—— (tr.) 1967. *The* Odyssey *of Homer.* Chicago, IL.

Lefkowitz, M. R. 1981. *The Lives of the Greek Poets.* London.

Lombardo, S. (tr.) 2000. *Homer: The* Odyssey. Indianapolis, IN.

Lord, A. B. 2000. *The Singer of Tales.* Second edition of original 1960 edition. Cambridge, MA.

Louden, B. 1999. *The* Odyssey: *Structure, Narration and Meaning.* Baltimore, MD and London.

Malkin, I. 1998. *The Returns of Odysseus: Colonization and Ethnicity.* Berkley, CA.

McAuslan, I. and P. Walcott (eds.) 1998. *Homer.* Oxford.

Morris, I. 1997. 'Homer and the Iron Age', in **Morris** and **Powell** 1997.

Morris, I. and B. Powell (eds.) 1997. *A New Companion to Homer.* New York.

Morrison, J. 2003. *A Companion to Homer's* Odyssey. Westport, CT.

Moulton, C. 1975. *Similes in the Homeric Poems.* Göttingen.

Murnaghan, S. 1987. *Disguise and Recognition in the* Odyssey. Princeton, NJ.

Nagy, G. 1996. *Poetry as Performance: Homer and Beyond.* Cambridge.

—— 2004. *Homer's Text and Language.* Urbana, IL.

—— 2009. *Homer the Classic.* Cambridge. MA.

Olson, S. D. 1995. *Blood and Iron: Stories and Storytelling in Homer's* Odyssey. Leiden.

Osborne, R. 2004. 'Homer's Society', in **Fowler** 2004.

Page, D. 1973. *Folktales in Homer's* Odyssey. Cambridge, MA.

Parry, M. 1971. *The Making of Homeric Verse: The Collected Papers of Milman Parry.* Oxford.

Peradotto, J. 1990. *Man in the Middle Voice: Name and Narration in the* Odyssey. Princeton, NJ.

Powell, B. B. 1997. 'Homer and Writing', in **Morris** and **Powell** 1997.

—— 2007. *Homer.* Malden, MA.

Raaflaub, K. A. 1997. 'Homeric Society', in **Morris** and **Powell** 1997.

Rozokoki, A. 2001. 'Penelope's Dream in Book 19 of the *Odyssey*', *Classical Quarterly* 51: 1–6.

Russell, D. A. and M. Winterbottom (eds.) 1972. *Ancient Literary Criticism.* Oxford.

Russo, J. 1992. *A Commentary on Homer's* Odyssey. Vol. 3. Oxford.

Schein, S. (ed.) 1996. *Reading the* Odyssey: *Selected Interpretive Essays.* Princeton, NJ.

Segal, C. 1994. *Singers, Heroes and Gods in the* Odyssey. Ithaca, NY.

Shapiro, H. A. (ed.) 2007. *The Cambridge Companion to Archaic Greece.* Cambridge.

Shay, J. 2002. *Odysseus in America: Combat Trauma and the Trials of Homecoming.* New York and London.

Shelmerdine, C. W. (ed.) 2008. *The Cambridge Companion to the Aegean Bronze Age.* Cambridge.

Silk, M. 2004. *The* Odyssey *and its Explorations,* in **Fowler** 2004.

Snodgrass, A. 1998. *Homer and the Artists: Text and Picture in Early Greek Art.* London.

Souyoudzoglou-Haywood, C. 1999. *The Ionian Islands in the Bronze Age and Early Iron Age 3000–800 BC.* Liverpool.

Stanford, W. B. 1959. *The* Odyssey *of Homer.* London.

—— 1968. *The Ulysses Theme.* Second edition of original 1963 edition. Oxford.

Steiner, G. 2004. *Homer in English Translation,* in **Fowler** 2004.

Sutherland, C. 2001. 'Archery in the Homeric Epics', *Classics Ireland* 8: 111–20.

Vivante, P. 1985. *Homer.* New Haven, CT and London.

Wace, A. J. B. and F. H. Stubbings (eds.) 1962. *A Companion to Homer.* London.

Wells, R. (tr.). 1989. *Theocritus: The Idylls.* Harmondsworth.

West, D. (tr.) 1990. *Virgil: The* Aeneid. London.

West, M. L. 1997. *The East Face of Helicon: West Asiatic Elements in Greek Poetry and Myth.* Oxford.

—— (ed. and tr.) 2003. *Homeric Hymns, Homeric Apocrypha, Lives of Homer.* Cambridge, MA.

—— 2007. *Indo-European Poetry and Myth.* Oxford.

West, S. 1988. *A Commentary on Homer's* Odyssey. Vol. 1. Oxford.

Zajovi, V. 2004. 'Homer and *Ulysses*', in **Fowler** 2004.

Acknowledgements

The authors and publishers acknowledge the following sources of copyright material and are grateful for the permissions granted. While every effort has been made, it has not always been possible to identify the sources of all the material used, or to trace all copyright holders. If any omissions are brought to our notice, we will be happy to include the appropriate acknowledgements on reprinting.

Texts
p. 82 *The Idylls*, Theocritus translated by Robert Wells, Carcanet Press Limited, 1988; p. 99 Reprinted by permission of the publishers and the Trustees of the Loeb Classical Library from *Plutarch: Volume XII*, Loeb Classical Library Volume 406, translated by Harold Cherniss, pp. 497, 499, Cambridge, Mass.: Harvard University Press, copyright © 1957 by the President and Fellows of Harvard College. Loeb Classical Library® is a registered trademark of the President and Fellows of Harvard College; p. 107 *Inferno: The Divine Comedy I* by Dante, translated by Robin Kirkpatrick (Penguin Classics, 2006), translation copyright © Robin Kirkpatrick, 2006, reproduced by permission of Penguin Books Ltd; p. 130 'Prologue', copyright 1952 by Ralph Ellison, from *Invisible Man* by Ralph Ellison, used by permission of Random House Inc.; p. 160 From *Ion and Hippias Major* by Plato, translated by Paul Woodruff, copyright © 1983 by Hackett Publishing Company; p. 181 excerpt from *Omeros* by Derek Walcott, copyright © 1990 by Derek Walcott, reprinted by permission of Farrar, Straus and Giroux, LLC.

Images
Cover: Ulysses and the Sirens (oil on canvas) by Belly, Leon-Auguste-Adolph (1827–77) Musee de l'hotel Sandlin, Saint-Omer, France/ Giraudon/The Bridgeman Art Library; pp. 11, 64 © The Trustees of the British Museum; p. 13 Attic white-ground lekythos decorated with a woman playing a cithara (glazed terracotta) by Achilles Painter (fl.c.470–425BC), Ashmolean Museum, University of Oxford, UK/The Bridgeman Art Library; p. 29 Vova Pomortzeff/Alamy; pp. 32, 164 akg-images/Erich Lessing; pp. 42, 57, 131 The Granger Collection/TopFoto TopFoto.co.uk; p. 78 Cup depicting Ulysses and his Companions blinding Polyphemus (ceramic) by Greek Bibliothèque Nationale, Paris, France/Flammarion/The Bridgeman Art Library; p. 81 Kevin Fleming/Corbis; p. 89 Lebrecht Music and Arts Photo Library/ Alamy; p. 94 Drinking cup (kylix) depicting scenes from the Odyssey, by the Painter of the Boston Polyphemos, Archaic Period about 560–550 BC, place of manufacture: Greece, Attica, Athens, Ceramic, black figures, height 13.2 cm, diameter 21.7 cm, Museum of Fine Arts, Boston, Henery Lillie Pierce Fund, 99.518; pp. 108, 133 akg-images; p. 111 The J. Paul Getty Museum, Villa Collection, Malibu, California, Fragment of an Apulian Red-Figure Bell Krater attributed to the Black Fury Group, about 375–350 BC, terracotta, 19 × 18.5cm; p. 120 Tibaldi, Pellegrino (1527–1596): Ulysses's Companions Stealing the Oxen of the Sun, Bologna, Palazzo Poggi, © 2011, Photo Scala, Florence; p. 125 The Art Gallery Collection/Alamy; p. 134 Attice red-figure skyphis – detail (Penelope at her loom), Chiusi, Archaeological Museum, © 2011 Photo Scala, Florence – courtesy of the Ministero Beni e Att. Culturali; p. 149 SuperStock; p. 171 The Art Archive/Agora Museum Athens/Gianni Dagli Orti

Artworks on pages iv and 161 by Peter Simmonett

Printed in Great Britain
by Amazon

33890433R00106